Hidden Lives
My Three Grandmothers

Hidden Lives
My Three Grandmothers

by Carole Garibaldi Rogers

SERVING HOUSE BOOKS

Hidden Lives: My Three Grandmothers

Copyright © 2013 Carole Garibaldi Rogers

ISBN: 978-0-9858495-5-9

Cover design by James Norton

Cover photograph Girl at Door, New York City Tenement, by Lewis W. Hine

Maps by Bill Nelson

Serving House Books logo by Barry Lereng Wilmont

Published by Serving House Books, LLC
Copenhagen, Denmark and Florham Park, NJ

www.servinghousebooks.com

First Serving House Books Edition 2013

For all my families

past, present, and future

Books by Carole Garibaldi Rogers

Penny Banks: A History and a Handbook
How to Collect: A Complete Guide
Poverty, Chastity, and Change: Lives
    of Contemporary American Nuns
Great Ideas from Great Parishes
    with Mary Ann Jeselson
The People's Prayer Book
    with Mary Ann Jeselson
Fasting: Exploring a Great Spiritual Practice
Habits of Change: An Oral History of American Nuns
    (revised and updated edition of
    Poverty, Chastity, and Change)

Table of Contents

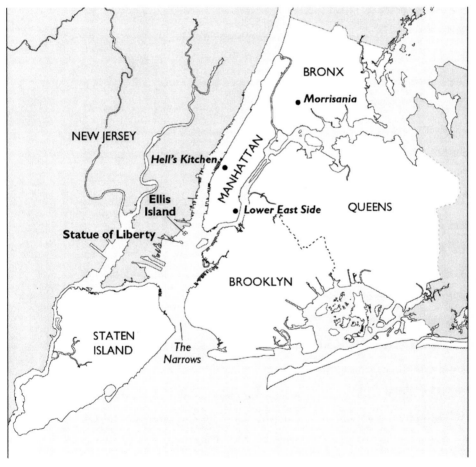

An Immigrant's New York
Early 20th Century

Prelude:
Empty Spaces

My father and I were heading north on Main Street in Concord, New Hampshire. It was late on a Sunday afternoon and the stores were closed, except for the Coffee Mill, but even there only a few stragglers remained. Fortunately, there was little traffic. I was driving us back up to the lake house where three weeks earlier my mother, at the age of 86, had had the first of two heart attacks and then two strokes.

Four weeks ago she had been the healthier of the two. In the unspoken language of families, we all expected to be facing end-of-life issues with my father long before my mother. He had the more critical and debilitating illnesses. But there we were, sitting on the porch after dinner, when my mother began to have trouble catching her breath. Earlier in the day, she had interrupted our grocery shopping to sit on a bench just beyond the checkout lines. I had never known her to do something like that and later I could never shop at that supermarket without seeing her there.

But that afternoon the spell, as she called it, passed quickly and we continued with our errands. In the evening, at dinner, she was perky and talkative, filled with plans for their summer. But as we watched dusk lower its filter over the mountains, her distress returned. I could see only her profile against the fading light and so I could not see fear in her eyes. I saw it in her hands. The next few moments set in motion the events that had led us to Concord.

Against her wishes—"It's nothing...I'll be fine in a minute"—I called 9-1-1. The path we followed had no detours: ambulance,

9

emergency room, local hospital, cardiac hospital, and, six weeks later, the rehab center in Concord. There, despite her aphasia, she could still express her anger at being where she was and how she was—able to walk and to talk, but not to make any sense to anyone else. Even for her to request one of those ubiquitous packets of jam required a sad version of Twenty Questions.

The car in front of us made a sharp turn into McDonald's. My father, staring straight ahead through the windshield, his cane propped between his knees, said, "There's something you should know." No horns blared but I instinctively checked the rear view mirror.

"The family you thought was your mother's family wasn't her real family."

Long pause.

"She was adopted."

And there it was. A truth so basic, revealed so late in her life, in my life, that I still wonder how we survived all those years as mother and only child without the secret erupting, slip-sliding, leaking out somehow. But the fact is: it didn't.

Such an ordinary moment. The road. The car. Halting conversations with my father. All were so familiar, but that moment, those three words, changed my life. I had grown so accustomed to not having grandmothers, or even stories about grandmothers, that I could not foresee I would want to spend years uncovering details about my mother's two mothers, one her birth mother and the other, her adoptive mother. Or that reclaiming the stories of those two women would lead me to a third, my father's mother—another grandmother hidden behind family secrets. That day, I did not feel anger or loss or deep sadness. The news was too stunning. Those would come later as I finally pierced my own protective shell.

I would discover that all three of my grandmothers had struggled to survive in tough New York City neighborhoods during the early decades of the twentieth century. Two things at least their families had in common: a fondness for keeping secrets, which can perhaps be tied to survival instincts or simply dismissed as typical for the era, and their culmination in one granddaughter who found those secrets painful and no longer acceptable.

At first I learned what I needed to know to claim my families. I read documents, searched archives, walked streets, connecting with people and neighborhoods and traditions I had not even known were part of me. But then I saw that I needed to do more. I deeply wanted to recognize and honor three women too long hidden from view, to give voice to the voiceless. For two decades I have been an oral historian, recording the voices of women who do not appear in history texts. Now these unknown women were my own grandmothers. I had to do more than fill in the lines of a genealogy chart as satisfying as that became. I wanted to not only unearth their stories, but share them. My personal need to know them morphed into public tribute.

This book would emerge because of a conflict between generations: those who could not or would not tell and those who must. In the tough times, I was pulled along by what anthropologist Ruth Behar has described as "duty-memory, the sense of responsibility that weighs upon the individual, as if an inner voice is saying, 'It is I who must remember'...." But whenever I paused to look back, I would conclude, over and over, that my work was not a duty at all. It turned out to be my privilege.

The short sentence my father uttered so calmly would change my life. Indeed it changed my basic assumptions of who I was. It led me down unfamiliar paths into the stories of three grandmothers. But as these women gradually filled the empty spaces my parents left, anger had to give way to acceptance. Telling their stories became my story, a long journey into healing, which began that afternoon.

"Why didn't you tell me before this?"
"We thought you knew."
"How could I know?"
I recalled a scene two weeks earlier. After the heart attacks but before the strokes, my mother could still communicate and a visiting nurse was asking about her family, searching for history of heart disease. When my mother was silent, hesitating in her

answers, I rushed in, talking about the woman I had known as one of my mother's older sisters. "Remember Aunt Kate, Mom? She had heart problems." My mother said nothing. Neither did my father, standing off to the side.

With such a recent display of my ignorance, how could they have believed I knew? I pulled over to the side of the road and waited for his answers. But the conversation quickly disintegrated. He made little sense, stumbling over his words, defensive against my barrage of questions. He did not remember when he learned the story or who told him or when the adoption took place. He knew no names. He would not look at me.

"You know your mother."

It was his traditional fallback, his ultimate defense, one I had heard so many times. And, of course, I did. Her playfulness, her quick anger, her devious, if sometimes charming, use of facts were all familiar traits that my father and I had experienced for years. But this time the words banged around in my head. It seemed I did not know my mother after all.

And for a long time there was little opportunity to find any answers. My mother's illness took all of our energy. When the doctors said she was ready to leave rehab, my father decided we would close up the summer cottage and they would move from their home on Long Island to a continuing care community near me in New Jersey. There were four levels of care at Heath Village, and within weeks my mother had been in three of the four; she missed only independent living. Up and down she traveled, my father and I with her, moving photographs, bringing afghans, until she settled into a downward spiral that nothing could reverse.

A therapist told me that stroke victims often exhibit their least appealing traits once the veneer of social grace is taken from them and they have no inhibitions. She made no judgment, just stated a professional observation, but my mother was a difficult patient. She was dangerously erratic, an extension of her charming impetuousness, and violently angry. At the doctors, the nurses, the aides. A priest. A psychiatrist. My father. Me. She threw her wedding and engagement rings at my father. She hid in someone else's closet.

She deliberately stopped up a toilet. She yelled and bit. She found no peace. Her anger enveloped us. My father sat all day with her, coaxed her to eat, tried to keep her calm. I wheeled her up and down the corridors, fussed over her hair, bought her easy-in, easy-out clothes, styles she would never have worn a year earlier. It was far too late to expect answers for any questions I might have asked.

But my memory worked overtime, skittering through the decades looking for clues I had misread or opportunities I had missed. For all of my childhood I had heard the stories. She was the youngest of four young girls raised by their mother, a German woman who died before I was born. They were poor but happy. "Where was your father?" I asked many times, and early on I learned how many answers there can be to one question. For a decade in her later years my mother wrote a column for a New Hampshire weekly where she enshrined the stories. Shopping expeditions to buy new Easter hats. Making root beer. Front porches for eating gingersnaps. Screen doors leading to backyard gardens. They had a glow, those stories, the edges of poverty softened and burnished in the telling, family tensions erased. How did an adoption fit into the narratives my mother had spun? It didn't.

Throughout my childhood and teenage years, we had been best friends and she had been a delightful companion—imaginative, playful, filled with enthusiasm for any activity. When I was sick in bed one winter she gave up her beloved pastry board to create a frontier village with me, laying the board across my legs as we worked. Together we made snowmen in the wide side yard or hunted for wildflowers, pressing them between the pages of whatever thick book she had at hand. A lifetime later, when I had to clean out her bookshelves I found lumpy encyclopedia volumes with brown stained pages where fragments of flowers and leaves still lurked. She taught me how to apply mascara. We shared books and exchanged recipes. We shopped in the city together. But over the years, barriers rose up between us and she seemed to withdraw from any serious conversations. Still we worked at finding common threads— the escapades of her grandsons never failed—and we continued to talk on the phone almost every day. In those last days I was losing a mother I had deeply loved. But the other mother, the one I had never had a chance to meet, the one hidden by all the secrets, was also beyond my reach.

I told myself I wasn't angry, that anger was useless, wasted energy. And I believed that until late one summer night in our garage. The four of us, my husband, sons Doug and Matt, and I, had unloaded a small moving van and were sorting out the hundreds of items we'd removed from my parents' home. I came on a framed oil painting I had long ago given my parents. Done by a friend of mine, it was a view of the lake cottage and I had thought it a fine Christmas gift. For some reason which always escaped me, my mother took one look and put it aside. She never acknowledged the gift. My father had quietly hung it in a room where no one ever went anymore. When it surfaced at the bottom of the "What Do We Do With This" pile, my body knew what to do. I pried the canvas from its frame. I held the painting low to the cement floor and stuck my foot through, once, twice, I don't know how many times. I broke the frame into four sticks and tossed all of it into the trash. I escaped into the house with my sons' uneasy laughter following me.

As Christmas approached, my mother grew smaller and quieter. She knew me and called me by name, but all she said was "Carole, I'm so cold" or "Carole, I'm so tired."

I wheeled her down the hall to see the Christmas tree. This time, a sight that had always brought her such happiness, whether it was her own elaborately decorated ones, a giant balsam in Rockefeller Center, or indeed any other, small or large, elicited no response.

By a Saturday in early January, after enduring a few more strokes, she lay silent and peaceful at last. Her skin was as clear and unwrinkled as it had been decades earlier; her hair, gone gray again, was still curly and spread out on the now calm surface of the pillow. When she died, I was standing on one side of the bed; an aide who had known her for only the difficult months and loved her anyway, was on the other. My father, seriously ill with the flu, was in bed himself, banned from the nursing floor, unable to be at her side as he had for all the days leading up to this one. A woman I did not know came to pray over her; her words seemed loud and intrusive.

My mother was beyond words. She had finally found peace. Peace for me would be a while in coming.

The winter day my father brought a faded envelope to my house is as clear a memory as that Sunday afternoon when he first opened up my mother's story. He sat at my kitchen table and pushed an envelope toward me. "You may want to have these," he said. In the envelope were a prayer book, some holy cards, and my mother's baptismal certificate.

I had always known my mother was Catholic and spent her childhood in the Bronx so it was no surprise that she would have been baptized at Our Lady of Victory Church on Webster Avenue. But the words that filled in the blanks on the certificate shocked me:

"This is to certify that <u>Rita Hoefel</u>, child of <u>Benjamin and Minnie Schneider</u>, born in <u>New York</u> on the 31st day of <u>May, 1911</u>, was baptized on the <u>21st</u> day of <u>May, 1920</u> according to the rite of the Roman Catholic Church..."

I knew my mother as the youngest daughter of a German widow named Margaretha Hoefel. These were names I had never heard.

"Who are Benjamin and Minnie Schneider?" I asked my father. No response.

"Did mother know she was adopted?"

He smiled faintly. "One time she dragged me all over Sunnyside looking for a man called Gus."

"Who was Gus?"

"I don't know," he said.

"You mean you didn't ask?"

He shrugged. I tried to jar him out of his non-knowing. "Didn't you wonder if he was a former boyfriend?"

He shrugged again.

Familiar with the language his body spoke, I knew that he had withdrawn somewhere away from me. He would not tell me more then.

Months later, when I asked again about Gus, I received exactly the same answer. He did not know anything about him. Another time, my son, Doug, paging through one of my mother's small address books, which my father had brought to me, found an entry for August "Gus" Fischer and an address in Woodside, NY, a Queens town that borders the neighborhood of Sunnyside.

"Is this the Gus you meant?" I asked my father. He seemed surprised to see the name there in her handwriting. "I guess so," he said.

"Did you find him?"

"No," he said. "When we got there, no one was home." He added only one new morsel: he had asked my mother years later about that outing, but she said they had never done that. She had no memory of spending the day looking for Gus.

The mystery has remained, but I now believe my mother thought Gus might know something about her birth family. And I believe my father knew that. Why else, whenever I asked about her adoption, did he tell the story about Gus, a seeming non-sequitur? I remembered so many other conversations with my father—his maddeningly evasive or non-committal answers. He had learned early in his life to protect himself and was using those same skills to protect my mother from me and my too-late questions. I never found out from him what Gus Fischer knew and why he knew. It was the first of many dead ends.

When I went to visit Our Lady of Victory Church and wander its neighborhood, I discovered a 90-year-old Catholic parish that remains an immigrant church. The sign in front said Sunday masses are now said in English and Spanish. To the south were blocks and blocks of low income housing projects. To the north, open lots and storefront auto repair shops. Across Webster Avenue, a bodega and the entrance to Claremont Park.

A high iron gate protected the parish offices from intruders. I rang the bell, gave my name and heard multiple locks turn. Mario, an immigrant from Honduras, introduced himself as the parish's man-of-all-jobs and when I stepped into the tiny front office, furnished with an old scarred desk and a single hard chair, I showed him the baptismal certificate.

"Welcome home," he said.

He offered me a tour of the church, proudly showing off the ways the parish had adapted the interior space to accommodate two musical traditions, Spanish and English, which was now predominately African-American. When I asked if the parish might have any more information about my mother, he suggested I come back another day to visit with the pastor. Only he could show me original records.

Doug, home from his university for a week's vacation, came with me to meet Father Peter Gavigan and, with his permission, see the original baptismal ledger. A fine gentleman with a hospitable heart, he was pastor to a very different immigrant community than the one that must have sheltered my mother, but he had a lively interest in local history. Imagine what it was like here, he said, before they built the Cross Bronx Expressway! He knew that the neighborhood in my mother's era was both German and Jewish. He still had a few elderly German parishioners among his English-speaking community. My mind wandered away to wonder if my mother ever sang here in a choir. Singing in German or English? Father Gavigan left us with Mario while he went to retrieve the ledger.

When he returned and we saw the dusty pages with faded ink entries, I was grateful for my son's research training as an anthropologist. I was emotional, involved in the moment, both anxious and exhilarated. It was he who noticed that all the entries were in the same handwriting. Clearly the ledger, spanning the years 1918 to 1934, had been recopied. It was he who found the index. "Hoefel," the name we were seeking, had been inserted on the line above another name, "Seidman." And when he turned to the listing for the proper date — May 21, 1920—we found the full names of my biological grandparents: Benjamin Seidman and Minnie Schneider. And we found my mother listed as Rita Rebecca Seidman Hoefel.

I had been preparing myself for new information, but I did not expect to see a completely different name for my mother: Rita Hoefel, the outer shell I knew, bracketing Rebecca Seidman, the core of her identity. And the Seidman name was totally unfamiliar; it had not appeared on the baptismal certificate my father gave me. Who was Benjamin Seidman? Who was Minnie Schneider? Were they from the neighborhood? Were they married? When had they died? And underlying all those questions was a significant one that these new names brought to mind: was my Catholic mother the child of Jewish parents?

By the time I had to confront that question and give it fair weight, I had long since finished 16 years of Catholic schooling. I was close to receiving a Master's Degree in Theology, adding two more years of Catholic education. And I could recall absolutely no connections to Jewish traditions.

From my earliest memories, my mother was devoutly Catholic. From the time I was in first grade, she took me with her to novenas every Monday afternoon. Her best friends in those days were the Dominican Sisters who taught me in early grammar school. She traded recipes with "Cookie," the sister who cooked all the meals for the convent, and she knew all their life stories, gleaned, I guess, from long conversations in the school yard while I played with classmates. My mother did not like crucifixes and religious art around the house so we had never had any. But for many decades she was totally involved in parish life.

I do not remember my mother as a writer before she began her late-in-life career as a columnist. But one piece of her early writing, a smudgy carbon copy of two typed pages, single spaced, has somehow survived. In an open letter to Princess Ann of Bourbon, Parma, who was about to renounce Catholicism to marry King Michael of Rumania in the Greek Orthodox Church, my mother displayed her own Catholic beliefs. My mother clearly believed that Ann would suffer in hell for her choice. She pictured Ann as she made her decision: "Surely Mary and the Angels walked beside her in her hour of trial—surely Satan too stood by ready to pounce on another soul!" I don't know if the letter was ever mailed. No matter my mother's disapproval, the wedding took place in 1948.

My mother's grasp on Catholicism waned in her later years. She stopped going to Mass. I did not know the reason. When I asked a few times, she was evasive, as always, and impatient. But Jewish? It seemed so totally impossible.

Two months after my mother's death, I called Ruth, the daughter of an old family friend. She was several years older than I, a friend of two older cousins who had died, and my only connection to information about Margaretha Hoefel. Ruth and I had met for lunch occasionally, talking easily, but broaching this subject was awkward.

"Would you know anything about my mother's early life?" I started the conversation hesitantly. "Could she have been Jewish?"

"Yes," she said. "My mother told me years ago that Rita was Jewish."

A straightforward answer to a question I had never dreamed to ask and information she had never thought to share. When I asked why my mother had been adopted, she said, "Rita's mother died and her father couldn't take care of her." She knew little more.

In the months that followed I often woke up in tears. I couldn't tell if they were tears of loss or of frustration, mourning my mother or all I couldn't know. How could I not know my mother was Jewish? That I was Jewish? To fill the holes, I wrote sweet scenarios in my head. Perhaps baby Rebecca had been born to a young couple who lived in the same Bronx neighborhood as Margaretha. Perhaps Minnie had died tragically when my mother was an infant and Margaretha had come to their aid. Or perhaps Minnie had died later, in the influenza epidemic of 1918, and my mother had lived seven or eight years in a Jewish family. That might explain why she wasn't baptized until 1920 when she would already have been eight, an unusual delay for Catholic families in those days.

My father assured me he had never seen a birth certificate and so I decided to confront the bureaucracy of The New York City Department of Records even though their website discouraged me. When I applied in person, I was told the certificate, which I could see just five feet away in the hands of an employee who stood behind the high intimidating counter, could not be released to me; adoption records were sealed. Following some whispered encouragement from another petitioner, I asked for the name of the director and put my petition in writing, giving all my eloquence to the request.

Three weeks later, by certified mail, came Certificate and Record of Birth Number 28599. I was home alone, sitting at the same kitchen table where I had first seen Rita's baptismal certificate, when I opened the envelope. Here at last would be definitive information about the baby who became the woman I knew as my mother. I wanted the truth, but once again I was so unprepared. The stories I had heard all my life and even my recent imaginings were obliterated by facts I saw on the paper in front of me.

Name of Child: Beckie Seidman.

Place of Birth: Jewish Maternity Hospital

Those last words, stamped in fancy italic script, swirled before my eyes. I put the paper down but picked it up again almost immediately, reading compulsively down the columns of information. My grandfather's name was Benjamin Seidman. He was 22. My grandmother was Minnie Seidman. She was 19. Her name before marriage was Minnie Schneider and she had no previous children. For each, their Birthplace was Russia; their Residence was 36 Orchard Street.

After months of speculation, the facts, shocking though they were, were oddly consoling. My mother had indeed been Jewish. I had two Jewish grandparents. I knew their full names, where they had lived and where they came from. What did that mean for me? I could not comprehend all the implications then—it would take years—and I could not imagine if I would ever learn more. I had no idea of the journey ahead, no idea that I would spend days wandering around the Lower East Side, finding buildings that still stand, and nights searching databases for information about Minnie and Benjamin.

In those early years of my searching, at lunch with some friends, the conversation turned to family memories. One woman had brought with her some letters from the nineteenth century. Her grandparents were famous; her mother kept everything and she had always cherished the stories she had heard since childhood. Another had been helping her husband clean out his family's home. Every room was filled with photographs and mementos. They found four violins, one of which, according to its bill of sale, had cost $800 in the 1920s. Another friend, a fine artist who had first learned to draw at her grandmother's kitchen table, said that in her native Iceland, everyone knows their ancestors. Women's last names are formed from a combination of their father's name and *dottir,* which means daughter.

I sat, numb. My friends had stories and photographs and memories. I had just learned my mother's real name and her heritage and her birthplace. I still knew nothing about my Jewish grandparents. I had no idea what other secrets might still be hidden. The conversation wrapped me and I had to make a great effort to breathe normally. In. Out. Steady. I kept my hands in my lap, when I was not twirling a spoon around and around my coffee, but my heart contracted with comparisons. I could not speak. As an only child, aloneness had surfaced often enough in my life. But the loneliness I felt at the table was as intense as any I had ever experienced.

Eventually, I recognized there was no way out but through and so I began to follow up leads, hesitantly at first but with more confidence as the details accumulated. My visits to the Lower East Side expanded to include more trips to the Bronx as I pursued the links between the two parts of my mother's childhood. Somewhere along the way I acknowledged that I was no longer searching only for her identity, but for my own. And I saw that I would have to pry open secrets about my father's family. They were a matched pair, my parents, protecting each other as well as themselves. My father had also kept significant family information from me. He was resistant, emotional when I pushed hard on either story. One sad night, in our kitchen once again, as my husband and he and I sipped wine before dinner, I stepped over the invisible boundary and asked too many questions. He broke down, sobbing at the table. My husband, furious at my insensitivity, turned on me.

"That's enough," he said.

Horrified at the sound of my father's sobs, I agreed and I stopped searching. I told myself to move on. Friends counseled me to move on. But deep down I couldn't. Reluctant to cause my father more pain, I returned to the search, but I told him few details. When I turned my attention to his family, I asked him to sign the letter requesting a copy of his mother's death certificate, and he did, but when he gave me the envelope I could tell he had not looked inside. I discussed our grandmother with some of my Italian cousins, but I shared only safe parts of those conversations with my father. He and I had seven wonderful years together after my mother died, but during that time I was following a family tradition. I was keeping secrets.

Eventually the time came when I once again spent my days saying goodbye to a parent. The trajectory of the closeness between my father and me was the opposite of my relationship with my mother. Perhaps that's inevitable with a three-sided family. For all those years when I was best friends with my mother, my father must have sometimes felt left out. Later, as he and I grew closer, I knew that my mother felt excluded from our occasionally lengthy early morning conversations. As the only child, I was the focal point of each of their attentions. I had never felt left out. But seeing the outlines of the secrets they had kept, I had to reevaluate my memories. Clearly, there had been a third side to those exclusive conversations, one that did not include me.

In the stereotypical suburban world where I grew up, fathers were absent a lot, working long hours, commuting on the Long Island Railroad, unavailable to chaperone class trips or plan children's birthday parties. They surfaced to teach us to drive, interview our boyfriends, and walk us down the aisle. But along the way my father had also taken me to his office on Saturdays and to Yankee home games, valiantly cheered for me at dreaded swim meets, tried unsuccessfully to teach me to throw a softball. He demonstrated over and over that he had faith in me.

He was a man of extremes. He smoked three packs a day. Then he would toss a full pack of Marlboros in the garbage can and quit cold turkey. He would go through two quarts of ice cream after dinner, gain 50 pounds, diet, lose 50 pounds, and go back to smoking. He would be back up to three packs within the week. We must have gone through that cycle two or three times while I still lived at home. My father suffered from frequent migraine headaches. He had a smoldering temper. I knew when to tiptoe around him. But he was also charming and courtly and I basked in his attentions as did my friends. He came into his own after he took early retirement and had time to be both father and grandfather. With the pressures of corporate life behind him, he drew on deep wisdom and humor and became a source of strength for me and his grandsons.

Now as his strength ebbed I saw all I was losing. His last months were not so turbulent as my mother's. He was depressed and would not leave his room, but he delighted in family visits. He still lost his temper occasionally, but then he'd apologize and tell me the whole story on my next visit. When a psychiatrist tried to help him with the depression, my father threw him out of the room. But they gradually became friends and fellow baseball fans. The doctor told me my father's last words to him were, "Go Yankees."

His last words to me, as he struggled to breathe, were, "I need all the help I can get." Help was coming, I assured him, rubbing his hand, keeping my voice calm, knowing the morphine was even then entering his system. He did not speak again. When he died 24 hours later, in his own bed by the window, I was for the first time in my life, despite husband and sons, truly alone.

After the long goodbyes, my research took on a new urgency and a new clarity. When someone you love dies, there is an empty place in your heart, but sometimes in that space you see more clearly what had been obscured by their presence. In my father's absence I finally saw Catherine, my Italian grandmother. Catherine Garibaldi joined my mother's two mothers, Minnie Seidman and Margaretha Hoefel, their turbulent immigrant lives running parallel, all three leading to me.

It was time to tell their stories.

Part I
The Lower East Side

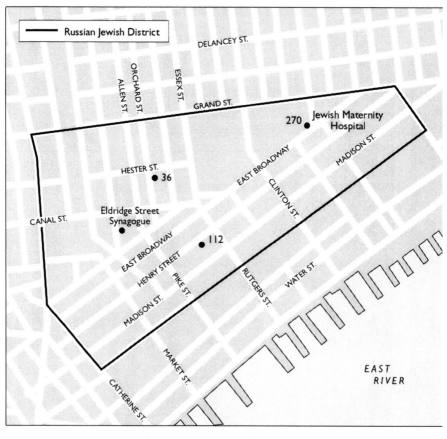

The Lower East Side, Manhattan
(looking north)

Chapter 1
Mindele

The first time I stood on the southwest corner of Hester and Orchard Streets, peering across at 36 Orchard, my mother's first home, I knew only the pathetically sparse facts I had just learned from her birth certificate.

All my life I had believed my mother's name was Rita, that she had been born in the Bronx to a German Catholic couple named Margaretha and William Hoefel. Yet there I was, struggling to grasp that my mother had actually been born Beckie Seidman, to Jewish parents, and that her first days of life were spent on Orchard Street in a tenement just across the street.

I stared at the building, allowing people to jostle their way around me while I wondered on which floor the small Seidman family lived and with whom. It was not likely that a family of three lived alone. In 1910, more than 500,000 Jews lived in the blocks surrounding this corner.

I imagined a June day and what it must have been like to bring a newborn home to 36. Like all the tenements on Orchard or Hester or any of the other Lower East Side streets, it would have been hot, crowded, noisy, smelly, dark. Probably by then, indoor toilets, two per floor shared by the families in four apartments, relieved the hardship of backyard outhouses. But in summer the small rooms would have been stifling. Did Minnie sit out on the fire escape with Beckie those first weeks? I focused on the fourth floor landing and saw a tableau there, two tiny figures crammed into the corner, rocking slowly.

The building looked much as it did a century ago. The decorative brick arches that topped the old tenement windows had been somewhat obscured by modern bay windows. Air conditioners had been inserted under the new windows, but the iron fire escape still bisected the façade of the building.

On that first visit, the street level of 36 Orchard, commercial space, as it probably was in 1911, was sealed, being refurbished for a mysterious tenant. Workmen could not answer my questions. On another trip, I watched through new panes of glass as three young men spackled and painted, transforming the ground floor rooms into an art gallery. They were dismissive, living only in the present, too busy to talk about earlier days. The neighborhood was once again changing. Still home to new immigrants, now Asian and Hispanic instead of Jewish, it was also becoming a chic outpost for artists.

I returned to Orchard Street many times. I wanted the building to tell me why my mother always hated dark living rooms. I wanted the neighborhood where so many women became seamstresses and worked at their machines for twelve to fourteen hours a day to tell me why my mother, who loved to knit, embroider, and braid rugs, refused to sew. And I wanted desperately to know my grandmother.

The search has taken many years and left me exhilarated at times but more often angry, saddened and frustrated. Paths that seemed to run straight detoured and ushered me into dead ends that required months to escape. At first, I went in person to libraries and archives. Later, as more and more sources went online, I spent long nights trolling databases.

The story of my Jewish grandmother was a classic immigrant tale. I just could not determine which variation on the theme was hers. I did not find a Minnie or any similar name at 36 Orchard Street in the 1910 or 1920 census records. I did not find a marriage certificate naming Minnie Schneider and Benjamin Seidman. I did not find a death certificate for Minnie Schneider or Minnie Seidman in any of the many variant spellings I checked. I could not choose one or another of the Minnies who arrived at Ellis Island.

As I came upon each new possibility for a grandmother, I optimistically tried on the description, looking for a match. A

Minnie Schneider arrived at Ellis Island with her mother in 1892; she was two years old and already a United States citizen. She would have been 21 in 1911. In 1900, another Minnie Schneider, age 9, arrived from Liverpool with her father and mother and three younger sisters. All were U.S. citizens. I wanted to think these were my family, great aunts and great grandparents, but the Minnie who was my grandmother was not a citizen. And if she had such a family, wouldn't they have kept her baby after she died?

Similar discrepancies stopped me from claiming as mine the Minnie Schneider who lived with her parents, a younger brother and sister, at 305 Madison Street. This Minnie was 24 in 1910 and had been born in New York. Then there was the Minnie, daughter of Joseph and Ellie, who lived on Hester Street in 1910. She was 20 that year and she spoke Yiddish—a possibility. But that family came from Austria.

When I turned to marriage certificates, I felt maddeningly close. Each time I followed up a listing in the Manhattan Brides Index, I expected to find my grandparents. One listing for a Minnie Schneider who was married in 1909 seemed a good possibility. But further research showed that this Minnie was a 20-year-old bride who married Michael Viner in a Catholic ceremony. I even searched for a "late" wedding when Minnie would already have been pregnant with Beckie. A Minnie Schneider was married on April 23, 1911, but the groom was Henry Hutter. Another Minnie married on April 18, 1911, but she was a widow marrying James Callahan at City Hall.

Late one night, pursuing one more fruitless search through the Ellis Island database, I understood that my grandmother was one of those thousands of women whose lives had slipped through the cracks. I might never find the information about her that I craved. But I couldn't just quit. I accepted a charge, what Patricia Hampl has written: "For we do not, after all, simply have experience; we are entrusted with it. We must do something—make something—with it. A story...is the only possible habitation for the burden of our witnessing."

I sought consolation among facts and statistics and in other immigrant's narratives. I immersed myself in stories of *shtetl* life in the Pale of Settlement. I followed the risky overland journeys Jewish families took across borders to reach a ship, of nasty trips in steerage, of arrivals at Ellis Island, and finally of life on the bleak and crowded Lower East Side. I lingered over the stories the survivors told, trying to conjure my grandmother's experiences. Gradually, I teased out scenarios that made sense, that fit with what facts I had, corralling them into a cohesive story that might very well have been my grandmother's.

Minnie was, of course, my grandmother's American name. Before she came to New York, her given name was probably Mindl, a popular Hebrew name for which Minnie was often the Americanized form. Her family might have affectionately called her Mindele. Her last name could have been spelled Schneider, as I saw it on my mother's birth and baptismal certificates or it may have been Schneyder or Schneader or any of the many variants. The name means "tailor" and somewhere in my family's history, there was no doubt a tailor or two with steady loyal customers, both Gentile and Jew. In the generations before Mindl, life was not easy, but artisans with a steady business could be comfortable enough.

My grandmother was Jewish and she was Russian. That meant she lived in the Pale of Settlement, a swath of land in Eastern Europe between the Baltic and Black Seas, corresponding to what is now Poland, Latvia, Lithuania, Ukraine, Moldova and Belarus. Catherine the Great had created the area in 1791 as a place to confine Jews living in the Russian Empire.

For a while, in the Pale, life was difficult but bearable. My great great grandparents could have lived in a small wood house with the tailor shop in front and rooms for the family in back, with fruit trees and fields surrounding their *shtetl*. They made enough money to buy chicken and fish for their own Sabbath dinners and give to those less fortunate. They could have had a few luxuries like a silver menorah and linens for festive meals. They could put aside rubles for dowries.

But by my grandmother's era, the end of the 19th century and the very beginning of the 20th, life in the Pale was dire. Economic changes through Europe, government restrictions on Jewish residents and increasingly burdensome taxes drove more and more Jews out of their own businesses. Newly arrived Jews, who had been hounded from other areas of Russia, squeezed into the *shtetlekh*, the crowded Russian and Polish towns where Jews were forced to eke out their survival. Towns that had one or two tailors suddenly had ten and there was not enough business for any of them to survive. This generation of Schneiders, like all their Jewish neighbors, saw their lives grow ever more harsh.

My imagination faltered. No matter how many facts I absorbed, how many faded photographs of *shtetl* life I examined, the details of my grandmother's early family life remained opaque. These were my ancestors, but I felt no emotional connection.

Until one Friday morning when I made Challah. I am my mother's daughter and long ago she taught me how to work with yeast recipes. But I had never made Challah and I surely knew my mother never had. There would be no recipe in her box of cherished clippings. So I asked two Jewish friends.

One recipe was Grandma Rosie's favorite; another was a prize-winner. I needed a third to learn how to do the braids. And I needed hours alone in my suburban kitchen to move beyond my mother, who adopted New England farm recipes as her own and used both lard and Crisco in her baking, to understand the traditions behind what I was doing. To remember why I couldn't use lard in an egg bread.

But I was still in my head, trying too hard to make up for a lifetime devoid of Jewish experience. I followed precise measurements, using dry packaged yeast and flour bought in a supermarket—a far different experience than *shtetl* baking. Not until after the dough rose for the first time and I turned it out for kneading did I move from my kitchen into my great grandmother's space. It was early morning for me, but not the pre-dawn hours when she would have worked at this task. I pressed the heels of my hands into the dough over and over, turning one quarter turn as I had learned as a young baker. I had no idea if that's the way earlier generations would have worked, but it felt right and my hands provided the link my brain could not. When the dough got too sticky I added more flour and

I let clumps cling to my fingers. I put the dough away for a second rising, punched down and again kneaded my way back to the Pale.

The room was always dark when my great grandmother arose, but on Fridays she started her day even earlier. She had the dough for several loaves of Challah already set aside for rising before she roused the children.

"Mindele, hurry. You must help with the kneading."

In the *shtetlekh* childhood for girls was fleeting. Only a few years separated babyhood from adulthood. By the time she turned eight, my grandmother's days of playing tag outside in the spring or indulging in make-believe during long winter days were over. She was expected to take responsibility for chores at home and to care for the new babies. By the time she was nine or ten she was in the market, helping all day at the family's stall.

That sturdy bundled figure kneading the dough, my great grandmother, was, I think, older than other women when she married. Before their lives had turned so harsh, her father had allowed her a few years of study. First, as was tradition for many families with daughters, she learned Hebrew, memorizing from sacred texts, studying with a *rebbe*. Since gifted young *rebbes* taught only boys who might go on to Yeshiva and bring credit to their teachers, a *rebbe* who taught girls would not have been among the smartest of the Jewish scholars. He would have been poorly dressed and always hungry; his school room dark and damp and tiny. But perhaps when my great grandmother showed promise in her studies, she was allowed to continue on with the village's secular teacher. From the *lehrer* she would have learned to read Yiddish and some Russian and easy arithmetic. Reading became her most prized possession.

But the world was changing and there was no more time. The *shadchan* had tried several times to make a match but without luck. She came again, suggesting a tailor named Schneider. When the two families agreed, whatever my great grandmother wanted, her days of studying were over. Her love of reading disappeared, seeping deep into her genes, not to surface again until her granddaughter Beckie came of age.

Like most of the other men he knew, my great grandfather lost his shop and was forced to take to country roads selling his services wherever he could. His wife, alone most years from Passover to the High Holy Days, managed the children and eked out small sums from her baking and knitting, items she sold at the markets. Like so many of the women in the *shtetlekh*, my great grandmother, in her own quiet ways, broke down the walls of Jewish male dominance. With her husband gone for months at a time and her own abilities to earn a living essential for the family's existence, she assumed a greater role in decision-making.

Her hands were rough and scarred, her knuckles protruding, her nails short, blunt, and dirt-encrusted as she kneaded, but she had a gentle touch with the dough. It was this she tried to teach Mindl as the little girl stood beside her, shifting from one foot to another on the cold floor. She wanted her to take pride in her work, particularly in chores that prepared for the Sabbath. This was what Jewish women could contribute to their faith; they kept the domestic traditions. Kneading was their prayer, a Sabbath *mitzvah*. Braiding, for Mindl, was more fun than duty. At first her only task was to seal the ends of the braid, but soon enough she learned to braid three strands and then mastered six. Before long she would be old enough to remove the loaves from the oven while her mother went early to the market.

After the loaves went into the oven, Mindl and her mother cleaned the house and set the table for the Sabbath meal. No longer were there silver candlesticks to provide light as they prayed and ate. They had long since gone to the pawnbroker. Small tin candle holders were all they had. Like thousands of other Jewish women throughout the Pale, Mindl and her mother would return early from the markets in order to light Shabbat candles before sundown. On the table, under a crocheted doily that my great grandmother had carefully washed that morning, the Challah lay hidden until the blessings.

Anticipating the Sabbath meal made Mindl happy all day. She only half listened to the women as they talked at the market. They kept their voices low; the news was never good. She ignored the taunts of the Gentile boys she passed on her way to do her mother's errands, including another *mitzvah*, delivering Challah to one of the newest families in town.

By the time Mindl was born, in 1892, there was not only severe economic hardship, but anti-Semitism had become an epidemic spreading rape, murder, and destruction through the Pale. No Jewish family, no matter how faithful they were to their religion and how much comfort its rituals and prayers offered, lived without a sense of desperation. The choices were stark. Families who stayed risked being imprisoned or beaten or murdered with their houses and businesses set aflame. Or they could leave their homes and risk the journey to another land. In the worst years, from 1881 when Tsar Alexander II of Russia was assassinated, triggering increasingly repressive regulations, to 1914, the beginning of World War I, two million people, one-third of the Jews living in Eastern Europe, decided to leave. The overwhelming majority of them chose to come to America.

In 1906, the peak year for emigration, 153,748 Jews entered the United States, most of them landing in New York City. I think my grandmother was among them. She would have been 14 that year and probably traveling alone.

What family calculations allowed a young girl to leave her world and risk the dangers of the unknown? Perhaps one day shortly before Passover that year an opportunity arose that changed Mindl's life. Several years earlier, the father from a *shtetl* family they knew well had gone to America. His letters promised he would send for his family and the prized steamer tickets had arrived—one for his wife and one for each of his children. But, in his absence, the *shadchan* had, against all odds, found a husband for the eldest daughter, who was Mindl's age and her good friend. Despite her mother's tears, the girl refused to leave. She would stay with her grandparents and marry in the fall. The family offered the ticket to the Schneider family for Mindl—with conditions. My grandmother would help care for the younger children on the journey and once she was earning money in New York, she would have to repay the family for her passage.

Mindl's father, a devout Jew, optimistic and traditionally myopic, opposed the trip. On his travels through the countryside he had heard the news of ever more violent pogroms, but he closed his ears.

"Life will get better," he said. "Wait a bit and see."

Like so many other Eastern European mothers, Mindl's mother was the practical voice. There was precious little free time or energy in her days, but she remembered how she had once loved to read. The new and foreign did not frighten her as much as it did her husband. It was too late for her to escape; her husband would never consider such a journey. But she wanted more for her daughter than *shtetl* life. She knew the odds were stacked against her Mindele having any luck with the *shadchan*. There were so few opportunities to marry in their town; the young men had all been conscripted into the Russian army or left for the cities. Mindl was her constant companion at home and working at the stall. She would miss her terribly; worse, she understood what her daughter could not: the separation would last a lifetime. But she saw that her daughter had skills she could bring with her. She could cook. She was a tailor's daughter and very good with a needle. She certainly had experience caring for children. Her Mindele was a steady, sober girl, not too pretty, not too plain. She calculated her daughter would have a far better future in America.

Other families in the *shtetl* had heard good news from relatives in America. At the market women read aloud letters from husbands and children who had made the long journey.

"My son says there is plenty of food. Fish you've never heard. Everybody eats."

"There is plenty of work, my son says."

"Mirel sent rubles again. See?"

"The children are all in school. Can you believe that?"

Townspeople called the United States "the Goldene Medina," the Golden Land. But Mindl's father was sure that she would lose touch with her religious practices. No one talked about keeping kosher in America. He had heard America called "*Treyfene* Medina," a ritually unclean land.

What did my grandmother think? She was a sensible girl. She knew the risks of the journey. But she also knew that her prospects were indeed dismal. In a neighboring town, Russian soldiers had raped some young girls. If traveling would be dangerous, she reasoned, staying home was also perilous. She did not like the idea of leaving her family but with the optimism of her years she did not believe it would be forever. Her father would change and soon her family would all join her in America. Somewhere deep inside her, in a place she had not ever encountered, an adventurous streak overcame her fears. If her parents allowed it, she would go.

Back and forth the discussion flowed. As Mindl lay in bed with the other children, she was no more than a few feet from where her mother and father spoke in hushed voices. She knew the conversation was about her. Once in a while she heard her mother say "Mindele" but the rest was inaudible and she drifted off to sleep. One night she awoke to the sound of crying. At first she thought it was one of the little ones, but the sobs were strong, if muffled, and she knew it was her mother lying close by. As her eyes searched out the dark she could see a body curled and shaking. Mindl lay frozen in bed, afraid to move, wondering what it meant.

In the morning she looked carefully at her mother. The familiar face was impassive. Mindl could read no message from it as her mother moved about doing her usual tasks. Not until evening when the family sat at table together did her father tell her the decision. She would be allowed to go to America. Her mother cried openly then; so did the other children who were learning for the first time about Mindele's future. Her father did not, at least where Mindl could see. He abruptly left the table. Mindl cried, too, at the thought of the separation to come, but as the days went by, she consoled herself and her mother by envisioning their reunion in America.

"I will earn plenty of money. I will send steamer tickets for all of you." She was sure that by the time her family came she would have a husband who loved her and a baby daughter of her own to welcome them.

When families left on their long journeys out of the Pale, the entire *shtetl* turned out to say goodbye. Mindl had been the center of attention for weeks as the final preparations were made. Aunts, uncles, and cousins from neighboring *shtetlekh* all arrived at the Schneiders' door. My great grandmother, her kerchief often askew, alternately cried and smiled with pride.

"Mindele," she would say after a little while. "Come sit with my second cousin Hannah."

Mindl, despite being the center of attention, remained demure, as she had been taught. But she was happy to be dismissed because often the conversation turned critical of her parents. How could they allow a daughter to leave and travel alone? Still everyone wanted to see the steamer ticket, to feel it and examine the lettering even though no one understood English. And everyone wanted to offer advice and dire predictions.

"Be sure you warn Mindele about white slavers....Where have you sewed her money? ....Give her 10 pounds of zwieback for the steamer. She won't have kosher food for days and days. She might starve....How do you know this family will keep her safe in America? You better start saving money to bring her back...." The questions repeated themselves and her parents' answers were never satisfactory.

When the visitors left, Mindl had learned, her mother and father would be short-tempered with each other and with her. It was best to have an errand planned or to take a walk to visit her new family. There, too, departure preparations consumed everyone. There the mother—call her Itke—would leave and the daughter would stay. It didn't make for any less tension. Mindl discovered in those last days that she was happiest alone where she could indulge her growing excitement.

Finally one evening, it was the Schneider family's last meal together. The *drosky* would depart early the next morning and there would be little time for private talk among the crowd that would gather. But at table they found there was nothing left to say. Her father said the blessings in a choked voice and sat morose and silent.

"Mindele, eat," her mother said. But neither could. Mother and daughter got up to clear, both hunkered down in their own thoughts.

Many a night I held that image of my family in my head as I

tried to fall asleep. I imagined them that last night, wondered what the two women were thinking, and ached to know more. Why had the stories been kept from me? And how many more were there?

Chapter 2
Mindl

In the darkness, Mindl clutched her bags and bundles under both arms. She was wearing two coats, her father's last gifts to her. Her mother had slipped in some crocheted doilies and extra head scarves and carefully sewed a few rubles into her undergarments. Surely they would be well hidden there. As Mindl passed through her family's door one last time, she stretched up to kiss the *mezuzah* as she had every day of her life. She wanted to run her fingers once more over the familiar surface, but she had no time to linger. Outside she was surrounded by wailing and shouting from neighbors and friends who had gathered to say goodbye. The horses stomped. The children in her new family called out impatiently. Suddenly she was very afraid. She dropped her parcels and clung to her mother. But her mother was not crying. Her features had not crumbled like Mindl's.

Then she embraced her daughter and her tears came, too.

"Shalom, Mindele," she whispered.

Gently she pushed her daughter toward the waiting *drosky*. Someone grabbed her parcels. Itke grabbed her arm and pulled her up. With two young children climbing immediately onto her lap, my grandmother had no clear view of her parents as the carriage started up. She tried to wave but she had no room to move her arms. Her eyes grew so blurry with tears that she no longer knew which figures were her mother and father. No one would again call her Mindele, the affectionate name only her family used. As she traveled with her new family, she would sometimes still hear Mindl, but officially, until she arrived in America, she would be nameless, another woman's daughter. Once safely in New York, she determined, she would reclaim her own name.

I, too, moved on. At the library, I returned my stack of books about *shtetl* life and replaced them with accounts of immigrants' journeys to America. I was drawn to the personal accounts, those that fed me with details I could never know from my own family's memories. Just behind many a young woman's words, often anonymously recounted, I saw my grandmother and traveled with her.

The women and children bounced along muddy roads through *shtetl* after *shtetl* until they arrived in a city, probably Minsk. Mindl was fortunate. The letter from America had included not only the valuable steamer tickets but also enough money to pay for the family's train tickets to a city near the German border. Although they rode in third-class accommodations, sitting upright on wooden benches for almost three days, they had a far easier trip than many other women who walked the same distance, usually in groups to protect themselves from dangers on the road. Even on the trains, women had to be careful. When they stopped at large stations, at least two of them in their group stayed to watch the bags while the others searched for food and toilets. When it was Mindl's turn to leave the train, she was so worried that it would depart without her that she had no time to be afraid of the ruffians she saw on the crowded platforms.

Once near the border, travelers without passports, like Mindl and her *shtetl* companions, whether they had arrived by train or on foot, had to make contact with one of the many professional smugglers who helped Jews cross out of the Pale into Germany. They had to pay a steep fee for his assistance and there was no guarantee of success. The closer they came to the border guards, the greater Mindl's fear. It was not hard to hoard her day's portion of food because she could not swallow.

They crossed at night in a canvas-covered wagon. The smugglers, most of them young men not much older than Mindl, had told them to hide under the hay between the sacks of flour and not make a sound. The border guards were alert to crying children and coughing adults. One of the smugglers used a branch as a rifle to demonstrate what would happen if they didn't keep the children quiet. Itke and Mindl were told to roll up small cloths and stuff them into the children's mouths. They cradled them and soothed their fears while they themselves struggled not to cough as they breathed in flour dust. The hay scratched their faces but they dared not move. The wagon came to a stop and from the muffled sounds Mindl guessed they were at the border. She almost stopped breathing. The children, wide-eyed and terrified, cuddled close to her. She heard the driver tell the guard he was carrying flour. No one came to the rear of the wagon to lift the canvas. Then she heard what she thought was an exchange of coins and the wagon rolled on. They had crossed into Germany.

As the wagon picked up speed through the countryside, the children finally slept. Mindl could not. Her back and shoulders were bruised from lying all night against the wagon slats, holding children tightly on top of her. Each bump over the rutted roads caused her sharp pain but what kept her awake was reliving her fright at the border. She had already experienced more of the world than either of her parents and she was no longer so confident about the future.

In Hamburg, Mindl's group waited several weeks for their ship to arrive. They struggled to conserve their meager provisions; they slept in rows of cots under dirty blankets. Every day they were easy prey to all varieties of thieves and con artists, many of whom spoke Yiddish and knew exactly how to take advantage of these latest refugees. Rumors of white slavers, searching for young women to sell into prostitution, circulated through the small groups of women who clung together day and night. At home Mindl had heard the whispered warnings from her mother's relatives and felt herself tingle with excitement. Now the dangers seemed much more real and she was constantly afraid. She could not talk to Itke. She felt no closeness toward this woman who was not her mother and who did not treat her as a daughter. She made herself wait until the little children fell asleep; then she gave in to tears, wishing she were home in the *shtetl* in the dark smoky room with her own family. If only the real journey would begin, she could concentrate on the future and put fear and homesickness behind her.

The days dragged on as they sat in a large hall waiting for their names to be called. They were herded this way and that, lined up, counted off, separated from their baggage, inspected, scrubbed, disinfected, vaccinated. The steamship companies took every precaution not to allow passage to someone who would not pass the rigorous medical examinations at Ellis Island and have to be returned to Hamburg at company expense. New friends heard their names and with hasty teary goodbyes left for their steamer. Mindl grew thin and pale as she waited for her turn. But eventually the day came when she, too, boarded a ship.

She stood on the deck and looked around her as others jostled for a place at the rail. This would be her world for the next ten days and she was curious to explore. But they were quickly hustled below decks by narrow slippery ladders into their steerage compartments. Poor Jews traveled in third-class accommodations at the very bottom of the ship where they felt every movement of the waves. In the dim light Mindl saw rows of narrow cots, each no larger than two feet wide, stacked three high. Once night came and the fading light from the sky no longer traveled through the hatch above her head, it would be pitch black.

She watched the others place all their belongings on the cots where they would sleep. They would use their bundles as pillows. That was the only safe option. They were issued thin blankets which she would soon learn did nothing to keep her protected from the chilling sea air. She felt a rolling beneath her feet as the ship left the dock and steamed up the Elbe toward the North Sea. Itke lay on her cot. Mindl gathered the children and went up the ladder to watch.

She was about to have her first glimpse of the open sea and nothing she had imagined prepared her for the gray waves rolling so far below her and endlessly out to the horizon. She had never seen sky so immense. At home in the *shtetl* it ended over the woods on the other side of the crooked brook where, even in winter, the women had washed the laundry. On the journey by *drosky* and train she had glimpsed fields larger and rivers wider than any she had known at home but this view from the deck of her ship grabbed at her breath. She turned to look back at the river and the city they were leaving behind. What would America look like if this was just Hamburg?

A damp cold wind chased them below. From all around her, she heard moans and wails and curses as the dreaded seasickness began to hit. The North Sea churned all night and few in steerage were spared. Once, when Mindl thought to make her way in the dark to the women's washroom, she slipped and fell as water and vomit sloshed through the passageway. She learned to stay on her cot and avoid all movement which only made the nausea worse. She was sure she would die there in that dark putrid place. She wished she would. For two or three days she did not eat or drink. Her skin grew dry and her eyes sunken. A neighbor from the next bunk, feeling better, brought Mindl sips of water and, eventually, a bit of Zwieback.

As she recovered her strength, she began to tune in to her surroundings. Her companions had discovered that on this steamer they were unlucky. Despite what they had been promised in Hamburg, the food sent down to them in pails was not kosher. Clearly the cooks did not know the fine points of Jewish dietary laws. Or they did not care. The women asked for hot water and they all lived on tea and the biscuits and crackers they had brought with them.

Mindl became ashamed of her appearance. In Hamburg, she had taken off one of the two coats her father had given her and packed it away. Now, sitting on her cot, she took off the stained, smelly one she was wearing and switched to the other. She changed her kerchief for a new one from her bag. She wanted desperately to wash herself and her dress free of the smell of vomit. In the *shtetl* her mother would make her way to do laundry in the stream even during the coldest winter weeks, saying, "We may be poor, but we don't have to be dirty." But she was too modest to change more than her coat in those crowded rooms and she dared not leave anything, even dirty smelly clothes, lying around for someone to take. When she went again to the washrooms she was distressed to find that there was no soap and the sinks had been used as slop basins.

It did not help that everyone else was as dirty and tired and unkempt as she. Her only consolation was going up on deck and she spent every free moment there. Steerage passengers were allotted only a small portion of deck, usually right below the smokestacks.

I examined stark black and white photographs of immigrant men and women crowded together on a ship's deck, coaxing warmth into their bodies after days in steerage. I looked closely trying to see Mindl there. Was that she? The young woman with her kerchief off and a single braid down her back? Or this one here, pinched face turned up to the sun? Or over there, in the background, slightly out of focus—was that Mindl?

I know the sun and sea breezes must have revived her spirits. When she had the children with her, she sought out a cramped corner where they could play some games. When she went alone, she made her way through the tightly bunched crowds, drawing close to some of the younger travelers. Too shy to talk much, I think, she would have watched and listened. A few were turning pages in books. The women were wearing *shtetl* clothes and she wondered how they had learned to read and she had not. Mindl knew that her mother had once learned to read and write, but there were no books in the household by the time she was growing up. There was no discussion of sending her to the *rebbe*, even though she knew her two younger brothers would study with him. Her father read from the Torah and she and her mother prayed from their memories, but she had never considered reading was a skill she could have. Sitting alone in the sun, watching her fellow passengers, she must have hoped she could still learn and added that to her list of dreams for her life in America.

Sometimes when groups broke out singing, stomping their feet and clapping their hands to the sounds of traditional folk songs, Mindl drew near to them. But mostly my grandmother would have kept to herself. She drew courage to take off her head scarf as some of the other women did and felt the breeze through her hair. She was fortunate. The weather stayed fine for most of her journey and as long as the sun shone during the day, she could endure the minimal food, the filthy toilets, and the long noisy nights when she was confined below on her tiny cot.

Mindl was down in steerage when she heard the first shouts from above. In the pre-dawn light, passengers had spotted land and soon everyone was clambering up the ladders trying to find a place near the railings. It was a while before she could see anything. Men and women in front of her had hoisted their children on their shoulders to see America.

The steamer approached New York along the southern shore of Long Island and entered the Narrows, making its way between Staten Island and Brooklyn. Ahead, off the port side of the ship, the Statue of Liberty came into view and the tired passengers knew for certain they had arrived in America.

Almost a century later, I stood at the pier on Ellis Island, looking out over the water. Tour boats and ferries crisscrossed the bay, their loudspeaker announcements audible on shore. The Verrazano Bridge spanning the Narrows glistened in late afternoon sun. But it was surprisingly easy to wipe out those modern touches and imagine a steamer filled with anxious immigrants coming toward me. I struggled to see Mindl at the rail, just as she no doubt struggled to see New York, the city that held her future.

Even before their feet touched firm ground, men in uniforms shouted at them in many languages. The travelers streamed down the gangplank, up the path and through the double doors just behind me where more officials shouted.

"Bags and boxes here."

"Men this way."

"Women and children over there."

My grandmother was a fourteen-year-old Jewish girl, her eyes wide and darting round, trying to follow the confusing instructions. The medical inspection card she'd received on the ship was gripped between her teeth. She had been told to keep it handy for the doctors, but her arms and hands were filled with bundles. As they piled their luggage in the center of the room, wondering if they'd ever find it again, her group of women and children was herded toward the stairs at the end of the room.

They did not know that climbing the many steps to the second-floor Registry Room was their first medical test. Immigration doctors stood at the top looking down as the tired women, children clinging to their skirts, trudged up the flights of stairs. Any sign of weakness, stumbling, shortness of breath might merit a chalk mark on the person's coat lapel. Other teams of doctors evaluated each immigrant's face, eyes, neck, and hands. A code of chalk marks indicated pregnancy, scalp infection, trachoma, and other medical conditions. Each mark required a further examination before the immigrant was cleared. Historians say that because the crowds were so vast, each medical exam lasted no more than six seconds. And only 2% of immigrants were ultimately denied entry to America. But stories of the inspections had taken on outsized proportions and every woman was terrified of being sent back or being separated from her child.

What the immigration officials couldn't evaluate was their deep embarrassment as a stranger in this new country examined their bodies in public. That feeling must have been intense for a sheltered young girl like my grandmother. But Mindl passed the medical inspection, her health certificate was stamped, and she moved down the lines in Registry Hall.

As I walked down that cavernous space, almost empty in late afternoon, I had time to look up at the arched tile ceiling and down at the highly polished brick floor. Three large half-moon windows punctuated each side wall. The view out the left was toward open water and the immigrants' past, the world they had left behind. Out the right was the skyline of Manhattan, where their future lay. Straight ahead were the high desks where they were to be inspected one final time. Behind those desks lay the door to a new life.

Before the travelers had boarded their steamer back in Hamburg, the steamship company had asked them a series of 29 questions and recorded the answers on the ship's manifest. The officials seated on high stools behind the desks could ask any of the 29 questions to confirm the immigrant's identity and worthiness to be admitted to the United States.

Because the questions for each immigrant covered facts like age, place and date of birth, names of parents and next of kin, skills, amount of money being carried and whether or not a job was waiting, I would know so much more about my grandmother if I had been able to find a manifest entry for her. But I felt her anxiety as she approached the desk. She had rehearsed her answers many times. She knew what she had told the steamship officials back in Hamburg, but she worried she would make a mistake and the official would determine her real identity. She would be sent back to the Pale, perhaps even imprisoned.

An interpreter standing beside the official translated for her. She answered two, three, maybe four questions. The official had only two minutes to make his decision. He nodded at her, waved her through the turnstile. Someone pinned a landing card on her coat and Mindl found herself facing the steep divided staircase known to generations of immigrants as the Stairs of Separation. Immigrants headed for trains to western destinations descended the right staircase toward the railroad ticket offices. Those who were to be detained on Ellis Island were separated from their families and shepherded down the center. Mindl and all the others headed for New York City were instructed to use the stairs on the left and pass through the door at the bottom.

I walked down the same black steps, now worn and uneven, through the same door. Mindl, like almost every other immigrant, past and present, faced a difficult and uncertain future. But at the moment she walked through that door, she must have been exhilarated. She had finished the miserable sea voyage. She had passed the tests. She had crossed into the promised land. She could not have guessed what I know. Her hard-earned future would not last long.

Chapter 3
Minnie

There she was, my grandmother, wearing her *shtetl* clothes, carrying her few possessions, trying to banish the motion of the ship, watching where she stepped to avoid the horse manure and rotting fruit, assaulted by strange noises, smells, and sights, bewildered, hungry, anxious but excited. She had made it to America.

Unlike some of the other women she had met in steerage, she had a place to stay. Wherever it was, however small, Mindl expected to be safe. But it did not take long for her to recognize that her role had changed. She felt her isolation immediately as the small group walked through the maze of streets from the docks to their tenement. Husband and wife wanted to catch up on years of news that their letters could not convey. She had no part in that conversation. The children transferred their allegiance from her to their father, tugging at his sleeves and dancing through the crowds to catch his attention.

Everyone they passed, men, women, and children, shouted, pushed, and shoved. Mindl had to struggle to keep her balance, but as she adjusted to the din, she found she could grasp much of what everyone was saying. She had arrived in the Tenth Ward of New York's Lower East Side, the most densely populated place on earth. Hundreds of thousands of Eastern European Jews had come before her and settled on these streets. Like other newcomers, she was terrified of the crowds, but she took solace in the familiar language.

When they reached the dark tenement rooms, Mindl saw just how her status had changed. She would be more boarder than daughter. Itke assigned her to sleep in the kitchen where at night her bed would be a board resting between two chairs. The parents shared the only real bed with the two littlest ones. The older children slept together in the parlor. The kitchen, in the middle of their three-room, cold water flat, which would have totaled no more than 325 square feet, was dark and oppressive. She consoled herself, recognizing that at least for the nighttime hours, she would have some privacy.

When she woke the next morning, she found little else to console her. If she looked out the grimy side window of their tiny apartment, she saw across an airshaft to another tenement's brick wall. If she looked out the parlor window toward the street, she saw dirt and garbage and narrow buildings jammed together as tightly as the double rows of pushcarts. She was stunned by the height of the buildings, the maze of congested streets, the tumult of carts and wagons and people. Already she longed for the sunlight and open spaces she had left behind in the *shtetl*. Dirt roads ran through their town and the woods grew thinner and further away each year, but in her memory they were still thick and beautiful. She wondered how she would ever live without sun and fields. Seward Park, only a few blocks east of where she lived, seemed small comfort. Later, I think, she and Benjamin would find it a refuge, a place to walk and talk by themselves.

Gradually Mindl discovered she loved the hustle and bustle of life on the streets. Even in those first days it was an escape to leave the apartment where already husband and wife were fighting. The energy surrounding the pushcarts, the rows and rows of unfamiliar merchandise in shop windows, the crowds of children at play made her optimistic about her own future once she too became a part of America.

Very soon Mindl would have set out to find work. The family, worried about her contribution to their rent, gave her the name of a man who needed unskilled labor and even pointed her in the right direction. Mindl walked up dark narrow stairs shortly after six in the morning and entered a room filled with the harsh noise of machinery. She had not eaten breakfast, but she had been told to bring a roll for lunch in case she was hired. Seven or eight other young girls, already at work, barely looked up from their sewing. The men who operated the machines ignored her, too.

Eventually, one man separated himself from his work and gruffly questioned her. When Mindl said she could sew, he grumbled, "We'll see," and cleared a place for her at the table with the other girls. He gave her a pile of men's jackets and told her to baste the lapels. All day, she worked side by side with the other girls. No one talked or even looked in her direction. Occasionally, the boss came over to check her work and, eventually, he added to her pile. At the end of the day, he told her to come back tomorrow. "Be here earlier." She was expected to work from 6am to 6pm. Her wages would be $3 a week—but she would be fined if she was late or talked while she worked or broke a needle or spent too much time in the bathroom.

She left the shop exhausted and hungry, horrified at the prospect of the days that stretched before her. When she had been home in the *shtetl* with her own family and making the decision to leave, she never envisioned the work in America would be so hard. But a small part of her was also elated. She had found her first job. She could send word home and claim success in her new life. Perhaps she would even make friends with the other girls around the table. And surely she would be able to find better work soon.

I like to think that one of the things Mindl did with her first wages was set out to buy new clothes. On Grand Street she had watched young women walking down the wide sidewalks, wearing hats instead of kerchiefs, shoes instead of boots, and shirtwaists in styles and fabrics she had never seen. Even their hair was worn so differently. She found a shop where she heard familiar Yiddish. Nervous and shy as any greenhorn, but resolutely remembering her mother at the *shtetl* markets, she haggled over the price—successfully she thought. She did not know quality nor could she have afforded it if she did; she was delighted with her few purchases. She could not have seen the shop owner and his wife smirk as she left. She would learn to make friends with the men who sold hats and shoes and fabric from their pushcarts; there were far better bargains to be found once she knew her way around the neighborhood.

When did Mindl change her name to Minnie? Was it difficult for her to let go of her old identity? Or as easy as buying the new clothes that helped her blend into her new surroundings? When I was first researching my family, I read that Ellis Island officials deliberately changed the immigrants' names because they could not pronounce so many foreign surnames and given names. Historians say that's only partially true; the officials worked with the names written on the ships' manifests. Poor handwriting certainly accounted for the many variant spellings of names and impatience with illiterate foreigners contributed to the confusion. But many immigrants changed their own names as they tried to adapt to life in their new country. They sometimes changed them several times; often they kept two names, one spoken and heard only in the family and one for the outside world.

The girls around her sewing table told Mindl that she should claim an American name. What was taking her so long? They had become Anna and Rose and Bessie. A neighbor down the hall in her tenement told the story of another Mindl, from a village not too far from hers, who had become Minnie. There was no one to affectionately call her Mindele anymore now that she was so far from her family. In the tenement they called her Mindl only to shout at her. So one day my grandmother announced to her companions around the table that she was now Minnie.

But the change in name didn't change her situation in the sweatshop or in the tenement. She rose and dressed each morning in the dark. Even when sunrise had happened in the outside world, no light reached the kitchen. It smelled of unwashed bodies and boiled cabbage. No matter how early she slipped out into the dank hall, there was a line for the two bathrooms that all occupants of the four apartments on the floor shared. She waited, leaning against the wall, cold and impatient. On days when she was menstruating, she was embarrassed to be carrying her overnight rags. She was expected to put on the kettle and clean up the kitchen before she left for work, but some days she was too late and she sneaked out of the tenement, running to be on time.

When she slid into her chair just as the bell sounded, one of the burly men who operated the machine across from her leered and raised his eyebrows. She blushed, ducking her head over the pile of jackets in front of her. Her fingers toughened; they no longer bled as she pushed her needle through the heavy fabric. But with increasing speed came more pressure. The boss now knew she could sew and he tossed higher and higher piles in front of her. Like most beginners, she worked by the hour; speed was everything and there were no breaks in the routine. The girls were friendlier, but they were not free to talk much and at the end of their day they were all too tired to linger. Many days she went back to the apartment with a headache. She was still expected to scrub the torn linoleum floors, peel potatoes, bring in the wash from the line, whatever Itke had not been able to finish while she sewed at home and cared for the youngest ones.

Minnie discovered that her weekly $3 earnings were vulnerable. Fines were unpredictable—whenever the boss chose, it seemed— and when orders slowed down, she was the first to be told to "stay home tomorrow." No matter how fast she worked, she was not yet as good as the other women.

During those "stay home" days she devised ways to escape Itke's demands and spent hours roaming the neighborhoods. The Lower East Side that Minnie saw was a mixture of many neighborhoods. In her time, no one used that familiar urban term, which now delineates such a large swath of Manhattan real estate. There were no formal boundaries. Crowded tenements, narrow congested streets and slum-like conditions pervaded not only the Russian Jewish district but also the Hungarian and Galician and Rumanian areas as well as the Chinese, Irish, and Italian blocks.

The Russian Jewish neighborhood extended from Grand Street to Monroe to Jackson, a teeming blunt-edged triangle. Within its casual borders were parts of Hester, Orchard, Eldridge, and Canal Streets, providing enough variety to keep Minnie's walks exciting. She did not need to venture into dangerous Gentile streets.

Everything in her new country was an education. The English alphabet puzzled her. The names of the streets intrigued her, but she had no way to learn about the early Americans whose names they bore: Lieutenant Eldridge killed in the War of 1812; Hester Rynders, the daughter of a lieutenant governor of New York; James deLancey, chief justice of the New York Supreme Court. His graceful orchards would have been unimaginable to the tired women who had to haggle for every apple at the pushcarts lining the street.

If Minnie walked one way, she passed landmarks that had already changed the lives of many of her fellow immigrants—the Henry Street Settlement House, the Educational Alliance, the Seward Street Library, the Jewish Maternity Hospital. Another way she saw the Grand Theater, the Thalia Theater or the Eldridge Street Synagogue. Right in the throbbing heart of her neighborhood were the markets along Orchard and Hester.

These were her favorite destinations. Minnie recognized chickens and geese, but there were also varieties of meat, fish, fruit, vegetables, and bread she had never encountered. Bananas, apples, herring, horseradish—the smells mixed together and hovered over the crowds. On Friday mornings, in preparation for the Sabbath, the corner of Hester and Ludlow Streets swarmed with even more shoppers at the Pig Market—ironically named because it did not sell pigs. She wondered sometimes what her mother would think about these streets, in some ways similar and yet so different from market days in the *shtetl*.

But there was more than food and housewares and clothes to catch Minnie's eye on these walks. In the crowded space that had become her world, all life, even its most private moments, was on display. No private zones existed when large families and their boarders lived together in three rooms. In summer everyone slept together on roof tops or fire escapes. On the streets, she saw children playing, but also young couples stealing kisses. She heard women cry out in childbirth and sing to their infants, but the same women had harsh voices to berate their husbands and the peddlers who tried to cheat them.

One day, hungry and increasingly anxious, she understood that she could not patiently wait to be called back to work. She had to find a place in another shop. This would have happened to her again and again; it was a typical immigrant woman's story.

Eventually, as she gained experience and made some friends, she found a place where she could work by the piece instead of by an hourly or weekly wage. If the shop's boss was tolerable, that made her a little happier. Whether she sewed hats or ladies' shirtwaists or men's suit jackets, the work was the same—monotonous and tiring; the conditions as bad—poor sanitation, dim lighting, and stagnant air; and the opportunities for harassment from the boss or male workers unchanging. With piece work, there was less pressure from an irascible boss but she still had to work fast to earn enough to live. There was competition among the women, all of whom needed more money, but there was also camaraderie. They talked more and sometimes laughed and Minnie gradually made friends she could see in the evenings or on her half day off. She learned to smile again.

Her loneliness began to fade, but her relationship with the family from her old village grew worse. They wanted her out. Her income was undependable; she got home so tired that she was no help with dinner or the children. She lingered in bed too late in the morning. She wasn't paying off her debt fast enough and she was brazen enough to buy an occasional trinket from one of the peddlers. Many immigrant families preferred male boarders; they were certainly more numerous and their wages were usually higher.

Minnie moved from one tenement apartment to another, seeking a cheaper rent or less crowded conditions or a better landlady. My grandmother had few other options. Living on her own in a tiny apartment, as I did so many years later, was not a possibility. She could never have afforded the rent. But, more important, it was so scandalous that someone would surely have sent news back to the old country and it would have reached her *shtetl*, shaming her family. She might have found a place in a public rooming house, but they were not deemed safe for nice young women. Or she could have moved in with another girl, perhaps someone she met at the shop. If they each earned $3 or $4 a week, they could have afforded to rent a one-room apartment and buy food and even save a bit for small pleasures. One young woman whose memories are anonymously preserved shared a room with a friend. After listing their expenses, which included basics like tea and potatoes and bread, but also meat and laundry, she added, "Of course, we could have lived cheaper, but we are both fond of good things and felt that we could afford them."

Minnie probably had five years between her arrival at Ellis Island in 1906 and the birth of my mother in 1911. I like to conjecture that she, too, grew fond of good things, at least for a while. I see her buying fabric from a peddler who had saved some remnants for her and learning to make stylish blouses for herself. She bought a couple of straw hats for ten cents each and a good pair of shoes on sale for 50 cents. She moved in with a friend and together they talked and laughed as they cooked, speaking mostly in Yiddish but practicing a few English words, too. They splurged on trips to the ice cream parlor and the candy store, indulging a new taste for chocolate.

When and how did Minnie meet Benjamin? I have looked at photographs of my mother as a young woman and tried to envision my grandmother at 17 or 18. I have learned that Benjamin was unusually tall for a Jewish man in that era. So I think Minnie was short, like my mother, perhaps buxom, too, like her. She was not a head-turner, but prettier than her mother thought back in the Old Country, with dark curly hair that escaped whatever hat she wore. Her face was drawn, with working and worrying and poor choices of food and her skin sallow. But her eyes, large, dark and wide-set, near-sighted, like my mother's, would have shown a sharp interest in everything around her. She would have had a slow but genuine smile and a high lilting laugh whenever she let it loose.

Perhaps they met at a dance hall. In 1907, there were 31 dance halls between Houston and Grand Streets, east of Broadway. The most popular attracted between 500 and 1200 young people on a single evening. The young women, arriving together with their friends, paid as little as five cents admission; the young men paid ten cents. *The Forward* warned frequently about the dangers of white slavers among the dance "professors," but like most of her contemporaries, eager for a break from hard work and cheerless apartments, Minnie now laughed at the warnings. She loved the music and high spirits of the evening. And she would certainly have welcomed an opportunity to meet a young man.

I imagine Minnie and Benjamin falling in love, trying to spend time together. But in the congested environment around them, there was no privacy anywhere. They talked as they walked the cluttered streets, getting to know each other; they lingered and kissed under streetlights or in hallways. They went to the nickel show and they sat on benches in Seward Park, anonymous among the old men reading newspapers.

As I walked along Essex Street, which still forms one boundary of the small park, I erased the high rise Seward Park Houses dominating the skyline north and east. I erased the colorful slides and climbing bars destined for this generation of immigrant children. I relaxed into the late winter sun and tried to summon up what happened next to the young Jewish couple who became my grandparents.

Did they make plans for a wedding? Did Benjamin bring her to meet his family or keep their love a secret? Did he take advantage of her naiveté? Did they lie together on a rooftop late one September night—when cool weather had already sent the others below to crowded kitchens and parlors?

My mother's birth certificate says her mother was Minnie Seidman, maiden name Schneider. But perhaps, like many other couples, they did not tell the truth. Because I cannot find a marriage certificate for them, I cannot allow myself images of a proper Jewish wedding. I cannot see Minnie making or buying or even renting her wedding dress; I cannot envision them standing together under a velvet canopy while a rabbi performs the traditional ceremony. No ring, no wine, no broken glass, no wedding guests crying "*Mazel tov.*" Saddest of all, no photograph to capture and preserve a moment in a family's history.

But there was a baby. Some time between September, 1910, and my mother's birth nine months later, Minnie and Benjamin moved to 36 Orchard Street. They did not live there in the spring of 1910 when the census was taken; but there they were, with newborn Beckie, one year later.

The building has remained inscrutable; I have not been able to penetrate its façade nor find any trace of Minnie, Benjamin, and

Beckie. I followed an intriguing lead I discovered in a 1930s photo of the building. The first floor shows a tailor shop, selling dresses and boys' suits, and the sign says "Jack Schneider & Bro." The coincidence promised more, but my hope, that Jack Schneider and his brothers were family to Minnie, evaporated as I looked further. No such business was located at 36 Orchard in 1910 or 1920 or even in 1925.

Compared to other tenement streets, this address, so close to the intersection of Orchard and Hester, must have been among the least desirable. Both streets were market streets—crammed with wagons and pushcarts from first light. The noise and dirt and stench of the market would have permeated all the apartments. Most of the families living in apartments at 36 Orchard in 1910 were no longer "greenhorns," the term the immigrants themselves used to describe the latest to arrive; they had arrived in 1906 or 1908, some as early as 1904. But they were still perched precariously on the lowest rungs of immigrant society. The men were peddlers or "stand keepers." The daughters worked in a "factory" on "ladies waists" or "millinery" or "cloaks." Elie Schnick and his wife Matl had six sons. William Rabinowitz and his wife had two daughters, ages two and seven months. Israel and Mollie Lustgarten had five children and three boarders, all named Pell. The Huidman family had two young children and four boarders, all men. One of Sarah Huidman's young daughters was named Beckie. Did my pregnant grandmother visit Sarah, play with her little girl? Is that how my mother's name was chosen?

Some of the 1910 census pages are missing—or the census taker gave up one day—because I could only find these four families for an address that would likely have housed at least 16 families plus boarders, in four apartments on each of the four floors. So it's possible some missing records would show that my grandparents had set up housekeeping there, but, more likely, Minnie and Benjamin moved into 36 sometime after they learned of the pregnancy in late 1910 or early 1911. Whoever welcomed them—or at least offered them shelter that winter—will remain a mystery.

Whenever I wandered the neighborhood, the entry door to

the small foyer for the upstairs apartments remained locked; the mailboxes and door buzzers for ten apartments were visible but tantalizing out of reach. No one came or went so I could not beg a visit. Once a For Rent sign hung on the door, but when I called the agent, the apartment had already been taken.

I occasionally stopped in the sleek art gallery that occupied the ground floor. I told one of the interns that in 1911 my grandmother brought her newborn home to an apartment upstairs and she mused on how buildings change. "This space used to be a Buddhist temple," she said. "See how the floor tilts upward toward the back? That's where the shrine was." She wandered away and I walked through the gallery, my mind on the past, wondering what changes have taken place upstairs. Yes, air conditioners and better plumbing. But what odors slip through the walls? Have all the *mezuzahs* been removed from the doorposts? What accented English echoes in the hallways? Are there any babies crying? Slowly I focused on the exhibit. I was surrounded by large photographs without an image. I was expecting windows onto other realities but their silvery time-exposed sheen reflected only my own out-of-focus features.

It is curious that Minnie had her baby at the Jewish Maternity Hospital. In her neighborhood, in the early twentieth century, women preferred to have their babies at home with a midwife present. The Jewish women living there were not unusual. In 1905, 42% of births in the city of New York were attended by midwives. Young immigrant mothers, whatever their nationality, trusted one of their own. A midwife knew the traditions and remedies of a shared past from the Old Country; she spoke the same language; she served as friend and advisor as well as provided medical care. Often she stayed after the birth and visited regularly to help the young mother. As important, a midwife charged far less than a doctor and hospital.

But if there were complications with Minnie's pregnancy, the midwife could have suggested a doctor and he, in turn, insisted on the hospital. For women like Minnie the hospital was a place to fear, where people went to die. And yet the Jewish Maternity Hospital, at 272 East Broadway, only a few blocks east of Seward Park, was a welcoming place for Jewish women. A biographer of the dancer Jerome Robbins noted that although his parents lived on East 97th Street, he was born at Jewish Maternity Hospital because his mother sought a place where the doctors spoke Yiddish and they served kosher meals.

The hospital provided good medical care but also a measure beyond. When 50 babies arrived in one week during early 1911, just a few months before Minnie gave birth to Beckie, the nurse in charge instituted a new method of identifying the infants by numbered and lettered bracelets so that a mother "has the satisfaction of knowing positively" that it is "her own little morsel of humanity she is kissing." The *New York Times* account added, "Even the three sets of twins are properly marked for identification."

In 1912, the paper reported the births of "three male children, weighing about five pounds each" to a Russian Jewish couple who "have been in this country only two years." The attending doctor planned to "notify Col. Roosevelt of the arrival of the triplets by telegraph." He also prevented the mother from walking home some five hours after giving birth.

Minnie would have been well cared for—and comfortable. The rooms were clean and certainly larger than back on Orchard Street. The hospital corridors were quiet to ears so accustomed to street noise. What a pleasure to have good plentiful food served to you. The doctors and nurses were strict in their instructions, but they were friendly, too. She learned to trust them with her baby.

How long did Minnie stay in the hospital? Who paid the bill? Was there anyone to help her when she returned home? All my questions resist answers. I can guess that Beckie was a healthy baby; certainly she survived her earliest days and sometime within her first years arrived at a foster home in the Bronx. But something more tragic happened to Minnie. Either she never recuperated from childbirth or she succumbed to infection or disease in the months after she left Jewish Maternity Hospital.

So many young girls who worked in the factories and sweatshops and lived on meager rations suffered from anemia or pneumonia or, worse, contracted tuberculosis, known as "the white plague" or "the tailors' disease." Serious diseases like scarlet fever and typhoid were treated at home. Cleanliness was an impossible dream. Jewish women who followed religious traditions were required to take *mikveh* baths within seven days after menstruation. Many baths were located in basements of tenements and the water, rarely changed, became foul. Given the conditions—too much work, too little food and fresh air, abysmal sanitary facilities at home and at work, food that rotted in the streets, rodents that ventured out from cracked walls, overflowing sewers and gutters—illness kept the upper hand.

Over and over I returned to the only memory that had been passed on to me: "Rita's mother died and her father couldn't take care of her."

Friends tried to help me find evidence of Minnie's death. One reminded me of the tragic fire at the Triangle Shirtwaist factory when more than 140 young women like Minnie died at their sewing machines. "I think it happened in 1911," she said.

And so it did—but on March 25, two months before Beckie's birth. I found myself perversely wishing that Minnie had died in the Triangle Fire. Then, I told myself, I would at least have details about her death and a community of mourners to join. Another friend suggested she might have died in prison and that such deaths would not be noticed. I did not want to imagine the crime, but I checked it out. Death certificates for prisoners were filed. Or, depressed and ill, Minnie committed suicide. In those years, many young women "took the gas," *genumen di gez,* as the papers wrote. Perhaps one more such suicide was just overlooked. But Minnie had a baby. And Benjamin was either husband or boyfriend. Did he desert her? The Yiddish papers also wrote of many such desertions.

More likely, I have concluded, Minnie left New York City. If she contracted tuberculosis, she would have been sent to one of the many sanitariums in upstate New York that cared for thousands of Jewish patients in the early decades of the twentieth century. The death certificate would have been filed in one or another upstate county and burial might have been there, too. The trail grew impossibly cold. But I am haunted by not knowing. Was anyone there to sit *shiva* for her? Who sent word to her small family?

I believe that, married or not, Benjamin mourned Minnie. I have uncovered oblique evidence that he loved her. But with no money and no help from his family, he decided he could not care for their baby and he found a way to place Beckie in foster care. My grandmother left behind no family treasures, only a baby, who will grow up thirteen miles to the north, still in a tenement, but worlds away in family, culture, and religion.

Whatever end I conjured for Minnie, I could not evade a tragedy. The past is "filled with jagged edges," historian Elizabeth Ewen has written. She was describing large contexts; I am chronicling one family's narrative. A mother died. A baby, placed in foster care, grew into a woman who kept the story a secret for 86 years. The edges have remained jagged through generations.

Chapter 4
Benjamin

It took me a long time to turn my attention to my Jewish grandfather. I wanted to linger with Minnie, mourning her early death, trying every avenue to find her. But Benjamin Seidman must have been the parent who placed my mother in foster care, setting in motion her transformation from Jewish baby to Catholic girl. I wanted to understand why. I discovered that, unlike Minnie, Benjamin had left a long paper trail and, to my joy, the search led to living voices, Jewish relatives who have filled empty spaces in my life.

The right man was at first elusive. Among several Benjamin Seidmans, I began to focus on one—a Jewish man originally from Minsk, who, in the 1930 census, was married to a woman named Sophie. They had four children by then and lived in Brooklyn. Some of that sounded wrong, but his date of birth was approximately that of the Benjamin who was my grandfather. One intriguing detail lodged in my mind. This Benjamin had a daughter named Minnie.

Gradually I assembled more documents about him, building a paper portrait. On his Social Security application, dated 1939, his place of birth matched. From his death certificate, where again birthplace and date matched, I learned that his father was named Louis and his mother, Sarah. Those could be my great grandparents. That new information thrilled me, but so many dashed hopes during my search for Minnie had taught me caution. I could well be sleuthing the wrong family.

The need for caution became even clearer when I retrieved this

Benjamin's marriage certificate. He was married to Sophie Kasden in 1916 at the age of 26. Both bride and groom attested that it was a first marriage. I had wanted to see "second marriage" for Benjamin, proving my case for his earlier marriage to my grandmother Minnie and tying all the evidence in a tight knot. But the link remained tenuous at best. Still, the date of the wedding left an opening. My mother had been born in 1911; Benjamin had come to New York in 1906 and married Sophie in 1916. There would have been time for an earlier marriage or relationship, producing the child, Beckie, whom he placed in foster care.

I had to move beyond the documents if I were ever going to know more. When I looked again at the 1930 census I noticed that Alvin, the son who had signed Benjamin's death certificate in 1968, had not yet been born. That would put him in his 70s. I called an Alvin Seidman in Florida and wrote to another on Long Island. Nice men, both, and approximately the right age, but neither had a father named Benjamin. Finally, it occurred to me that Alvin might have died—and indeed he had, at the age of 45, only seven years after his father. His death was reported in 1975 by his wife, Rosalind Seidman, living in Brooklyn. Benjamin's wife, Sophie, died three years later. Her death certificate was signed by her daughter, Minnie, also living in Brooklyn.

These two women, Rosalind and Minnie, if I could find them, could challenge or confirm my hypothesis. Their memories could enhance the sterile portrait I had pasted together from documents. Or they could tell me positively that I had the wrong man. I worried about how they would react. What would they say to a total stranger, a Catholic woman from New Jersey who, without much proof, says she might be part of their New York City Jewish family?

One December, shortly before the holidays, I wrote to Rosalind, Benjamin's daughter-in-law, inviting her to contact me. Within the week, she called. I sensed I was talking to someone smart and decisive but also friendly and curious. I was edgy, talking too fast, spinning out too many details, stumbling over facts. But her calm questions were insightful. She grasped the complicated relationships I was describing.

"Benjamin was a handful," she said, "even in his later years when I knew him. I wouldn't be at all surprised if he is your grandfather."

We had jumped over the niceties and landed so quickly at a conclusion that I was left breathless.

Although she had no proof, Rosalind believed it was certainly possible that Benjamin had a child before he married Sophie. But she was dismissive of my key piece of evidence: a daughter named Minnie. I did not understand Jewish families, she told me firmly. Jewish people only named a child after someone who had already passed away. I was not quick enough then to share my conjecture: that my grandmother Minnie had been dead for ten years or more by the time Benjamin's second daughter was born. Rosalind also did not believe it at all likely that a man would name a child after a woman who was his former wife or the unwed mother of his first child. Later, Melanie, my son's partner, who taught women's studies, would tell me that in class discussions about naming, her students sometimes reported they were named "after my dad's first girlfriend."

Rosalind and I spent the rest of our conversation getting to know each other. She talked about her three sons and one daughter and five grandchildren, three of whom lived nearby in Brooklyn. She had been a widow and a single mother for more than 25 years.

She had called me because she was working on research about her own ancestors and was intrigued to meet a woman doing the same thing. I told her about the places I had visited—Ellis Island, the Lower East Side Tenement Museum, the Eldridge Street Synagogue. Perhaps we could meet, she said, go to the archives together.

At the end of the conversation—perhaps after she had become comfortable with me—she offered that she was no longer close to many in the Seidman family. She was an in-law and not very welcome. But she was in touch with one niece, Ellen, Benjamin's granddaughter, a woman who would therefore be my cousin.

Shortly after the holidays we talked again and she gave me a phone number for Ellen. I was welcome to call. It would be many months before Rosalind and I could arrange our schedules to meet in the city, but within days I called Ellen in Florida, where she was caring for her mother who had had an incapacitating stroke.

Ellen's voice was embracing. She had spoken to Rosalind; she thought it would be wonderful if it turned out we were cousins. And she was delighted to have an opportunity to talk about her grandparents. Her early childhood, like mine, had happened against the background of World War II. Her father was in the military and her mother worked long hours so Ellen practically lived with her grandparents.

"I remember those years in Technicolor," she said.

She described her grandmother as "a mythic character" and, as I will learn, Ellen had absorbed her spiritual dimensions. While Sophie got positive reviews, not so Benjamin. Sophie may have had a mystical strain, but Benjamin had a rebellious one. Ellen tried hard to give me a balanced portrait, but we started with her conclusion.

"It wouldn't surprise me if Benjamin had a previous wife and daughter."

Her words were stunningly similar to Rosalind's. But she filled in many more details about Benjamin's personality and she bolstered her descriptions with narrative. In one hour, on a Sunday evening, we reached across silences and secrets, allowing me to know the man who was probably my grandfather, whose name I had not heard or seen until after my mother had died.

When I hung up the phone and looked at my scribbled notes, I was amazed I had been able to write anything. Both hands were trembling. Downstairs my husband was reading the last of the Sunday papers. But before I went down to share my news and reenter the everyday, I lingered at my desk, wanting to laugh aloud and dance. I wanted to put aside anger and sadness and puzzling questions and simply revel in the good news: I had connected to my grandfather and I had found a cousin who already felt to me like a sister.

The Benjamin who matured into a family man several years after my mother had been born and sent to live in the Bronx was a man of contradictions. He was not pleasant or particularly kind to his children or to outsiders, although he was deeply in love with Sophie. They were married for 52 years. He was a rebel and a drinker, but even in his adult years he had allowed his father to dominate him. He was an observant Jew, leading prayers at home on the Sabbath and at the Seder, but he did not faithfully follow many of the Jewish customs. *Mitzvah* did not come easily to him.

My grandfather, I now know, was exceptionally tall and fair, with reddish hair and light skin. He wore large hats. Whenever he was out in the sun, he had to sit under an umbrella. And, contrary to Jewish practice, he had tattoos. Both his daughter-in-law and his granddaughter told me about the tattoos. When Rosalind first met Benjamin, he was wearing a sleeveless shirt and his tattooed arms shocked her. As a child, Ellen worried that her grandfather could not be buried in a Jewish cemetery because he had abused his body with the tattoos.

Benjamin read and wrote English and he loved reading the newspapers. He preferred to speak Yiddish at home, but he didn't talk much to his family. The Seidman women agreed: he was a hell raiser. He was hot-tempered, a law unto himself, preferring to do things his way without consultation or compromise. He liked to fight, which was unusual for Jewish men in those days. He was a brawler, a stubborn man who was also selfish, a physical presence who did not hesitate to climb over fire escapes to continue a fight or puncture an argument by tossing someone down a flight of stairs.

In the apartment buildings where the family lived, first on the Lower East Side and then in Brooklyn, the limited supply of hot water had to be shared by all the tenants. Benjamin loved to take a long hot bath—his *bagna,* he called it—at 4:30 in the morning and he did not care about the rest of his family and the neighbors in the other apartments. If no hot water was left for them, that was their problem and he ignored all complaints.

Benjamin's trade was painting houses, inside or out. But he did not work steadily and he was not a reliable provider. The family moved around a lot. He was not an easy man to get along with—whether you were his child, his neighbor, or you wanted him to paint your apartment.

Ellen's mother had once recommended her father to a neighbor who wanted her kitchen painted. The woman chose yellow as the color and she then left the apartment. Benjamin painted it pink because, he said, he had pink paint. When she complained loudly enough for everyone in the apartment building to hear, he told her he knew she didn't want a yellow kitchen. Pink was the right color. Rosalind also told me the story of how Benjamin painted the woman's kitchen a color she didn't choose, but in her version the colors were green and blue instead of yellow and pink. Rosalind was surprisingly understanding. Maybe he was color blind, she said.

I had arrived into a new family and was hearing stories that had clearly been told before and had taken on lives of their own. It intrigues me how some narratives survive in families, told and retold, while others, contradictory or perhaps more revealing, remain dormant. That was true in my Italian and German families, too, as I would discover. This story became iconic—a way for Benjamin's children and grandchildren to convey the difficulties of living with him, and do so with some humor.

In our first conversation, Ellen and I shared more than stories about Benjamin, trying to become cousins quickly. We talked about our writing careers; our spiritual lives; our families. We agreed to meet when she returned to New York from Florida. In the meantime, she said, I should talk to Minnie, her aunt, Benjamin's younger daughter.

"She is a character but she is devoted to the family and I think she would like talking to you."

Minnie had never answered the letter I had sent her months earlier. But two days later, still delighted at my good fortune in finding the Seidman family, I called Minnie. I was ready with a polite introduction, but I got through only two sentences when she hung up on me.

The following week, I tried again. This time Minnie listened through—I had moved Ellen's name into my first sentence and told her quickly that I was not selling anything. She said abruptly that she was going out with friends, but allowed that I might call back.

I carefully selected what I hoped was a safe time—early on a Sunday evening—and called again. She was indeed more relaxed and open. I told her I was searching for my grandfather whom I believed was her father. She was amazed, not angry or defensive, but, she said, "It is not possible." Her mother would have told her. Sophie confided in Minnie; she told her everything.

We conjectured that perhaps even Sophie didn't know about the baby Beckie, who had become my mother. I asked if she knew why she was named Minnie and explained that my grandmother's name was also Minnie.

"There's nothing special about my name," she said in a tone that stopped further inquiry.

Minnie revealed herself to be a tough woman—the character Ellen predicted. She found it interesting that my mother became a Catholic and raised me Catholic, yet I was searching for a Jewish family. Why hadn't I called earlier when her mother was still alive? Sophie would have known the answers. I did not say how much I wished I had known enough to ask these questions decades earlier. Instead, I explained about the secrets my mother had kept. She understood, she said.

"My father was good as gold," Minnie concluded. He would never have abandoned a child. Besides, there was his family. They would never have allowed a child of theirs to be placed in a foster home.

Minnie's stories, contrasted to Ellen's and Rosalind's, held many contradictions. Was Benjamin good as gold? Or a brawler and a handful? If I had reached Minnie first, I might have concluded I had the wrong Benjamin. As I listened to her, it seemed likely that if this Benjamin were indeed my grandfather he had not married my grandmother. That could explain why the family didn't take in the child. If my mother had been born out of wedlock, as they said then, perhaps Benjamin never even told his family. And, if he did tell them, his father Louis, from what the women have told me, would not have been at all helpful.

Louis Seidman, my great-grandfather, was "a very, very mean old man." Those were Minnie's words, but Rosalind and Ellen agreed. If my mother had been put up for foster care or adoption, Minnie said, it would have been Louis' fault.

He was first a peddler and then went into the used furniture business. One time after he had repossessed a parlor set, he stopped by the apartment where Benjamin and Sophie were living. The furniture was in the wagon in the street. Sophie wanted the furniture because they had no furniture in their parlor and she would have loved a place to display her china. The set was heavy wood and the chairs had red plush seat covers. Benjamin asked his brothers to help unload the furniture from the wagon and take it up the stairs to his apartment. When Louis returned, he was furious. Who had told Benjamin and Sophie they could have it?

"We'll pay on time just like your other customers," they said.

"Where are you going to get the money to pay me?" he asked. "You don't have any money." He took the furniture set out of the apartment and back down to the wagon.

Louis was an Orthodox Jew, yet he was apparently married four times. That was a family secret, Minnie said when she told me. His first wife, Sarah, who would have been Benjamin's mother, my great grandmother, died. But what happened to the next three wives? If Louis had been widowed so often, why was it a family secret? Minnie told me Louis was "cheap"—he didn't give his wives any money. No money during their marriages? Or after *gittin*, Jewish bills of divorce? I asked Rosalind about divorce.

"No," she said without hesitation, "Jewish men didn't divorce."

My grandfather had an older sister, Rose, who was also tall. Rosalind told me she had never seen a woman as tall as Benjamin's sister. Rose may have been married when she came to America; she had three children, two boys and a girl. And, like her father, she too had multiple marriages—five, according to Minnie. Perhaps that was why Rosalind was so positive Benjamin's sister would not have taken a child.

"You have to understand a family," she said.

I was trying very hard to understand this family. Several weeks after our first conversation, on another Sunday evening, Minnie called back. She had been thinking.

"Do you remember asking me why I was called Minnie?"

My question had triggered her memory. "I always had a bone in my throat that I didn't have a name on my birth certificate. My brothers and sisters did. I was just 'baby.' Whenever I asked my mother why there was no name on my birth certificate, she sidetracked me." Minnie ultimately learned that her father wanted one name and her mother another. Together we conjectured that her father, who had named his first daughter Sarah after his mother, had wanted to name his second daughter after his first love. Sophie would have known the reason and resisted.

Minnie concluded, "I was my father's favorite."

And there it was—proof not in a legal document, but in a name. It was the strongest link I had found connecting that small threesome at 36 Orchard Street in May 1911—Benjamin Seidman, Minnie Schneider, and little Beckie—with the later Seidman family I have encountered almost a century later. Instinct and intuition overcame elusive facts: this Benjamin Seidman was my grandfather—a Jewish rebel who broke with tradition in many ways and dared to name a daughter after a first love, who was my grandmother.

I told Minnie how happy I was that she had called.

"We should get together," she said. "We might be sisters."

She had the generations askew—we were aunt and niece, not sisters—but the relationship was real and welcome. She had read about people finding long lost families, she said, and now it was happening to her.

And to me.

The early phone calls with Rosalind, Ellen, and Minnie led to longer personal visits with both Ellen and Rosalind. I did not have such good fortune with Minnie. A few weeks after our phone conversation, I called to arrange a lunch. Her phone was disconnected. I tried again intermittently for many months before I gave up. I sent off a card to the Brooklyn address; it was not returned but she did not call me. I asked someone skilled at investigative research to check on alternate addresses. We found several possibilities, even a few in Florida, but when I called, no one knew—or admitted they knew—a Minnie Seidman. When I asked Ellen, she gently warned me off. She would not say why—only that she found Minnie's living arrangements too sad to describe.

Much later, Ellen would call to tell me that Minnie had died. They did not sit *shiva*. There would be no memorial service, no opportunity to say good bye to an aunt I had never known. I would have to be content with one extraordinary phone conversation.

When Ellen invited my husband and me to join her for dinner in Woodstock, New York, her voice on the phone was as endearing as I remembered—soft, gentle, and tentative, too, in the way her inflection occasionally went up at the end of her sentences.

We met at Joshua's, a restaurant on the corner of Tinker Street and Tannery Brook Row in the center of the charming downtown that is Woodstock. She and her husband had started the restaurant many years earlier. They had arrived in town, driving up from New York City for a vacation with their two children in the back seat. It was so beautiful they wondered why they didn't just stay there. So they did. Joshua opened the restaurant, learning to cook as he went along. Ellen created the menu—a medley of Levantine delights. Now her daughter runs Joshua's.

Ellen met us in the narrow foyer. I felt our connection more than I saw physical resemblances. In person she was as nurturing a presence as I could have hoped—the ideal person to be my first new family in more than fifty years. She was carrying what she called her treasure. I had asked to see any family photos she had and she had brought a large framed photograph of Sophie, as beautiful as Ellen had told me, with pale gray-blue eyes filled with light. She had full lips and long dark hair. In the convention of the time, she was unsmiling, but even without knowing Ellen's stories, I saw a strong, warm and, yes, even mystical woman.

As we talked that night, trying to catch up on each other's lives, we were struck by similarities in our personalities. She had always been bothered by "the chosen people" aspect of Judaism. I have had the same problems with Catholicism's claim to be the one true church. She is not observant, considers herself a Taoist. I remain Catholic but can no longer identify with the institution. In many ways, we are both descendants of the rebellious Benjamin, but I doubt either of us could have stepped so easily over religious barriers decades ago when we were immersed in our traditions.

Ellen wanted to know my reaction when I learned my mother's heritage. In fact, she asked several times. I told her about my numbing anger at all the secrets.

"Did your father know?"

"Yes," I said. "He knew and he kept the secret, too."

She asked more questions and together we conjectured that my mother, vulnerable and abandoned early in life by both her parents, had been spoiled by her adoptive family. I knew they had loved her. Then along came my father, who dearly loved her, too, and who spent most of his lifetime trying to make her happy. As long as she kept the past buried, my mother had never had to come to terms with who she really was.

But it was Benjamin whom Ellen and I wanted to talk about and the conversation always circled back to him. She told me my grandfather had warm brown eyes with flecks of red in them. Her mother had the same eyes. "You do, too," she said.

During the meal, three of her four children stopped by our table. When her younger son was introduced as Ben, I raised my eyebrows in a question and she smiled.

"Of course."

Much later, when we met at an outdoor sculpture park, Ellen would tell me I was the gift of a cousin to her. She had said first what I also felt. We agreed that we talk often of each other to friends and always we smile.

That night Ellen gave me stories of my grandfather. But she believed we were equal. I had given her a chance to envision her grandfather at 22.

"You have told me a love story," she said as we walked out into a warm rain. "Benjamin had a woman he loved and a child before any of us even knew him."

Several months later, Ellen arrived at my house, bringing a DVD of old family videos. Her son had given it to her as a present and she had brought me a copy because, she said, "Your grandfather is here."

As we settled in to watch, it was clear that showing me these images was extraordinarily difficult for Ellen. Tears clouded her eyes. She believed she looked dreadful as a teenager. "Who didn't?" I asked, remembering my own glasses, pedal pushers and ugly two-piece bathing suits. But far more painful for her were the scenes from her wedding day. She found herself explaining to me not only who was who in our family but also why she married Joshua, why she never should have, why they had to divorce.

Later, on the phone, I would remember to tell her how courageous she was to confront those memories just to share Benjamin with me and how grateful I was for her trust. But as the grainy images crossed the screen, I said nothing, trying to absorb the cast of characters. There—we stopped the tape—was a clear shot of Benjamin, wearing an overcoat and fedora, smoking a cigar. It was probably taken sometime in the early 1950s. I studied the eyes, the line of his jaw, his lips. I could see nothing familiar in his features.

We came to the track of Ellen's wedding videos and we stopped again as Benjamin and Sophie walked together after the ceremony. He was leaning on a cane, talking intently to her. This was Ellen's favorite image of her grandparents; it captured, she said, the tenderness between them. We stopped again and again at scenes from the reception as Ellen pointed out all the family. I scrutinized Minnie and Sarah, Ellen's mother, looking for resemblances to my mother, but I found none.

At the reception, Benjamin sat at the head table with the bridal couple and it was he who gave the *hamotzi*, the blessing over the bread, before the meal began. I don't have many choices, but this photo of Benjamin standing beside the Challah invoking the blessing has become my favorite image of my grandfather.

Our grandfather, Ellen had told me, loved to pray. He read Hebrew. He once took her to a synagogue in Brownsville, Brooklyn. She was very young; she could remember only a squat building, crowded and noisy inside, with the women all upstairs and her grandfather downstairs with the men, devoutly praying.

But at family religious celebrations like Chanukah and Passover, he was fierce and demanding. During Seder dinners, he prayed for such a long time that the food would grow cold and the children impatient while they waited. He would be furious if someone interrupted or drank wine at the wrong time. But he could drink all the wine he chose—and he drank a lot. In Ellen's wedding photograph, I saw a benign old man enjoying the honor accorded him as respected elder in the family. But I do not have memories of a tyrant who ruined family Seders.

Everything I have learned from the Seidman women, even the video images Ellen shared, show me that Benjamin was greatly in love with Sophie. He was in his mid-20s when they met in Asbury Park, New Jersey. She was a tall, striking woman, who looked Russian, not Jewish. He saw her walking on the beach. She had come to America alone and was working as servant and sending back money to her family.

"You're the one I'm going to marry," he told her. His father would not approve because he did not believe she was Jewish. But she was.

For Benjamin, Sophie would always matter the most. He liked to be where she was. He would sit reading his newspapers and smoking a cigar while she cooked. When he had his final heart attack and was being carried out to the ambulance, he grabbed for her hand, saying, "Don't leave me." Whatever the stresses were in their marriage, and there were many, as I've learned, it lasted a lifetime.

But he was not a family man. His devotion started and ended with his wife. Ellen recalled that one of her uncles, thinking back about his father, once asked: "Do you think he ever loved any of us?" Rosalind, who always seemed to be trying to balance out the family stories she told me, remembered that Benjamin sent her husband a birthday card. And when Alvin was seriously sick with meningitis, his father, she said, had been very caring. But the bottom line remained: her father-in-law was "a tough man."

When I met Rosalind in the lobby of a New York hotel, I had no idea what to expect. The space was filled with people arriving, meeting, departing, but I walked directly toward a petite woman in elegant brown tweed slacks, a beige cashmere cowl neck sweater, and soft wool jacket. She had blond hair, strong blue eyes, and fine tanned skin.

"Carole!" she said. And I saw a warm friendly smile. Finding each other had not been at all difficult.

Her first question to me was by then familiar, the same question

Ellen had asked several times during dinner. How did I feel when I learned I was Jewish? But Rosalind followed up with other rapid-fire questions.

"Have you told your sons?"

"Do you understand that because your mother was Jewish, you are Jewish, that your sons are Jewish?"

"Yes," I said. One answer had to do; we were evading a speeding taxi as we crossed Seventh Avenue.

"Did you have a Catholic school education?"

I acknowledged I did. She could tell, she said.

"How?"

"Because you are organized and methodical."

I laughed. "And I have good handwriting."

"I have a lot of Catholic friends," she said. "They do, too."

In the short time it took us to reach a Bagel Maven and settle in with our coffee on the deserted balcony, I somehow passed muster. Her youngest son had asked her to find out what I wanted. Was I looking for money? She smiled easily as she recounted their conversation. She had told him not to worry, she said. I sensed that same question was in her mind, but I never had to answer because she never voiced it. Instead, we became friends.

In the two hours we spent together she told me much about herself. She had become a widow at the age of 44, when her youngest son was ten. Alvin was the only one in the Seidman family to die young. "Smoking helped that along," she said. She described herself as a realist, sometimes a cynic, about people. As an in-law, married to Benjamin's youngest son, Rosalind came to the Seidman family late and she was clearly hurt by the family. With the Seidmans, she said, it was always the other spouse's fault. In retrospect, she said, she wished she had reached out more to some in the family, but I could hear the pain and guess at the turmoil of her life as a young widow.

I showed Rosalind a photograph of Ellen and me that my husband had taken at our dinner in Woodstock. I had brought a camera again and I asked for a photograph of the two of us. A waitress obliged and we ended our first meeting. She was going to walk across town to price out some cashmere sweaters; I was leaving for New Jersey.

A year later, we met one more time, at the YIVO Institute for Jewish Research on West 16ᵗʰ Street. That day we were trying to go back another generation. She was determined to help me find Benjamin's ancestors. We looked at documents together. She was positive that *this* Leib Seidman became Louis, my great-grandfather, and *this* Boruch became Benjamin, my grandfather. "These men are your family," she said.

When we had a late lunch at the deli on the corner of Sixth and 16ᵗʰ, Rosalind, like Ellen, wanted to talk about my mother. She had been thinking about her—the young Jewish girl who grew up in a Catholic home. She wondered what she knew and when she knew. What must it have been like for her?

Rosalind remembered her own experiences in public school. "Some of my friends said the Jews murdered Christ. I said, 'Who's Christ?'" She wondered how my mother would have felt if that had happened to her. "How troubled she must have been," she said, "Who could she talk to?"

And she felt sorry for me, too. How sad that for all those years my mother didn't tell me we were Jewish.

"Do you have any idea of what you've missed?"

Another year went by, with cards exchanged, and just as I was beginning to think about having lunch again with Rosalind, Ellen called.

"I have sad news," she said. "Rosalind has had a massive stroke."

I was not prepared for how sad the details would be or for the emotional wave that crashed into me. The stylish, bright, and lively woman I had only met twice but so enjoyed could no longer move or talk. She would not go again to the Metropolitan Opera on Saturdays or shopping for cashmere bargains.

Rosalind Seidman and I were not related by blood. Her husband, dead for more than 30 years, would have been my uncle; her children, whom I have never met, are my cousins. But it was

Rosalind who first accepted me as a Seidman and I quickly came to think of her as a friend as well as family. She grasped the complicated facts I shared, asked the right questions, told me emphatically when I was wrong, talked to me confidently as if she'd known me for years.

Ellen's news left me as bereft as if I'd lost an aunt I'd known for many years. Don't be so desperate for a family, I chided myself. Don't oversimplify. I knew full well that a longer deeper relationship would have brought disagreements. We veered close enough during our two afternoons together. But I wanted to celebrate my amazing encounters with Minnie, Ellen, and Rosalind. At any age it is rare to meet new people who accept us and respond to us as we are, even rarer when those new people turn out to be family. During the time Rosalind and I spent together we had formed a unique bond and that connection was what I mourned.

Chapter 5
Boruch

Somewhere in the midst of listening to Minnie, Rosalind, and Ellen tell stories about Benjamin, I came upon Rachel Naomi Remen's book, *My Grandfather's Blessings*. There I found the Jewish grandfather I wanted as mine. Remen's grandfather was an Orthodox Jew, a rabbi and scholar of the Kabbalah, the mystical teachings of Judaism. He died when Remen was seven, but his wise stories and sayings and blessings remained with her. "The Kabbalah teaches that the Holy may speak to you from its many hidden places at any time....My grandfather taught me how to listen."

From Remen's grandfather I caught a glimmer of Jewish mysticism, a place that lured me. And for the first time I heard the ancient Jewish legend of the Lamed-Vov. During all the history of the world, there must always be 36 good people. If there are not, God says, the world will end. These good people, whom no one ever knows, even the Lamed-Vovniks themselves, respond with compassion to the suffering of the world. "Without compassion, the world cannot continue," Remen's grandfather explained.

It took a while to let the magic go. Remen's grandfather was not my grandfather. And Ellen's grandfather was not yet my grandfather. Yes, he was the same Benjamin Seidman. I was grateful for Ellen's memories, the good and the not so good, which brought him alive for me. But with no memories of my own, I craved information about the younger Benjamin. He would have been tall and fair and red-haired, probably religious, perhaps already sporting tattoos. But was the young man who courted Minnie and became the father of

Beckie as hot-headed and intolerant as the person he became 20 or 30 years later? Was he as unresponsive to my mother as an infant as he was to his later children? Is that why she wound up a foster child in the Bronx? Did Benjamin truly love both Minnie and Sophie?

I returned to prosaic, tedious genealogical research. I had already spent many hours on the first floor of 31 Chambers Street in the municipal archives of the City of New York, Mecca for anyone searching for ancestors in the five boroughs of the city. But I wanted more than Benjamin's marriage and death certificates. If I found naturalization papers for Louis Seidman, I could place father and son in their wider world and watch my grandfather grow up.

The archives of the New York State Supreme Court are on the seventh floor at the end of a long dreary hall. I opened a door into a set preserved from a 1950s movie. High metal shelves lined with dull gray ledgers filled three-quarters of the room. The large windows were so grimy that little daylight entered. Scarred wooden tables were crammed to one side by the door. At one, a skinny, balding man, holding the *Post,* his eyes squinting at the headlines, studiously avoided looking at me. Another, equally uninterested, worked a tabloid crossword. A clerk materialized from among the shelves, took my request form, hunted down a dusty volume. He turned pages, wordlessly slid the binder across to me. The men finally looked up as I pulled out a chair at their table, but they were no longer of interest to me. I was meeting my great grandfather.

Leib Seidman, 5' 4" tall and weighing 190 lbs, a block of a man, had blue eyes and grey hair. He was 54 years old in these documents, a peddler, living at 112 Henry Street, who had immigrated to the United States from Hamburg, Germany, in 1906. His last foreign residence was in Bobruisk, Russia, the city where he had been born. He declared his intent to become a citizen on August 25, 1910. In the official language of such documents, he attested that he was not an anarchist; he was not a polygamist, nor a believer in the practice of polygamy. It was his intention in good faith to renounce allegiance to foreign princes or potentates, "particularly to Nicholas II, Emperor of All the Russias, of whom at this time I am a subject" and to become a citizen of the United States of America. Below the obligatory "So help me God" was his signature. I ran my fingers over the neat, carefully formed letters, written almost a century earlier.

When the Seidman family arrived in New York on May 15, 1906, their ship had been on the ocean for eleven days. Flying the German flag, the Blücher had left Hamburg, made stops in Dover, England, and Bologne Sur Mer, France, and then crossed the Atlantic to New York. The Seidmans, a family of six, included Leib, husband and father; Sore, his wife; two sons, Ary, 18, and Boruch, 14; and two daughters Freidl, 5, and Rochel, 3. They traveled "Zwischendeck" or steerage.

The family had traveled to Hamburg from the city of Bobruisk, in the province of Minsk, well inside the boundaries of the Pale of Settlement. By the late nineteenth century, Bobruisk, one of the larger cities in Bylorussia, had a population of more than 30,000 people, 88% of whom were Jewish. Russian Jewish immigrants to the United States remembered Bobruisk in idyllic terms; one leader went so far as to say, "There is a little Bobruisk in each of us."

Bobruisk had probably experienced fewer of the violent pogroms that began in Elizavetgrad, well to the south, in 1881, and spread throughout the Pale. But as new laws forced more and more Jewish families off the land and out of the *shtetlech*, all the cities of the Pale became more crowded and living conditions more desperate. Bobruisk had additional troubles. A great fire in 1902 left 2500 families homeless and 15 schools and synagogues destroyed. As the economic troubles continued and threats of persecutions grew, the men of the community staged street demonstrations and organized *boyukve* or armed self-defense brigades.

The 1905 Revolution, promising democratic reforms to Tzarist Russia, collapsed within days and throughout the Pale, Jews suffered not only a loss of hope but increasing persecution. In Bobruisk, the general strikes that labor activists had organized were suppressed. The activists became marked men. Many were forced into emigration. The Tzar's army began to visit Bobruisk, enforcing conscription. The Russian army had long claimed all Jewish men once they reached the age of 21, but new laws with harsher penalties closed off the creative methods Jewish families had used to evade the draft.

What combination of political and economic pressures impelled Leib to leave his home and take his family to America in the spring of 1906? The Blücher manifest listed Leib's occupation as *lehrer* or secular teacher. He could have been part of the Bund, organizing young men into strikes and protests against the increasing attacks on the Jews of Bobruisk. Or, more likely, he was just a bystander to political events, an ordinary family man who lost his teaching job and found no other after his school was closed or burned.

Ary and Boruch Seidman, at 18 and 14, would soon have become vulnerable to the draft. Perhaps their two older brothers, who did not travel to the United States with them, were already in the Russian army. The obstacles and dangers the Seidmans envisioned must have been overwhelming to force Leib and Sore to take two teenage sons and two toddler daughters away from their homeland. I wonder which was more difficult: to subject the children to the dangers of traveling across an ocean or leave two other sons behind. In 1906, Isadore was 31 and Isack was 28. Boruch also had an older sister, Rose. I do not know how or when she reached New York. Perhaps she traveled separately with her own family, leaving at the same time or soon afterward.

I see Leib and Sore saying goodbye to their Bobruisk families at night. Perhaps they did not even acknowledge the separation to their elderly parents. Sore would not have told the little girls where they were going. They were only five and three; it would not have been safe for them to know the family's plans. Ary and Boruch would have known. They were almost men, unwilling to show their feelings but excited at the adventure before them. Sore, I think, suffered the most. If Isadore or Isack were married, as they probably were, she was also leaving grandchildren behind.

To reach Hamburg, the family traveled overland more than 700 miles and crossed the dangerous border out of the Pale and into Germany. Leib had to pay for transportation and lodging as well as fees to their guides and bribes to the border guards. In Hamburg, he had to pay the ship's passage for six. Travel by steamship in 1906 was cheaper than the earlier long journeys by sail, but how did Leib save even that much on a teacher's salary? The Blücher's manifest lists a cousin, Israel Icuaschov, residing in Long Island City, as the family's sponsor. Perhaps he or other relatives already in America helped Leib with their fare, but Israel's name never again surfaced in any Seidman documents.

When the Seidman family passed through Ellis Island and settled into their new life, they had a few advantages that other Russian Jewish arrivals did not. Eight out of ten Russian Jewish men who came to America around the same time as the Seidmans were able to read and write. But a former teacher, coming from a city as large as Bobruisk, had more than basic skills—a facility with numbers, say, useful for selling and bargaining. Leib also had some relatives who might have smoothed the troubles that befell so many greenhorns. He had two sons who were already of an age to work and provide more income for the family. And the Bobruisk *landsmanshaft*, an organization of men from the same town or city in the Old Country, would have been large and well established and able to offer him plenty of advice and companionship. On the Lower East Side, *landsmanshaftn* often established their own synagogues, assisted with funerals, and provided whatever charity they could to their members. Where you came from in the Old Country was more important than what you did in the new.

But perhaps Leib's abilities or intelligence also made him dissatisfied and mean-spirited. Many an immigrant daughter recalled a mother, far from her beloved home and bitter at her poverty, whose tongue lashed family, boarders, neighbors, and tradespeople without exception. Why wouldn't the same be true for fathers like Leib who faced a life far different—and no less difficult—from the one they left behind?

Peddling was demeaning work, whether the man went door to door or operated a pushcart. Competition was fierce, no matter what you sold—fruits and vegetables, meat, clothing, pots and pans, furniture—and whether you sold for cash or on the installment plan. Despite the long hours, constant in humid summers as well as bleak winters, and plenty of help from family members, peddlers struggled to eke out a small profit. They were caught in a vise between wholesalers who claimed a substantial cut and shrewd housewives, adversaries as well as neighbors, who demanded bargains. Still, given a new immigrant's few choices, I'd guess Leib liked the independence peddling gave him. He did not have to report to a sweatshop boss; he was his own boss.

On May 11, 1908, just two years after she had arrived in New York, Leib's wife, Sore, called Sarah in her new country, died. She was 54. I do not know how or why she died, this woman who was my great grandmother. When I sent for her death certificate, providing even the certificate number, I was informed that it was "missing." The bureaucracy sent me a note of apology and a refund.

Sarah might have succumbed to tuberculosis or pneumonia or a virulent anemia, but whatever happened, her funeral was simple and her burial soon, most likely within 24 hours. The family would have relied on the assistance of their *landsmanshaft*. The women of the society cleaned her body with warm water, vinegar, and spices like coriander, and prepared it for burial. As the coffin was carried down to the street, the neighbors gathered to join the family in mourning. David Jacobson, Executive Director of the United Hebrew Community of New York, described the scene: "When someone died on the Lower East Side, the whole neighborhood came to a halt....the shops closed down and everyone came out onto the street to pay their respects and to follow the funeral procession." Some followed Sarah's horse-drawn hearse all the way to the Williamsburg Bridge as the procession made its way to a cemetery in Queens.

After the family returned from the cemetery they began the seven day mourning ritual called *shiva*. Who sat *shiva* at the Seidman home? Only the immediate family, excluding children, would have participated. So Leib and his teenage sons were there. They would not shave or bathe for the seven-day period. Was Rose in New York by then? She, too, would have sat with her father and brothers. Friends and neighbors provided the mourning food—round objects like hard-boiled eggs, lentils and beans, to remind the family of the inevitable circle of life and death. The apartment was set up like a synagogue with prayer books, a torah, and prayer shawls. Neighbors had covered the mirrors and provided low stools for the family to use.

My grandfather was 16 when his mother died. Mourning continued for eleven months. Boruch, like other dutiful Jewish sons, would have recited *kaddish*, the traditional and ancient Aramaic prayer, each day during that time. Sarah's death was most likely the first great loss in his life. There would be several more. I cannot know how he grieved in those early years, but I do know that decades later, when he was married to Sophie, he would insist that his first daughter be named Sarah.

Boruch did not have much time to adjust to life without his mother. Only four months after Sarah died, her replacement stepped into the household. On September 15, 1908, Leib married again—a widow named Breina Feldman, who was 48 years old. Once again I am left to imagine how Boruch might have felt and how she might have behaved toward her new sons.

When Leib married Breina, he lived at 112 Monroe Street and she lived nearby on Pike Street. Within two years, by the time he declared his intent to become a citizen, he had changed his name to Louis and Breina Feldman was listed as Charlotte Feldman and the Seidman family had moved a few blocks away, to 112 Henry Street, still in the heart of the Russian district of the Lower East Side.

Another two years went by before Louis petitioned for naturalization on May 27, 1912. On these documents he listed four children: Israel, born in 1875, Rose, born in 1880, Ary, born in 1888, and Boruch, born in 1890. His petition was denied because, like many another immigrant, he had not followed all the rules. One of his two witnesses was not a citizen.

Louis reapplied on February 11, 1913. He gave the same address and the same wife, Charlotte, but this time he listed seven children, adding Isack, born in 1878, who still lived in Russia, and two young daughters, Frieda, born in 1900 and Rachell, born in 1902. I was delighted at the reappearance of the two little girls, who had been listed on the manifest for the Blücher but not in the first application. Where had they been in 1912? And where were they in later years?

They did not surface in any other stories until Ellen arrived with the DVD of her wedding. There, in attendance, was her great aunt Friedl, Benjamin's sister. Ellen would also tell me that when her mother grew angry with her as a child, she'd often say, "You're just like Friedl. All you ever do is read." And there, in Ellen's fond memories, I found another link between paper documents and my grandfather's family.

This second application was successful; Louis Seidman took the oath and became a United States citizen on June 5, 1913. I began to feel a connection with this short, overweight, aging peddler. He had been widowed and had remarried. He struggled with a new language, omitted or confused facts, and got the rules wrong. But he was stubborn. He had persevered in his intent to become a citizen.

The riveting piece of information on all these documents for 1910, 1912, and 1913 was the Seidman family's address: 112 Henry Street. It was the same address I had seen on Benjamin's marriage certificate, where he lived when he married Sophie in 1916 and where the wedding actually took place. This address provided the written documentation I craved. Boruch, son of Leib from Bobruisk, was Benjamin, husband of Sophie. In between, incredible as it seemed, there was Minnie Schneider and my mother, baby Beckie.

Benjamin must have moved there with his father and stepmother sometime around 1910 and probably he lived at 112 while he courted my grandmother. All the places I have envisioned Minnie are only a short walk away. I wonder how much time Benjamin spent there after Minnie died and their baby became a boarder in the Bronx. He must have left 36 Orchard and come home to live with his family— for a while anyway. Perhaps he was treated as the black sheep of the family, a son who had disgraced his father. But his daily routine, as difficult as it was, went on. He worked as usual and he prayed as usual, but at some point either he or his father must have decided his life needed to change. Benjamin went to live in Long Branch, New Jersey, a community along the ocean near the beach town of Asbury Park, where he met Sophie, the woman he married in 1916. He came back to 112 to marry and to live with his bride.

The building has been demolished, replaced by P.S. 2, Meyer

London School. When I stood on the sidewalk in front of the school's institutional gray doors and looked across at 111 and 113 Henry Street, which are as they were, five story brick tenements, I imagined the newly married couple looking out their windows, seeing what I saw almost a century later. Sophie had difficult in-laws. Did they make her cry—or make her angry? Benjamin hurried about his new life, trying to make a living, but, in the evenings, did he wonder about Beckie or mourn for Minnie? Did his bride Sophie even know that there was a Beckie? I could see them, standing together at the window, he tall and fair, she tall with that cascading dark hair. They loved each other. They could not know, either of them, if that would be enough to get them through.

Henry Street is a long street on the Lower East Side, famous through the years for the Henry Street Settlement House, which is still located in Federal and Georgian style row houses at 263, 265, and 267 Henry Street. To the south and west, as the house numbers decrease, the buildings do not have such grand pedigrees. In the early twentieth century, this end of the street housed both greenhorns and those moving up the economic ladder; some families had servants while others still had boarders. Some of the men called themselves business men; they ran stores, shops, and small factories. Others, like Louis, were peddlers.

In those years the average income for a Russian Jewish man in New York was $520 a year. Leib would have counted on extra income from his sons and his wives but even with that boost, the family could not have reached $800 a year—the income economists of the time deemed necessary for a decent standard of living. When I read that figure, it nudged at my memory, more than a random statistic, but it was a while before I connected it, reluctantly, to the story I'd heard at lunch with friends about other New York City grandparents, a family who had been able to pay $800 for a violin in 1920.

As sons of a *lehrer*, Boruch and his older brother would have known how to read and write when they arrived in America. Fortunate for them—because there would have been little time for schooling in their new lives. Their working days began as soon as they arrived in New York. Perhaps my grandfather was a newsboy, hawking tabloids with other young boys. Or, at 14, he could have started right away in a factory. Or he worked with Louis peddling fruit or household necessities. For as long as he remained unmarried, he was expected to contribute to his family's income. No surprise that Louis did not welcome Minnie and Beckie.

At some time during his teens, even while he still lived at home and gave money to his father, Boruch stepped out into his own life. He changed his name to Benjamin. That would not have been the usual translation for Boruch or Borukh; more likely a boy would have become simply Baruch or even Barney. The Old Country Yiddish name that morphed into Benjamin was most often Binyamin or Benyamen. So I am left to wonder why the teenage Boruch chose this particular name. Only the first letter provides a clue, linking his past and future.

In 1911, on his daughter's birth certificate, Benjamin listed his occupation as "waiter."

Maybe he worked at the Garden Cafeteria in its earliest days, long before intellectuals like Isaac Bashevis Singer made it famous. When his customers ordered their blintzes and tea, he served them and punched their tickets. They lingered, talking, shouting, arguing with each other, then paid at the cashier as they left. Or maybe he was one of the infamously rude waiters at Rattner's where in later decades gangsters and entertainers hung out. Rattner's served huge crowds; 1200 might come on a Sunday morning, waiting in line behind velvet ropes to be admitted. I envisioned my grandfather, at nineteen or twenty, hustling among the tables, serving *kreplach*, exuding the in-your-face rudeness that came to characterize the restaurant's staff. I had once again succumbed to sentimental yearning, seeking a tangible connection to a grandparent whose early days will remain a mystery to me. Far more likely, the nondescript cafeteria or restaurant where Benjamin worked, serving the Russian Jews of his neighborhood, had no lingering reputation and was decades ago replaced by similar havens for newer immigrants.

None of the Seidman women had any memory of Benjamin working as a waiter. So this could have been a temporary interlude from peddling with his father or working in a factory. Or a young man's rebellious break from his family's wishes, a way to hang out with friends. Or the only job he could find that year. As it happened, his daughter was born that spring, and a temporary occupation was preserved forever on an official document, leaving his granddaughter to conjure scenarios.

When I first started walking around the Lower East Side, I did not know much about synagogues and I did not yet understand the history of storefront *shuls*. My grandparents had lived at the corner of Hester and Orchard. The Eldridge Street Synagogue was only three blocks away and so I thought it logical that my grandfather worshipped there. More than 1000 people attended services on High Holy Days during the first decades of the twentieth century.

The Moorish, Gothic structure is a magnificent synagogue, built for Eastern European Jews in 1887, as a testament to their success in their new country. After decades of serious deterioration—collapsing stairs, decaying foundation, and leaking roof—the building has, over a 20-year period, been restored to its former appearance. The Sunday I first visited, early in 2000, structural work had been done, but the sanctuary remained a faded, if evocative, remnant of what it was. There, on the carpet were threadbare spots worn away by the feet of generations of cantors. The wooden bench where I sat was scarred and worn and showed water damage from the ceiling that leaked. There were not yet crowds of tourists clustered around a guide.

I picked up the fund raising literature for the restoration, which asked Jews from around the country: "Did this synagogue help shape your life?" For someone who had not grown up with any awareness of a Jewish heritage, the answer was No. Or was it Yes? I stood in the silent dark interior, envisioning a grandfather I never knew praying here on *Yom Kippur* and felt comforted. The journey ahead seemed somehow less frightening as the first intimations of "Shalom" soothed my soul.

I revisited the synagogue many times, noticing progress in the renovations. The last time the spectacular new stained glass east window designed by Kiki Smith had just been installed. I sat dutifully with a guide in the *ezras nashim*, the upstairs gallery reserved for women. And downstairs, in the restored *beth hamedrash*, I made my way through the row of interactive displays about the neighborhood. I absorbed the facts, as I thought I should, but nothing again affected me the way standing in that still-decrepit sanctuary had.

In the interim I had learned about neighborhood *shuls*. The number of synagogues on the Lower East Side, during the years Louis and his sons lived there, grew to 1000. Peddlers like my great grandfather would not have been able to afford even a rear seat at the Eldridge Street Synagogue. Most likely, my ancestors prayed in a small *shul* in a storefront or basement somewhere on Henry Street or perhaps just around the corner on Pike Street. Men from Bobruisk would have brought a Torah scroll with them from the Old Country. That gave their space its holy dimensions. Technically, any space could have been a synagogue as long as there was enough room for a *minyan*, ten men, to gather for prayer.

The Seidman men not only fulfilled their religious obligations at the *shul*, but visited with other men from Bobruisk. Perhaps this was a place where Louis, away from his family, known to men from his old city, unhampered by the heavy and monotonous work of peddling, could relax. And Benjamin? Perhaps he, too, found companionship and solace in services he remembered from earlier happier days.

As I imagined my grandfather in his late teens, turning 20, I had to confront a still gaping hole in his story: how he felt about the young woman named Minnie. I have long hoped that he loved her. I see him taking her to an ice cream parlor, buying her a chocolate soda, sipping through the same straw. Did he bring her little gifts—with money scraped out of his meager wages? More importantly, did he bring her home to 112 Henry Street and introduce her as the woman he wanted to marry? With his mother dead, did anyone present Minnie with the prenuptial ball of knots that many a Jewish bride was expected to untie? By custom in those days, that role was assigned to a mother-in-law; she would observe how the young woman worked at her task and judge if she were industrious enough and patient enough to marry into the family. I cannot know if Charlotte cared enough to carry on that tradition.

And I still do not know definitively that my grandparents married. But because I do not wish to imagine my mother as the result of a casual encounter, a September night tryst that had a troublesome result, I choose to believe Benjamin loved Minnie and was bereft when she died so soon. My cousin Ellen's words—"You have told me a love story"—comfort me. So does Benjamin's decision many years later to name his second daughter Minnie. That must suffice.

The other question that remained was how he made the decision to board out his baby girl. If he went for help to a Jewish social service agency, did they warn him she could wind up in the home of a Christian woman in the Bronx? If I conjecture that he wanted to keep the child and sought help from his family, I hear only angry words in the Seidman home. What insults did Louis hurl at his son? And Charlotte. What role did she play? With no extra money or space or time in her life, she might well have said, "He's not my son. His baby is not my responsibility."

My grandfather and my great grandfather did not have easy lives. Besides the expected immigrant struggles to earn a decent income, they both lost significant people in their lives. First, there were two women, Sarah and Minnie. Later there would be Ary.

In one of my two conversations with Minnie, she told me that one of Benjamin's brothers had died young in a tragic accident. She described how Benjamin got drunk that day "because he was so sad." She saw him when she came home from school. "It was the only time I ever saw him drunk," she said. That conclusion contradicted the memories Rosalind had shared, but it was a new glimpse into Benjamin and it gave me a clue to pursue.

One day I randomly searched for a death certificate for an Ary or Aron Seidman, sometime after 1930, guessing that Minnie would have been six or so by that year, in school, and able to remember what she described. I found him.

Aaron Seidman, aged 44, died on January 24, 1930, from a fractured skull and ribs and shock. The death certificate says the place of death was "the sidewalk in front of 2 Delancey Street." He was married, living in Brooklyn, and working as a brushmaker. His birthplace was Russia; his father was Louis; his mother Sarah. And although the official notice in front of me didn't add any more detail, I knew two more facts: he had a younger brother named Benjamin and he was my great uncle.

Aaron died on the northeast corner of Delancey and the Bowery. When I visited so many decades later, the Bowery Restaurant Supply store occupied the corner building and stretched along Delancey. Its windows, piled high with dusty stockpots, woks, and sets of blue and white tea cups, distracted me as I wondered what kind of accident gave Ary a fractured skull that day. A car swerved off the Bowery and ran into him. A bus jumped an icy curb. Or there was a fight. Or he fell into a construction site. The list of possibilities went on. I marked it down as one more mystery I could not solve.

And I wanted to cut Louis and Benjamin some slack, to allow them to be who they were—sad, difficult, and sometimes bitter men. I would like to have known my grandfather. But if the Seidman men were so difficult, perhaps my mother was ultimately better off among loving women. William, the troublesome Hoefel man, had already died by the time Margaretha and her daughters would welcome young Beckie into a household of women. But what if she had been allowed to remain with her father? No matter how uninterested he might have been, the hole in her soul, and in mine, might have been a bit smaller.

Coda:
Shalom

Shabbat Shalom! I heard the greeting in a totally new way late one afternoon when I was driving home through a bleak January landscape. It was very early in this story and I had tuned by chance to the weekly radio broadcast of Friday services from New York's Temple Emmanu-El. The words resonated deep within me. I knew nothing about Shabbat services and the word *Shalom* meant little more to me than a two-syllable version of "Peace."

As I was to learn, the Hebrew word expresses a wish for the deep peace that only God can provide. Its root verb means "to be complete, perfect and full." For the prophets, the word carried rich meanings of wholeness, health, tranquility, and harmony. Early in the Book of Genesis, as Abram struggles to accept God's vision for him, the Lord promises him: "...you shall go to your ancestors in peace." In the Book of Numbers, the Lord teaches Moses a blessing that ends, "the Lord lift up his countenance upon you and give you peace." In both these passages, the Hebrew word is "Shalom."

As time went on, I learned something else. *Shalom*, said in the silence of the heart, soothes and consoles. The word became my lifeline as I worked to reconcile two parts of my identity: decades as a Catholic woman, rooted in those traditions, versus months as a Jewish woman, still unconnected and uninformed.

Now, after more than ten years of "knowing," I am still struggling to understand what it means for me to learn that my mother was Jewish. What has changed in my life now that I know I have a Jewish mother and two Jewish grandparents? The simple answer is that nothing has changed; the more complex—and more honest—answer is that everything has changed.

I had learned of my heritage with certainty on what Christians have long called Palm Sunday, the Sunday before Good Friday, the year I was 59. Until that night when Ruth said, "My mother told me Rita was Jewish," I had only inconclusive, tentative truth. Hearing it said calmly in a brief declarative sentence was far different from guessing at fragments, as I had been doing, basing my conjecture on a shrug of my father's shoulders or on the names "Benjamin Seidman" and "Minnie," as I found them on my mother's baptismal certificate.

"In the Jewish tradition, whose history *is* its memory, to be Jewish is to remember being Jewish," according to the French historian Pierre Nora. What could it mean for me to be Jewish when I had no memories? No deeply rooted communal ones. No tender personal ones.

In her collection of oral histories of ordinary people like me who were raised as Gentiles and discover as adults their Jewish heritage, Barbara Kessel asks what it is that makes a person Jewish. Is it "memories or genes? Blintzes or biochemicals? Consent or descent?" She lists the factors that mattered in the narratives she heard: lineage, culture, theology, community, education, Israel, the Holocaust. They sound familiar. Five of the seven are actually the elements that made me Catholic.

Otto Maduro, a sociologist and philosopher of religion, has suggested that finding possible Jewish roots helps people face their discomfort in "being *just anybody* in an anomic, anonymous place." His is a nuanced position not claiming empirical data. But it does not explain my search. I have had an identity, just not a Jewish one. It does not explain many of the stories in Kessel's book; nor does it explain well-known people who uncovered a Jewish past that had been hidden from them. Joyce Carol Oates, Christopher Hitchens, and most recently, Madeleine Albright have written of their Jewish heritages. It seems unlikely that any of them felt they needed a corrective for being "just anybody."

Albright was 59 and being vetted for Secretary of State in

1997 when a reporter from the *Washington Post* revealed her Jewish ancestry. Both of her Czech-born parents were Jewish; three of her grandparents and many other relatives perished in the Holocaust. Her family tree, Albright would later write, was stripped bare. Albright, her brother, and sister, all returned to the Czech Republic to make connections to their past. She has written movingly of her experiences while researching her family's years at Terezin.

The similarities in our stories struck me. We were both 59 when we learned of our Jewishness for the first time. Our parents, approximately the same ages, had tenaciously kept the secret until their deaths. Both sets of parents had raised their children as Catholics. A skeptical press did not believe Albright could not have known something so important; some friends did not believe me, either.

But, more important even than her fame, there are other major dissimilarities between Albright's experience and mine. She lost close relatives, including both grandmothers, to the Holocaust. My Russian Jewish grandparents, difficult as their lives might have been, were safely in New York City during both World Wars and the Holocaust. Albright's father, a diplomat, professor, and writer, left his children an unpublished novel, which Albright believes can be read as memoir, and several published books. Her mother left a long letter and family photographs of grandparents, aunts, uncles, and cousins. I have no written family records, no photographs, and scant personal memories of my Jewish ancestors. Finally, Albright had a brother and sister with whom she could share the stunning revelation and subsequent family reunions. I have not had that consolation, but my husband and both sons have read the documents, visited New York City sites with me, and been a part of every chapter in this story.

Many times I had to ask myself why I pursued these stories of my grandparents. Why did I choose to tell their stories and in the process reveal my mother's Jewishness when she had chosen not to? The search has not provided escape from discomfort, as Maduro suggests. On the contrary, it has forced me to grapple with complex emotions like anger and guilt and love.

But I found the courage I needed in what Simone Weil has written: "To be rooted is perhaps the most important and least recognized need of the human soul....To be able to give, one has to possess: and we possess no other life, no other living sap, than the treasures stored up from the past and digested, assimilated and created afresh by us." My grandmothers' stories are living sap and it became essential for me to digest, assimilate, and create afresh.

When I began my task, the implications of my new identity overwhelmed me. Wherever I turned, my predictable world had been disturbed. I had no idea when or if calm would ever return. The present was unsettling enough. But what if I had known at earlier stages in my life? What would I have done differently? Would I have been willing to acknowledge my Jewishness then? Would I be an observant Jew now? There were no answers to the hypothetical questions that crowded in on me. I might have married Bentley, the serious and charming Jewish medical-school student I met the summer between my junior and senior years in college. We cared for each other, but we broke up dutifully. He told me his mother could never accept a *shiksa* in the family. And I, rooted so deeply in Catholicism, couldn't imagine living my life as a *shiksa*. But suppose I had been able to trump his mother's judgment with news of my hidden Jewishness?

Allowing my memories to go further back, I searched for ambiguous family conversations or awkward encounters. Which should I have interpreted differently? I do not recall any overt anti-Semitism in my mother or my father. But I cannot overlook the central fact: they kept my Jewish heritage a secret from me. I believe they thought they were protecting me. The question is: from what?

From the time I was nine we lived in a town that slowly became predominantly Jewish. The Reform Jewish Congregation grew apace, moving from fire hall to schools, eventually building its own temple on the main avenue through town, across the street from Curé of Ars Roman Catholic Church. That parish grew, too, and we were very involved in parish life. I went to a Catholic grammar school and traveled by train to a Catholic high school. I had no Jewish friends even though the development of large modern homes built behind our row of modest Cape Cods was almost totally filled with Jewish families. My friends lived on my street or went to school with me. It was a parochial existence, not all that unusual for suburban life in the 1950s.

I was born into Catholicism and baptized as an infant. I was educated in Catholic schools by sisters from a variety of communities and I have no memory of being taught that the Jews killed Christ, as Rosalind Seidman mentioned and as I know many Catholic children were. Perhaps I wasn't attentive enough, but especially in the early grades, we mostly spent our time on the basics of church practices— how to go to confession, how to receive Holy Communion, what to do during Lent. We did not study Bible stories. Perhaps that dismissiveness alone could be read as anti-Semitism, but more likely it reflected the dismal lack of Scriptural knowledge among our teachers, once again not uncommon for most Catholic adults during the 1950s. On the other hand, the prayers I learned, the words we heard during Mass and the liturgical services on Good Friday in particular certainly sent subtle and not-so-subtle anti-Semitic messages. Even the way we referred to the Old Testament and the New Testament implied that we believed Christianity had rightfully supplanted Judaism in God's plan.

My family didn't discuss national or international events at the dinner table. And my high school history courses, lingering on early explorers like Vasco de Gama or myriad Civil War battles, never made it into the twentieth century. So it is not surprising that I did not learn about the Holocaust until college. But long ago it became unacceptable not to know. I have been playing catch-up for years. I face the facts differently now, not as I did in earlier decades when I wondered if my German relatives wore Nazi uniforms. Now I understand I would have been classified a *Mischling* by the Nazis, the term they used for people like me who have both Aryan and Jewish blood.

In 1935 Germany, as a result of the "Law for the Protection of German Blood and Honor," *Mischlinge* were identified by the number of Jewish grandparents they had. I would have been classified as a half-Jew with two Jewish grandparents. My sons would have been quarter-Jews, with only one Jewish grandparent, and they would have been able to retain their rights as German citizens—but only until 1942 when the rules changed again. After that time, most *Mischlinge*, whether half-Jews or quarter-Jews, wound up in the camps.

I found myself imprisoned—belatedly—by thoughts of the Holocaust. Then I came on Susan Jacoby's memoir, *Half-Jew,* and read her father's words: "....I think it's a dead end to consider yourself a Jew because Hitler would have sent you to the ovens along with all of the full-blooded Jews. ....it's like letting Hitler define the terms. Holocaust, Holocaust, Holocaust—well, it seems to me that being a Jew has to mean something more." I let Jacoby's father guide me out of narrow definitions of identity.

But what was the "something more" for me? The parameters of my identity remained elusive. Many of Barbara Kessel's interviewees who were "suddenly Jewish" had a frisson of memory when they learned their true identity. They recognized their inner Jew. They talked about "coming home"; about "a lightbulb" going off; about "looking in a mirror." I have had none of those feelings. Although I am comfortable claiming my Jewish heritage, I have come to accept that, no matter how I might try to learn customs and rituals, I cannot be religiously or culturally Jewish.

Certainly, there are myriad ways I could behave and still be Jewish. "There are six million Jews in America and six million Judaisms," according to Jacob Rader Marcus, the grand historian of American Judaism. That assessment illuminates my idiosyncratic sampling of mostly Reform Jews. One friend never goes to synagogue on Yom Kippur; another always does. One sat *shiva* for her father; another didn't. One cares deeply about Jewish history and Israel's future; another is as politically uninvolved as an adult as I was in my teenage years. One distains being observant and prefers Unitarian fellowship; another is proud of his faithful attendance at Friday evening Shabbat services. The women no longer light Shabbat candles although they remember the tradition from their childhoods. A few still light a menorah each December. All are adamant in describing themselves as Jewish. They all get Jewish jokes and can easily slide into Yiddish colloquialisms. But their diversity has shown me the ambiguity of being a modern American Jew.

Orthodox and Conservative Jews agree that I am Jewish if my mother is Jewish. Jewish heritage is matrilineal. Reform Jews will accept someone as Jewish if either parent is Jewish and if she chooses to identify with the faith. In Israel, the Law of Return allows a Jew from any country to come to Israel and become a citizen. In the context of this law, to be Jewish means to have a Jewish mother or have converted to Judaism. But conversion in Israel is a political issue as well as religious one and to be granted legal status as a Jew can require attendance at a state-run conversion institute and appearance before a conversion court presided over by rabbinical judges. My mother may have been Jewish, but were I to seek citizenship in Israel, I think many of the requirements for a convert would probably also apply to me.

Rules don't exist in Judaism without rabbinic interpretation, even in the United States. I have chosen not to consult a rabbi, but a few things seem clear to me. I am Jewish by lineage. If I want to identify myself as Jewish, I may. But to be honestly a Jew, I would have to make my own personal commitment to the Jewish community, to Judaism's wisdom, history, culture, ritual.

And there I reach the heart of my dilemma. My memory, my imagination, my language are deeply Christian. I cannot summon up memories of my Bat Mitzvah the way I can of my First Communion. My mother did not make chicken soup with *kreplach* or bake Challah. The mother I knew was Catholic in the kitchen as well as in church. When it was my turn to pass on traditions to our sons, the candles we lit in December were in Advent wreaths, not in Chanukah menorahs. We bought them sparkly Advent calendars, not colorful handcrafted dreidels. I have been to Seder dinners and felt most welcome. But a few years ago a Jewish friend invited me to join in Sukkoth festivities at her home. I found I could not go; that was too far out of my comfort zone.

When I began wandering around the Lower East Side, searching for connections, I stopped into a Judaica shop on Essex Street, one of the last to remain, and on impulse bought a *mezuzah*. Inside is the traditional rolled parchment with the verses from Deuteronomy, known as *Shema Yisrael*, from its first words, "Hear, O Israel." Now as I pass through the doorway where I have properly affixed the *mezuzah*, I occasionally brush it with my fingertips. But I do not say the words of the *Shema*. I do not know them. Observant Jews, who say the prayer morning and night, learned the words as toddlers. From my childhood, I hear instead the words of the "Hail Mary."

I am Catholic. I am Jewish. The tension between the two is subsiding. I cannot linger on what might have been. My Jewish identity is not unwelcome, just unfamiliar. And since it has come so late in life, it will probably always feel strange. Still, I'm finding ways to look beyond fragments. I am delighted to have found complexity where once there was a vacuum. I have long been uncomfortable with barriers and fond of ambiguity. Now I lightly place the blame on my mixed genes. I have hated secrecy, not even knowing what I did not know. It is time to ignore the dichotomy of "either/or" and live in the happy tension of "both/and," yearning like all of us toward wholeness.

It has taken me years to reach the point where it feels honest to send the greeting, *Shalom,* to someone. The first message goes to Minnie, my Lower East Side Jewish grandmother. I have imagined her life but I can never know her. I cannot know what kind of work she did or where exactly on the Lower East Side she lived or how she met my grandfather. But I do know some things. I know she felt the sun on her face and sometimes a breeze through her hair. I know she struggled to get up each morning in cold dark rooms. I know she wore high button shoes and shirtwaists. I know she prayed and cried and laughed. I know she felt a bloody newborn slip between her thighs and sighed in relief. I know she did not want to die so young.

Someday I may find a marriage certificate and know without a doubt that Minnie Schneider became, if only for a little while, Minnie Seidman. Someday I may find her death certificate and know where her body rests.

I've learned that my grandfather was a prayerful Jew. I can only guess that my grandmother would have been equally observant, especially had she had time to grow old. She could have shown my mother, and then me, how to light Shabbat candles, connecting us to Jewish women through the ages. Probably I would have let the tradition lapse as I have so many Catholic traditions from my school days. But the choice would have been mine. I will never know all Minnie might have taught me. The loss will remain. Still, I can remember.

Shalom, Minnie.

For Benjamin, my Jewish grandfather, genealogical research was so much more fruitful. I've even found the names of my great great Jewish grandparents—Abraham Saidman and Ribeky Monin. Someday I may visit Bobruisk where they raised their son, Leib, my great grandfather, who left for America with his family in 1906. Abraham and Ribeky said goodbye to their grandson, Boruch, too, on that spring day. He grew up to become Benjamin, my grandfather, linking me to them in ways neither they nor I could ever have imagined.

When I think of the video of Benjamin giving the blessing over the bread at my cousin Ellen's traditional Jewish wedding and compare it to my own Catholic ceremony, I can only wonder at how one wrinkle in the rigid New York City foster care system, almost a century ago, transformed my life.

In the memories shared by the women of his second family, Benjamin has taken on concrete characteristics, both good and bad. He is more than a name on official documents. I know who he was to Minnie, Ellen, and Rosalind—a complex difficult man who dominated their family landscape. And I have imagined who he was to Minnie and to baby Beckie. That must be enough because it is all I can have.

Shalom, Benjamin.

My mother was separated from her Jewish family as a toddler, perhaps even as a baby. She would never have had time to absorb the heritage of her Jewish birth. The part of my mother that was Jewish was buried beneath all her experiences of growing up German Catholic. But I am convinced she knew of her Jewish roots. Sadly, she was never able to reconcile the two or open her Jewish heritage to me. Her story does not fit neatly into religious categories. Her loss of her Jewishness cannot be blamed on assimilation, on parents who wanted to pass as Americans, denying their Jewish heritage. Nor can she be described as a convert to Catholicism with all the implications of a personal decision. Her transition from Beckie to Rita, from one faith to another, was caused by family tragedy and facilitated by strangers, without any effort or choice on her part. She accepted her German Catholic identity by the age of eight and for the rest of her life she lived out of that identity.

I am grateful for my German grandmother's sturdy Catholic faith and for my mother's diligence in passing on that heritage. But that does not lessen the pain I feel that I did not know my Jewish grandparents, that there was no one to teach me to cherish my Jewish birthright. I know now what I have missed.

At first, I told family and friends that my mother's death had come on a Saturday. Then one day I understood with a shock that she had died on the Sabbath. "Judaism teaches us to be attached to holiness in time.... The Sabbaths are our great cathedrals." I learned from Rabbi Abraham Joshua Heschel that although my mother died in a nursing home at the end of a turbulent illness, she died in a cathedral of sacred time.

Saying *Shalom* to her is a way of saying goodbye to the mother that, despite our lifelong closeness, I never knew. It is a way of letting go of my anger that she did not share her Jewish heritage with me. It is a way to express my confidence that she is now whole and safe, living in harmony, somewhere, somehow experiencing a peace that only God can give.

Shalom, Beckie.

Part II
The South Bronx

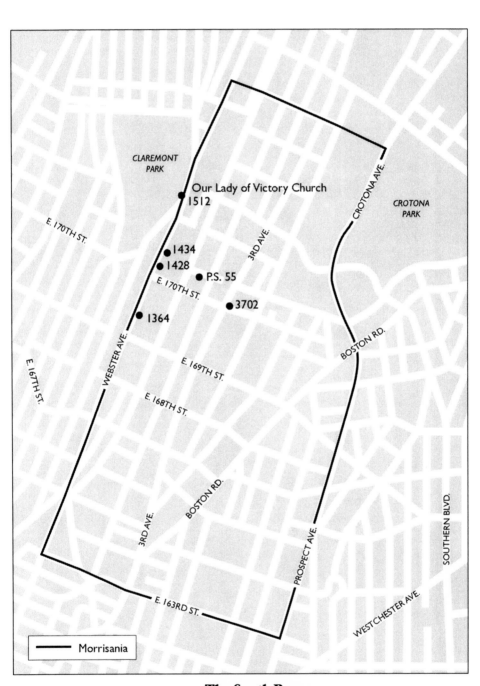

**The South Bronx
(looking north)**

Chapter 6
Margaretha

Years went by before I opened the carton and found the letter addressed to my mother and mailed from Germany in 1940. I had seen it once before, after my mother's death, when my father and I packed away the contents of the bottom drawer of her old mahogany secretary. But I did not remember the two slits, top and bottom, or the two swastikas on the back of the envelope. One had been stamped in red; the other, larger, in bold black. Above the symbol, within the same circle, were the words *Obercommando der Wehrmacht*. On the front of the envelope, my mother's married name and her address and the postmark: 6.9.40. In the lower left corner, in fading pencil, were the numbers 1683.

I opened the letter through the slit across the top. The single-page letter was unharmed and, no surprise, written in German. A small photo fell out. I stared at the three women and one man carefully posed on some rocks outside what seemed to be a small log house with a porch. Large trees darkened the background. I turned the photo over, hoping for names, and found only, "Love to Rita and all from Marie and all!" written in English.

By the time I read those words, I had learned that my real grandparents were Benjamin Seidman and Minnie Schneider. They had called my mother Beckie and they had come from somewhere in Russia, not Germany, where this letter had been mailed. I had also learned that my mother was baptized Catholic and given the name Rita, in May, 1920, at a Catholic church in the Bronx. Somewhere between 1911, when Beckie was born to Jewish parents on the Lower

East Side, and 1920, there must have been a legal adoption. How else could one explain baptizing a young Jewish girl? But those intervening years had been impossible to penetrate. Had she been adopted as an infant? Or later in the decade?

It would take much more research to piece together what happened to my mother in those nine years. But Marie must have been a German relative who, in 1940, knew my mother as Rita. As I looked more carefully at the letter, I noticed that it was written in a different handwriting than the English words on the back of the photo. And at the end of the writing, at the lower left of the page, appeared the pencil numbers 1683—the same numbers as appeared on the envelope. So the letter must have been read by a censor and that aroused my curiosity. What did the *Obercommando der Wehrmacht* allow to cross the Atlantic in 1940?

I asked a friend to translate for me. And what we discovered totally amazed me. In the midst of all the pleasantries he typed out for me, I read, "25 years ago when you visited us, you used to like riding bicycle with him." So my mother went to Germany around 1915—a totally new piece of information for me. She met at least two of the people in the photograph—the man, Michael, who looked to be in his 40s, and one of the women, Marie, who wrote the letter.

The letter was remarkable in itself. A woman whose country was again at war remembered a peaceful scene where two children from different worlds, American and German, Jewish and Christian, rode bikes together—just before an earlier war had engulfed her country. But the words of the letter also gave me a major piece in the history of my mother's adoption. I could positively place her with the Hoefels as early as 1915 when she would have turned four.

One night I tried the Ellis Island data base, searching this time not for Minnie, an arriving Jewish grandmother, where I had had no luck, but for returning travelers. And there I found three Hoefel women—Margaretha, 49; Anna, 17; and Becky, 3, who arrived in New York on the Noordam on October 2, 1914.

I was fascinated by the simple progression of what I saw before me. In 1911 my mother was Beckie Seidman; by 1914 she had become Becky Hoefel; in 1920, transformation complete, she would become

Rita Hoefel. In 1914, with anti-Semitism only slightly below the surface and Germany already at war, my mother was a tiny Jewish girl traveling across the Atlantic with two unrelated German women. She rode bicycles, laughed and played for a while with German "cousins" and then returned to her life in the Bronx.

Who were Marie, Michael, and the others in Weiskirchen? In 1914, Margaretha, newly widowed in 1911, had no obvious source of income. Who paid for this trip for Margaretha, Anna, the youngest of her three biological daughters, and Becky? Why did Margaretha go? Beckie had left her Seidman name behind and as Becky Hoefel was part of a new household. But why did Margaretha take her to Germany? Perhaps she wanted to introduce this little girl to her family. More likely, she had no one to care for Becky while she was gone and she did not want to lose her back into the foster care system.

"As the baby of the family, I was the tail end of that history and by the time I would try to make sense of it, it had been erased by my elders." The words are Helen Fremont's as she searched for her own mother. But the anger and frustration are also mine.

By the time my father told me about my mother's past, I, too, was at the end of the family line. Margaretha, my adoptive grandmother, had died before my parents married. So had Barbara, the oldest Hoefel daughter, and her husband, Arthur. Margaretha's second daughter, Catherine, died in 1950 and my mother lost contact with her husband and her children.

The key to the history should have been the youngest Hoefel daughter, my aunt Anna, a kind, indulgent woman, who served as a surrogate grandmother to me. Anna was on the trip to Germany in 1914; she was the only godparent at my mother's baptism in 1920. She was my godmother many decades later. She, her husband, Andrew, and their two sons, Jim and Vincent, were our closest family during my childhood and adolescent years.

Here's a family story. Two boys, supposed to be minding their new cousin, pushed the baby carriage sedately up and down a driveway in Queens. It was a hot summer day. They were 12 and

10—and bored. No neighbors were in sight. They stepped apart, then further and further apart. They shoved faster and faster, propelling the carriage back and forth between them. The baby slept peacefully. Or the baby cried.

The ending always depended on who was telling the story. When Anna remembered, she was tolerant, amused, the mother of young boys. The baby was safe, oblivious. When Rita, chagrined new mother who stepped inside for a few minutes, told the story, the baby was crying. Jim and Vincent laughed. I remembered nothing. I was in my role: the baby in the family.

By the end of the 1990s my aunt, uncle, and two cousins had all died, and after my mother's death, when I started my research, I had only three women, none related to me, whom I could question about all I did not know. It turned out that the secret of my mother's past had been well kept.

Ruth had been the source who confirmed my mother was born Jewish. Now I wanted to clear up the German side of the story. Ruth's mother, Anna, had been a good friend of my aunt Anna. The two women with the same name, distantly related through ancestors in Germany, and their husbands, both named Andrew, had known each other since before their marriages. I asked Ruth if everyone was in on the secret but me. She did not know, she said, but she assured me that she had never discussed it with Jim and Vincent, my cousins who were her contemporaries.

Joan, one of Vincent's longtime friends, was eager to tell me how she had first learned my mother's story.

"Sometime in the late 80s, after we both retired, we were having lunch in the CityCorp building, sitting side by side. 'I have something to tell you,' Vin said. 'My father just told me that my Aunt Rita was adopted.'" Apparently, Vincent had not known about Rita's adoption nor had any hints about her Jewish past until a few days before that conversation.

"He was totally shocked," Joan said.

Yes, he would have been. Vincent had never married. In my early memory of him, he was a charming older cousin, a talented musician who tried first the priesthood, then the Army, then banking, never quite finding his way. I was still a young woman when I understood that he was always going to be a lost soul. After his years in the seminary and in the army, he dutifully lived with his parents and, after my aunt's death, stayed on in the same apartment with his father. He only moved when, alone, he could no longer afford the rent. Rita had always been his favorite aunt, his confidante and family cheerleader. They talked on the phone for hours. He depended on her. He would have thought he knew her well.

According to the story Vincent told Joan, his father showed him "a paper," which had apparently been stored in the safety box in their apartment. Vincent needed to know, his father had said, but it was still a secret. "Rita does not know she was adopted."

My progress was one step forward and two back. I was more than a decade behind in learning the news. Could it be that my mother really didn't know that she was adopted? Did she not know that she was born Beckie Seidman? What was the mysterious paper? And where did it go?

Joan conjectured that after Vincent died, the paper went to his brother. But Jim died three years later. When I called his widow, Helen, she was totally surprised to learn that Rita had not been a "real Hoefel." Jim had never said anything to her, Helen assured me. But as I asked questions, she remembered aloud: After Vincent died, Rita told Jim that in the safety box in Vincent's apartment there was an envelope with a paper. The paper would show that she was older than John, her husband of more than 50 years, and since he didn't know that, she wanted Jim to please bring it to her "on the sly." Jim did that, Helen said, and she was sure he never looked in the envelope.

Dead end. If the paper had been delivered to my mother, as it must have been, she would have destroyed it. In my childhood, one of her favorite ways of getting rid of paper she didn't want was to tear it into tiny pieces and scatter them in the toilet. I envisioned the same fate for this document. Certainly it was not with any of her papers and my father confirmed he had never seen it.

I have come to believe my mother did know she was adopted. Certainly my father always knew her correct age. In fact, I will discover that he changed his own date of birth on their marriage

license to make himself older than she. That courtliness was typical
of my father just as the charming ruse my mother played on Jim was
typical of her. I can see it all and I can guess what really happened.
The paper my mother wanted kept secret was probably the official
adoption document, which would have remained with my aunt after
my grandmother died. My uncle, growing older and left holding
the secret after his wife died, told both Jim and Vincent about the
document before he himself died in 1987. Vincent, needing emotional
support, told his friend, Joan; Jim did not tell his wife.

But Jim knew the secret. When he filed for probate after
Vincent's death in 1994 he listed the four daughters of Margaretha
Hoefel in correct birth order—Barbara, Catherine, Anna, who was
his mother, and "Rita." Why did he put quotes around Rita? In the
text of his letter, the usage occurs again: "...all deceased except my
'Aunt Rita' and me." He hadn't needed to look in the envelope; he
already knew Rita's secret.

And he took the news in stride. Jim was a staunch family man,
a local banker involved in Rotary, Kiwanis, and the Chamber of
Commerce. For years, he coached Little League baseball teams. In
a cheerful, solid citizen way, he dealt with whatever life sent his way
and then turned his attention to the next thing. And when he had
done that, whatever it was, he played softball or went out on his
boat. Unlike Vincent who died alone in his apartment and was not
found for four days, Jim died on a baseball diamond, tossing balls to
his grandson. He was not into family drama; he and my mother were
not simpatico.

My frustration with family secrets grew as I worked my way
through the unidentified photographs at the bottom of the carton.
Some had obviously been ripped out of albums; bits of heavy black
paper still clung to the reverse sides. Some, showing a toddler with
curly brown hair and large dark eyes, were cut or torn in half. Were
these images of my mother after she became a Hoefel? Who would
have been in the other half? In some photos the same little girl was
one of two or three or four children. Who were the others?

In different snapshots, probably taken in the mid-1930s, I

recognized Anna and Andy with their two sons. And here were the same two boys, a few years younger, with an old woman. That must have been my adoptive grandmother, Margaretha. Feet planted firmly on the ground, shoulders square toward the camera, unsmiling, her body said tired. How sad that my mother never showed me these photographs. And, although she told me many narratives of her childhood, she never told me the true one—a most uncommon story of how Margaretha and Rita became mother and daughter and what this German widow really accomplished in the years after it must have seemed her life was over.

On May 26, 1911, just five days before Beckie Seidman was born at the Jewish Maternity Hospital on the Lower East Side, Margaretha Hoefel became a widow in the Bronx. Her husband, William, died at the age of 40, leaving not only his wife but also three unmarried daughters. Barbara was 19; Catherine, 17; and Anna, 14.

Margaretha was 45 that May, five years older than William. He had arrived in New York from Germany in 1888 at the age of 17. Margaretha Bauer had arrived a year earlier at the age of 23. She traveled on the same ship, the Fulda, leaving Bremen, as Philipp Bauer, 14, a laborer; Johan, 29, a farmer, Marie, his wife, 30, and their daughter, Angela. Were Philipp and Johan or Marie related to Margaretha? I will probably never know. It seems like too much of a coincidence to find several people with the same surname, even a common surname, on the same ship and believe they are all unrelated. But my mother always said her mother, meaning Margaretha, had no relatives in this country.

I would love to know how Margaretha met William Hoefel. Perhaps they were from the same home town in Germany. Or they were neighbors in their new city. I can only know that they married sometime in 1890 when William was 19 and Margaretha probably 25. Their first daughter was born a year later. William became a naturalized American citizen sometime between 1890 and 1900. As his wife, Margaretha would have received derivative citizenship, a footnote to their lives then, perhaps, but important a decade or so later when she would travel to and from Germany as a widow caring for young Beckie.

In 1900, Margaretha and William, with three daughters by then, lived at 1775 First Avenue, between 91st and 92nd Streets, in the midst of Yorkville, a lively neighborhood, then as now, and which used to be called *Kleindeutschland* or "Little Germany." While Margaretha raised the girls, surrounded by scents and sounds familiar from her own childhood, William might have worked at the Jacob Ruppert Brewery, a short walk away, at 90th and Third.

Sometime before 1911, the Hoefel family moved to the Bronx, to 3702 Third Ave, at the corner of 170th Street. In the decades before Prohibition, the Bronx, where other large enclaves of German immigrants had settled, was home to several breweries. The smell of hops hung over many a neighborhood and beer gardens lined many a street. When he died, William was a stableman at a brewery. So perhaps he worked at Hupfel's Brewery at 161st and Third Ave or at the Ebling Brewing Company, a large cluster of red brick buildings and towering smokestacks at St. Ann's Avenue and 156th Street. Both breweries maintained their own stables to care for the massive dray horses that still pulled delivery wagons filled with kegs along Bronx streets.

One of the causes of William's death was alcoholism. Did he drink at the brewery—during or after long hours wiping down the flanks of sweaty horses? Did he stop at a *biergarten* on his way home? Did the drinking absorb the family's money? Was he frequently out of work, moving from brewery to brewery, menial job to menial job? Or perhaps his alcoholism was no worse that many another man at Ebling's or Hupfel's and he kept his job at the brewery until his final illness. One of the other causes of his death was serous meningitis, highly contagious, which he might have contracted at work or anywhere in the neighborhood. In the days before antibiotics, death would have come quickly. My mother had a lifelong intolerance for alcohol. Early on, she would giggle over an occasional whisky sour and later came to enjoy her glass of white wine, but anyone who drank too much risked a rapier-like rebuke. As I tried to read behind the words on the death certificate, I had to wonder if my mother, little girl in a precarious household, had absorbed her attitude from Margaretha, widowed too early because of alcoholism.

Money was certainly tight for the Hoefel family even in those years before William died. The building where the family was living in 1911 was within stretching distance of the El, the elevated Third Avenue subway, a dreadful location whether your windows faced the Avenue or not. In a reminiscence about riding the subways in 1956, Gregory J. Christiano wrote, "A classmate of mine lived on the corner of 183rd Street and Third Avenue in a second floor apartment facing the el. You could reach out and touch the catwalk from his kitchen window. I was in his house many times and neither he nor his family ever complained of the noise or thunderous vibrations as the trains continuously rumbled past. The trains always came to a screeching halt because the station was at this corner." Where the Hoefels lived in those years was just one block from the 169th Street station. They, too, would have felt the constant vibrations as trains rumbled by and they would have known the sounds of a screeching halt every few minutes day and night.

At the time of William's death, two of his daughters, Barbara and Catherine, were old enough to work. So their wages would have helped support their younger sister Anna and their mother. For Margaretha, widowed at 45, speaking little or no English, what other sources of income were there? I remembered one other fact Ruth had told me: "Anna's mother took in boarders for money." And I wondered when that began. In 1911, shortly after Beckie's birth and William's death? Were there other foster children in the Hoefel home in those early years? Are those the children in the photographs?

Within a year, Margaretha and her daughters had moved away from Third Avenue and the El to the relative quiet of Webster Avenue. The tracks of the New York Central Railroad were only a block away, running parallel to Webster between Brook and Park Avenues, but at least those trains ran below street level, reducing the noise and dirt. On June 12, 1912, Barbara married Arthur Bochow at Our Lady of Victory Church at 1512 Webster Avenue. On her marriage certificate she listed 1364 Webster, a three-story building, deep and narrow, as her residence. The building was just north of 169th Street and only a few blocks west of their old Third Avenue apartment.

The apartment at 1364 was the first of four Webster Avenue addresses I found listed in Margaretha's name in the New York City Directory—and there may have been even more. Life for immigrant families in those early years of the twentieth century was "nomadic," as historian Elizabeth Ewen has written. "They move from tenement to tenement, drifting from poorer to better quarters and back again, according to the rises and falls in their fortunes." Vulnerable families like the Hoefels moved because they were evicted or because they wanted to live closer to relatives or they found a better, larger apartment or there was an increase or decrease in their income.

Families did the moving themselves, using pushcarts for furniture and carrying smaller household items in their arms. Everyone helped, including the children. The first move for the Hoefel women, from Third Avenue across to Webster, stretched a cumbersome distance. They would have walked four blocks west along 170th Street, crossed over the New York Central tracks, then trudged south to 169th. At either end of the walk there were flights of stairs. Was there anyone who might have helped with the moving, the carrying, the cleaning? The first of May was traditionally moving day in New York; so perhaps the women were fortunate, carrying and pushing their belongings under clear sunny skies.

Life would have been easier for a while. Barbara's marriage brought another salary into the household; her husband was a bookkeeper. The young couple continued to live with Margaretha, Catherine, who was not yet married, Anna, and probably young Becky, until at least 1914. By then, Barbara and Arthur had a daughter, Edna.

When I tried to imagine the Hoefel women during this period, I was once again confronted with years of evasions and erasures. I had no stories to wrap around the names, no details to warm any facts I assembled. I looked again at the photographs I had retrieved and tried to guess who was Margaretha, who was Barbara, and who was the young Kate. Whose wedding photograph was this? They were not pretty women, not like my mother was. But their faces were not unkind. I wished I had their early stories. Even if, as I now understand, my mother was so much younger, certainly there must have been family history she could have shared. I did know some later history; the 1930s would be a decade of loss for Rita. Barbara's husband, Arthur, died of heart disease in 1930. In 1935, both Margaretha and Barbara succumbed within months of each other, the first to a stroke, the other to cancer.

Catherine, my Aunt Kate, died the summer I was eleven, tall and bright for my age, but shy, bookish, with a taste for melodrama. When my mother told me Aunt Kate had died, we were standing in the kitchen of our new home on Long Island. It was the first death I had encountered outside of my books. I left my mother in the kitchen, ran to my bedroom, which was no more than a dozen feet away, and flung myself on my bed, crying hard, long legs dangling awkwardly off the edge. I fully expected my mother to come and comfort me—she had been quite composed when she gave me the news—but she did not come. After a time I got up and went back to the kitchen. Nothing more was said.

A few days later my father drove us to New Jersey for the funeral. No one said anything to me during the trip, except once when my Aunt Anna told me I had to behave myself because I had to uphold the honor of the Long Island branch of the family. Unspoken, but which I intuitively surmised, was that my New Jersey contemporaries, who would have been Catherine's grandchildren, did not behave.

What years of misunderstandings preceded the funeral, I could not know, but after it was over we quickly lost contact with Aunt Kate's family, although one of her daughters continued to send my mother Christmas cards for many years. They, too, have all died. Somewhere I have "cousins" of the next generation, Hoefel descendants, but without their last names, it is unlikely I will ever find them.

All the Hoefel women were still living together at 1364 Webster Avenue during the summer of 1914 when Margaretha and Anna and Becky set off for Germany. It is not clear when they left or on what ship, but in those years trips to Europe usually lasted a few months. The ominous backdrop of world history offers some clues. Francis

Ferdinand, the heir to the Austrian throne, was assassinated in Sarajevo on June 28, 1914 and the news made headlines in New York newspapers the following day. By the beginning of July, Germany had committed to joining Austria in its struggle against Serbia, which it deemed responsible for the assassination. Russia joined on the side of Serbia and by August 1, Germany had declared war on Russia. The United States was still on the sidelines, observing from across the Atlantic. So it seems likely to me that Margaretha, traveling with a young daughter and a toddler, set off early in June before anyone could know how dangerous Europe, and especially Germany, might become.

What was the ocean voyage like for a girl just turned three? Was she afraid of the endless sea around her? Was she sick? If they traveled both ways on the Noordam, as seems likely, she had lots of places to explore and several decks where she could play outside in the sunshine. The ship offered accommodations for 286 passengers in first class, 292 in second class and 1800 in third class or steerage. Did the women travel first or second class? Or have to endure steerage? The manifest for the Noordam, on the return trip, listed aliens traveling second class or steerage on separate sheets. But since all three Hoefels traveled as citizens, the manifest did not show the kind of accommodations they had. The one-way fare for first class was $100; for second class, $60; for third class, $40. I multiplied by two for the adults and added a child's fare, then doubled the total for round trip and conjectured— hoped— that the Hoefels traveled second class. There they would have had a small but private stateroom, a pleasant, if not luxurious, dining room, and decent food.

They were extremely fortunate that their return voyage, after Germany was at war, was uneventful. Not so for the two crossings that bracketed theirs. The Hoefels left Rotterdam on September 23, 1914. A few days earlier, on September 9, on its homebound journey, the Noordam had been captured in the Atlantic by the British and taken to Queenstown where German reservists on board were held as prisoners and cargo meant for Germany was impounded. Britain had declared war on Germany in August and the Noordam, even though sailing under the Dutch flag, was "carrying contraband destined for the enemy."

The Noordam was allowed to proceed to its home port and several days later the Hoefels boarded for the next scheduled voyage back to New York City. They arrived safely in New York on October 3. The Noordam left again for Rotterdam. On this return voyage, on October 17, around 11 am, as the ship passed Dover, it struck one of the mines the Germans had placed along the shores of Belgium and Holland. The crew readied the lifeboats, but the ship stayed afloat and after drifting for sixteen hours in the North Sea, two tugs brought her to safety through the Hook of Holland. By then, Margaretha, Anna, and Becky were safely home at 1364 Webster Avenue. The United States would not enter the war for more than two years.

What did the travelers share about their journey? Once they arrived in Rotterdam, they must have traveled by train to the Frankfort area of Germany. I doubt the family had access to a rare automobile; and I doubt the women traveled first class. So they would have endured a tedious train ride of more than 280 miles with many changes en route. When they arrived where they were to stay, all those strange faces must have startled a three-year-old. But probably there were new faces for Margaretha, too. I wondered if Margaretha's mother could still have been alive. Perhaps that's why she made the trip. Did she visit with sisters or brothers? How many children were around—nieces and nephews she had never met? Or was there only Michael with whom Becky enjoyed "riding bicycle," as Marie would write some 25 years later? And what was the relationship Marie and Michael had with the New York Hoefels?

I cannot guess how long it had been since Margaretha saw her family. Perhaps she had not visited since she left for America more than twenty years earlier. Certainly she would have seen changes in her small village as it sprawled ever closer to Frankfort. And I am sure the specter of war hovered over the reunion. The townspeople would have been alarmed by the news as it reached them. Perhaps men in the town, even in Margaretha's family, had already left for military duty on the Russian front.

The letter from Marie Sahm, dated 1940, appearing half a century later among my mother's papers, told me little about my mother's reaction to her German relatives. I wonder how much a young Becky could even have remembered. But she must have enjoyed herself, liked the family she met, and as an adult kept in touch with them. In the letter, Marie wrote, "I'm happy that you still think about me, too" and she suggested that she and Rita "can perhaps see each other again."

It still seems strange to me that my mother never spoke of her trip and I never saw any other correspondence from Marie. This letter probably survived not because of any special significance my mother gave it, but by neglect—just one other piece of paper in the drawers she never sorted and one other set of conflicting emotions she did not allow to surface.

I think now that Rebecca/Rita absorbed more of the surrounding politics of her era than I could ever have understood. During her childhood years, anti-Semitism had begun to permeate American society. National political arguments surrounded proposals for literacy tests for new immigrants; these were fueled in part by anti-Jewish sentiment. The bogus science of eugenics, a philosophy that advocated improving human gene pools by state control, provided intellectual cover for discrimination. Such ideas, launched in academia, seeped slowly but inevitably into gritty city neighborhoods like the South Bronx where the fatigue of poverty combined with overcrowding and competition had already made the ground fertile for prejudice.

Arthur Miller, raised in the Bronx in the same decades as my mother, has written of learning of world events "as they trickled down to my homeland, the floor"—meaning the years when he was a very young child. "The impact of things seen and heard from the carpet is red-hot and returns with a far greater shock of truth when recalled .... At the very time we are most vulnerable to impressions, we are least able to avoid outrageously misjudging what they mean."

Becky, a bright little girl, would have absorbed much red-hot information. She was a Jewish child surrounded by adults in a

German family in a mostly German neighborhood. Playing on the floor in the Hoefel apartment, she could have heard stories and comparisons and anti-Semitic remarks. Rooms were small; walls thin; families large; neighbors only a footstep away. Who came in and out of that household? What stories did neighbors share? What news events were discussed? What prejudices were conveyed in whispers with a nod or glance toward the child over there? Later on my mother would have found it impossible to reconcile what she learned that way. Although without question the Hoefel women loved her and accepted her, the undercurrent of those years can easily provide the reason Rita never allowed her Jewish identity to surface, even to herself.

But there was another layer of complexity. In April, 1918, when my mother was still only six, a different prejudice seized the Bronx. The entry of the United States into what had become World War I added patriotic rhetoric to the lives of all Americans. Store advertisements in the *Bronx Home News* include boxed notices that read: "Berlin thanks you—Every time You Eat a Slice of white Bread or Take an Extra Lump of Sugar." Or "Buy Liberty Bonds—It is for you to supply guns, shells and bayonets that mean decisive victory and freedom forever from slavery and barbarism."

Long lists of newly drafted local soldiers, including German-American boys, ran in the *Bronx Home News*. Headlines told of Austrians killed, of U-Boat raids. Households hung a square of white fabric with a blue star in their window; it signified that a man from the family was in the service. Neighborhoods raised money in Liberty Bond drives.

What kind of anti-German sentiment did the Hoefel family absorb? Were there also worry and sadness among the women as they thought of relatives they had so recently visited? Did any letters pass through the German censors of that era and reach Webster Avenue? As patriotism reached fever pitch, how did Margaretha react? Both her sons-in-law, American citizens, had registered for military service. Did Margaretha and her daughters stick together with their German friends? Were they proud and patriotic, too, suppressing their own worries and fears? From what I knew of my aunt Anna, and what I saw in the photos of Margaretha, Barbara, and Catherine, the Hoefel women were stolid, steady, resilient. It was my mother who brought roller-coaster emotion to the mix. And it was she, youngest and most vulnerable, who would have suffered the most.

World War I was a turning point in the history of the Bronx. "[S]omething had begun to change in the innocent world the people of The Bronx had known," Lloyd Ultan and Gary Hermalyn wrote in *The Bronx in the Innocent Years—1890-1925*. "One of the legacies of the war was a strong anti-German sentiment, so that it was no longer as respectable to claim to have come from German stock."

Waves of prejudice and intolerance would continue to wash over my mother. By 1940, when Marie wrote her letter, hoping that this latest war "comes to a good end," Rita would have been absorbing the anti-German, anti-Nazi sentiment of the days preceding and during World War II. Margaretha had died. Anna had married Andrew McDonald and wore an Irish surname. Rita had married John Garibaldi and wore an Italian surname. Deep within her, the shame of a German identity joined the shame attached to a Jewish heritage.

Chapter 7
Becky

The creased, torn clipping shows a cluster of children gathered under a banner for P.S. 55. One little girl stands out, at least to my eyes. She is wearing denim bib overalls, staring out from under a farmer's wide-brimmed straw hat. She is in the second row, almost dead center. Many of the other children are also dressed in costumes. There's a king with his homemade gold crown; there, a nurse; there, an Indian princess. My mother is not smiling, but then no one is. The women accompanying the children all wear summery dresses and floppy straw hats. Next to the P.S. 55 banner is another identifying the Bronx County Chapter of the American Red Cross, School Auxiliary. There is no caption and no story.

I determined that the clipping came from the *Bronx Home News*, but the year and the event were elusive, like so many facts of my mother's story. The newspaper ran an account of a "soul-stirring" Red Cross parade in May, 1918, but the photographs were different. This photo did not match the 1919 event, either. A librarian told me the files for 1920 were incomplete. But, given my mother's likely age, the summery clothes on the teachers and a gathering of children still together before the end of their school year, I surmise it was May, 1920, when a photographer snapped the picture and preserved one event from a mysterious childhood.

My mother never mentioned P.S. 55. She never described any of her school experiences or reminisced about classmates. What I do remember was her answer every time I asked about her life as a little girl. "I had a very happy childhood," she said. Sometimes the words came out defiant, sometimes gay. Sometimes she added, "My mother loved me very much." A psychiatrist friend told me: beware of sentiments expressed strongly and often, without any nuanced or contrasting feelings.

Despite the mystery still surrounding the circumstances of her relocation to the Bronx from the Lower East Side, this photo confirmed that my mother attended P.S. 55 on St. Paul's Place, just a few short blocks from the three Webster Avenue apartments, where I know Margaretha lived with her daughters in the years from 1912 until sometime after 1920.

By the time I traveled up and down Webster Avenue, 1364, 1428, and 1434 had long been replaced by the Butler Houses, a high-rise project with a heavy crime rate. The six 21-story buildings were surrounded by green space and playgrounds, but the lobbies, corridors, elevators, and stairs were sad and dangerous. Across the avenue were discount outlets, liquor stories, pizzerias, and check cashing storefronts. Residents of the neighborhood were primarily black and Hispanic families who gradually replaced the aging Jewish and German population, remnants of the early decades of the twentieth century. The housing developments have obliterated Brook Avenue for this stretch of several blocks, but the railroad tracks are still there.

The German neighborhood the Hoefels knew as Morrisania has come to be included in what is more commonly called the South Bronx. During the late 20th century, the name became synonymous with urban decay; it was shorthand for all that was wrong with public housing projects—crime, drug addiction, broken homes, high drop-out rates in its schools.

While violence and poverty still plague the neighborhood, in some small ways life is better. I saw the contradictions when I visited my mother's grammar school on St. Paul's Place. A five-story brick building, stretching from Park to Washington Streets, it enrolled close to 700 students in grades from pre-kindergarten to fifth. I walked through newly painted red doors into a lobby where the floors shone and the walls were bright white. Colorful murals adorned the stairways that led to the second floor. Auditorium doors, straight ahead, were flanked by framed photographs of baseball players. The hall ways were quiet; students were in classrooms. But, evidence of 21st century realities, a guard stood duty in the lobby.

In 2000, P.S. 55, renamed Benjamin Franklin School, was the worst performing school in the city. By 2005 after changes in administration, the school reported improvements in test scores and brought its average daily attendance rate up to 93%, the citywide norm for elementary schools. But no one hid the difficulties. All of the students live in one of two housing projects; it is the only school in the city school system to serve project residents exclusively. Learning happens for the children, but it is always at risk to the drugs and violence, which remain neighborhood issues. Teacher turnover is still high and parent involvement is still low.

I wondered how old Becky was when she started school here. Some of the women in the photo must have been Becky's teachers. I examined their faces, looking for signs of kindness, patience. Did they encourage Becky? She would have been a good student, excelling in arithmetic and reading and geography. Much later when I was in school, I was amazed to watch my mother list all the states and their capitals in less than three minutes. A generation later, when her grandsons were in grammar school, she astounded them with the same feat.

Becky might have gotten an A for effort and possibly an A for deportment, an important grade in those days. She would not have been a troublemaker. But perhaps she was a daydreamer. Or a talker. I could see her whispering and giggling with the girl in the next seat. Did she get impatient with the tedious routine of learning penmanship? Slow was never her favorite speed—for talking or writing. But she would have enjoyed the competitive speed that math flash cards demanded. I bet she did well in spelling bees, too. She could easily have been the last girl standing.

Who might have helped Becky as she learned to read? It could not have been Margaretha who had not yet learned much, or even any, English. Who helped with arithmetic homework? Probably it was Anna, who was in high school or at work. Barbara's husband was a bookkeeper. Perhaps after work, he sat with Becky. I cannot know if Barbara's daughter, Edna, was there at the kitchen table, doing her lessons, too; she would have been a year or two behind Becky in school.

Were any of the children in the photo Becky's close friends? Did she skip rope with the other girls in the schoolyard? I know, when I was in my skipping rope years, that my mother would rather have jumped than hold the end of the line. She was chagrined that I never mastered Double Dutch. I let my thoughts wander from the schoolyard. When she left its safe embrace, were there older children who teased her or frightened her as she walked the few short blocks home? Living where they did on Webster Avenue, the Hoefels were well south and west of the neighborhoods of Tremont and Bathgate where Jewish and Irish and Italian families intermingled. They were at the western edge of Morrisania, whose population was predominantly German. Did Becky walk her neighborhood streets as a Jewish child? Or, even though she had neither blue eyes nor blond hair, as a shy little girl with a German name who knew at least how to say *bitte* and *danke*? Which ethnic taunts reached her ear? Was there anyone to defend her?

Even a very young Becky, comparing her home life with some of her classmates, must have known her situation to be more precarious—on many levels. By 1920, throughout the Bronx, many families owned their own homes. These may have been modest frame houses, but the mere act of ownership placed these families higher on the economic ladder than the Hoefels and their Webster Avenue neighbors, who moved from one rental apartment to another. As a widow, Margaretha certainly struggled financially. She was also older than most other mothers in the neighborhood. There were no young brothers to pull Becky's hair or hide her homework. Instead she had two much older brothers-in-law, grown men who served in the Army, and, by 1918, already had young children of their own. In those early years my mother had no status in the family. She was still among them temporarily, a boarder or perhaps a foster child.

Decades later, it will become apparent that Rita was ill at ease around men who talked loudly, moved aggressively. Around gentle men, like my husband, my sons, a nephew or two, she was more relaxed. As she grew older she became angry at electricians and plumbers who came to the house. Her anger gradually spread to encompass parish priests, a lawyer, an unfamiliar doctor. Did her agitation reprise early encounters—or lack of them? The psychiatrist who examined her toward the end of her life asked my father, "Do you know why she hates men?" My own question, asked a few years earlier: "Was mother ever abused?" My father told the psychiatrist he had no idea. He told me he had often wondered the same thing. Together we shared clues, reviewed behavior patterns, and conjectured. But we found no answers.

The few stories my mother ever told me about those early years, in snippets and disconnected freeze-frame scenes, were woven, with greater detail, into the occasional columns she wrote for *The Weirs Times*, a New Hampshire weekly, when she was in her late 70s and early 80s. What I have learned from my research has reinforced what I had guessed as I read her articles, one by one, as she mailed them to me over the years. There was little basis in fact for most of the childhood stories she told.

My mother's writing career—or rather her published writings—spanned eleven years, from the time she was 76 until shortly before her two serious strokes at the age of 87. During that time she published more than 60 articles, writing consecutively for four New Hampshire newspapers. *The Evening Citizen*, a daily paper published in Laconia, gave her a first taste of success.

She called me early one morning to say she'd written this short article. She didn't think it was worth anything, but what should she do with it. I offered to read it, make some comments, whatever she wanted. I'd even type it for her. I had no idea what to expect. My mother had long wanted to write and had from time to time tried her hand at novels and poetry, but she had never published anything and to my knowledge she had not completed anything in decades. As it turned out, "One Woman's Spring" was charming, containing a hint of what was to follow in her future columns, and I encouraged her to send it out. I did not expect her to follow through.

But I can still hear the excitement in her voice when she reported a few weeks later that *The Citizen* had published her article and had paid her $25. She was hooked. The next time the paper ran one of her articles they attached a postscript describing her as "an occasional contributor to this newspaper."

She moved on to contribute to two smaller weeklies, which soon folded, and finally settled in as a Contributing Writer at a popular large-circulation weekly, *The Weirs Times*, where she stayed for six years, writing 39 articles. She had found her audience. The paper frequently ran her work on the front page accompanied by an appropriate full-color photograph and she was thrilled to receive fan mail. Sometimes she added recipes or a Christmas craft project to her seasonal columns. Always she blended her love of holidays with the natural world outside her window. She wrote of the present where storms destroyed property and woodchucks devoured gardens, but, as time went on, she more and more used the past as her reference point.

Like the stories she told me, facts about her past were imaginatively mixed with fantasy. As I reread them, I looked for clues I may have missed earlier. Certainly the family scenes she described were correct in one way: there was no father present. A strong mother, who would be Margaretha, dominated every scene she described. But the ages of the older sisters did not match what I had learned was the truth. By the time my mother was six, an age she often used in her writing, Barbara was married and had two children of her own. Catherine, soon to be known as Kate, was also married and a mother. Only Anna was still "at home" and she was 20 when my mother was six. Even the words "at home" took on puzzling connotations. In the idyllic, if poor, Christmas scenes Rita described, there were no crowded apartments or loud neighbors, no flights of dark stairs, no baby nieces and nephews underfoot, no brothers-in-law, no other young boarders—only a family of young girls laughing together in the kitchen or around a fireplace.

My mother loved *Little Women*. I have come to believe she unconsciously wrote herself into Louisa May Alcott's classic. The parallels were there—a family of girls, raised in poverty by a strong kind mother and an absent father—but the fiction obscured a reality so much more compelling. In the apartments on Webster Avenue in the Bronx, where my mother spent her childhood, there were no back doors that led to gardens, however small, and no screened front porches to sit with the neighbors and share gingersnaps. No family of four laughing daughters, all young together. Instead of the proper Protestant Mrs. March, there was a German Catholic widow who not only found ways to survive as her own daughters married and left the household, but also brought a young Jewish girl along with her.

That is the woman who is my grandmother. That is the woman I miss. She had no husband, no education, and no financial security, but she remained a "head of household" well into the 1920s. I circled back to what I had learned from Ruth, old family friend: my grandmother took in boarders for money.

It was no surprise that Margaretha thought about taking in boarders to survive. In those decades, that was a common way to make ends meet. One out of four immigrant families did so. Newly arrived families, with many young children, and only the most menial of jobs available to them, took in lodgers until their income increased. Sometimes it was the response to a family crisis like the death of a spouse. The lodger was often a single man or woman, perhaps a relative or someone from the village back home. Less frequently, the boarder was a child.

What made Margaretha choose to board young girls like Becky? Probably she decided it was safer than having single men in a home where she also had three young daughters. How did she make the arrangements? She could have simply boarded the children, providing food and shelter, or she could have actually become a foster mother. Neither option was unusual. In those decades, city and private agencies both placed children in foster homes. There were also private boarding arrangements. Classified advertising in the *Bronx Home News* had a specific category for "Boarders Wanted." Some advertisers requested babies; others, "children only." Some ads even included the fee to be charged—$10 a week.

There must have been other young girls boarding with

Margaretha during the years Becky was there. Ruth's simple sentence told me so, but the 1920 census has been the only hard evidence. And that information, listing as "boarders," three little girls, including Rebecca Seidman, all of whom seemed to be Jewish, would take years to parse.

Whatever their formal relationship, Margaretha and the children and assorted Hoefel family members lived in a series of tenement buildings, three stories high, narrow and deep. Light only entered through windows in the front or back of the apartments. When the windows were open for fresh air, dirt and noise and unwelcome smells blew in, too. Keeping a clean house, as Margaretha did, required unrelenting work. Clothes lines stretched out from the rear windows high about the ground. Winter or summer, the lines were filled with sheets and towels, men's shirts, and ladies' underwear. Some residents hung the bedclothes over their window sills. Those would have gathered even more grit as they flapped over the traffic on Webster Avenue.

On Wednesdays, women in the Bronx used to take a break from the heavy housekeeping chores to spend time with each other. Then Margaretha had time to visit with her neighbors, women who also spoke German. When the Hoefels lived at 1428 Webster, a German family from Frankfort lived next door. Whilimina Knobel spoke German; she, too, was in her fifties. This I learned from the 1920 census, and once again I have facts, not stories. "We lust after stories," Cynthia Ozick has observed. I plead guilty. I want to know what the women talked about Wednesday after Wednesday. I want to hear Margaretha's worries, know what made her laugh, who lent her eggs, and who walked with her to church. I want to eavesdrop when Whilimina and Margaretha traded news about sales on Easter hats. I'd like to know who helped the family move from 1364 to 1434 to 1428. The three buildings were nearby; Margaretha would have been able to keep her neighbors even as she changed addresses. No doubt her friends moved often, too.

I think my grandmother was probably a good cook—with a talent for baking, like my mother. Many of my mother's columns are rooted in the kitchen. But I have inherited no German recipes—

and only one memory that might connect to fact. For several years during my childhood, I came home from school on the day before Lent began to find that my mother had made "*Fastnacht Kuchen*," deep-fried doughnuts covered in confectioner's sugar. The recipe, she said, came from her mother and she remembered the sugary treats from her childhood. She gave me the name with its German pronunciation—which I mangled in my memory for years—and we didn't ever translate "Fast Nacht" into Shrove Tuesday, the day before Ash Wednesday. Not until I started looking through cookbooks on my own did I learn that *kuchen* is German for cake.

And not until after her death did I decide to try my hand at making *fastnachts*. I had often wandered through her file of recipe clippings, selecting one or another that appealed to me, but I went through once again, searching under breads and cakes, finding nothing for *fastnachts*. So I borrowed a recipe from a blogger who was in turn borrowing from his mother's old and nameless German cookbook.

My mother loved baking yeast breads, including sticky buns, and I can see why she took the extra time to make deep-fried *fastnachts*. They are light and crispy, sugar-coated but not too sweet on the inside. In texture, weightier than a puffy Dunkin and airier than an old-fashioned cruller. *Fastnachts* taste best when still warm. They were not, in any case, to be enjoyed in Lent, which began the next day.

Margaretha, like the other women in her neighborhood, would have been a canny shopper. Leaving her apartment on Webster Avenue, she turned right and walked several blocks uptown to Claremont Parkway and then turned east to the market on Bathgate. There she would have bargained for milk and flour and chicken or fish and the other everyday items she needed for a household with both adults and children. She would have bought day-old bread and over-ripe fruit. Back home, she relied on old German favorites like *spaetzle* and sauerkraut to stretch the evening meals. I wonder if any *krauthobblers*, the door-to-door cabbage slicers who were a familiar sight on the Lower East Side, also brought the fixings for sauerkraut to Margaretha's neighborhood. That would have made her life a little easier.

Third Avenue would have been her other shopping destination. At Christmas she shopped at Hearn's or McCrory's or Woolworth's, around 149th Street, shadowed by the El. She would have bought clothes for her girls at one of the large department stores like Blumstein's, at Third and Melrose. The store regularly ran full page ads boasting 50-cent sales. Cullen's, at Third and 121st Street, sold hosiery for 25 cents and women's suits for $9.95. Are these the stores my mother meant when in one of her columns, she described shopping for Easter hats?

"On a Saturday morning my mother took us shopping downtown. The first stop was the girls' millinery department. We chattered happily as we tried on Easter hats. We did not get a new one each year. Finally we agreed on large white straw hats with black velvet ribbons down the back. Our next stop was the shoe department. We sat in a row to try on the patent leather Mary Janes. There was no hesitation here. We all detested the practical brown shoes we usually wore. One of my sisters said she wished she was a princess and could wear Mary Janes every day! As we carefully walked back and forth trying out our new shoes we noticed the other shoppers were smiling at us (and so was mother)."

I can't guess who they were, those little girls sitting so primly in a row, but I linger on the image of Margaretha smiling, hoping that at least was fact, and wonder again how she managed. What was the source of her endurance all those years? Her three daughters had stayed nearby and helped out financially. She had her own gritty determination, forged by years of struggle. But I suspect it was also her Catholic faith that gave her sustenance. She would have gone often to Our Lady of Victory nearby at 1512 Webster Avenue, her parish church, where Barbara was married and Becky baptized. Immigrant Catholic women developed strong devotion to St. Rita and St. Jude, both known as women's saints, both patrons of hopeless cases. Thousands attended novenas in their honor whenever they were held at various Bronx churches. I can see Margaretha there in the crowded church, head bowed, German prayers on her lips. Perhaps she had a special devotion to St. Rita, her namesake. Perhaps that's why my mother, when the time came for her baptism, would become Rita.

I conclude that Margaretha was as good a foster mother as a widow in her 50s could be. I cannot know if she took Becky with her to the market and bought her a slice of apple strudel from one of the stalls. Or if she had the energy to walk with her to the Morrisania branch of the New York Public Library. Or allowed her to go with Barbara and Kate and their husbands to Niblo's Garden, a delightful destination just east of P.S. 55 on Third Avenue, where German families enjoyed *wiener schnitzel* and pigs' knuckles, danced, and sang along with the massive orchestrion. Like all the other children there, Becky would have been thrilled with the fabulous new wooden music machine.

Certainly Margaretha and the three Hoefel daughters loved Becky. Perhaps they loved the other boarders or foster children, too. But Becky was the one who stayed, who became part of the family. Whatever events or atmosphere clouded her early years, Becky knew love from the Hoefel women. Then she became Rita, my mother, a woman who censored memories, denied conflict and loss, and rewrote her history.

My sons were 6 and 4 the fall my mother called to say she was shopping for old fabrics. She would have been 68. She was, she said, her customary enthusiasm for a new project pulsing through the phone line, going to dress the doll she had just received from my uncle after my Aunt Anna's death the previous month.

My mind was circling on young boy things, not dolls, but I asked, "Whose doll?"

"Mine," she said. "From when I was a little girl."

Why did my aunt keep it all those years if it was my mother's? Why had I never seen it? It then became, somehow, my aunt's doll from her childhood. (My father's answer: a bemused smile, a shrug, and "Who knows?")

The doll was named immediately and I received periodic updates on the project of dressing her. My mother who, throughout my childhood, couldn't and wouldn't sew, who drove me to a Singer store through traffic she hated so I could take sewing lessons, which I begged her to take along with me, spent hours hand stitching undergarments and a lacy long white dress for Grace. She visited doll shops, bought red patent leather Mary Janes and a matching purse. Then she added a red sash to the waist of the white dress, a flamboyant touch but also strategic; it hid the stitching that joined bodice to skirt, which she preferred us not to see.

This was, she told me many times, a Madame Alexander baby doll. And Grace did have that typical delicately painted porcelain head and lovely brown hair. Her body was soft and stuffed but her arms and legs were also delicate porcelain—skin so pale and smooth it was clear she never saw sun or rough playmates.

After my mother had named her and dressed her, Grace came into her own—becoming a major presence in the family. She was ensconced in a comfortable blue armchair in the corner of my parents' living room where no adult and certainly no little boys should dare sit. "Watch out for Grace!" became a refrain during our visits. After sufficient teasing—or perhaps some worries about her safety—my mother eventually moved Grace to their bedroom, where she lounged on the double bed surrounded with pillows, while we visited.

When my husband and I went to close up the house, after my mother's disabling strokes, we had to choose what to sell and what to keep. Grace was in her customary place in the blue chair. It was not hard to decide on her fate: she received a green sticker—she was a keeper.

The mystery of Grace's origin was solved—or not—in one of the columns my mother wrote for *The Weirs Times*. Rereading it after her death, I could not be sure whose memories held, my mother's or mine. The column was so charming and the details so immediate that I was overcome with remorse.

"....I couldn't wait for Christmas that year. I was six years old and I was getting a new doll for Christmas. Shopping with my mother one day, there in a store window I saw the doll. She had long blond hair and brown eyes. Her dress was pink and her pink hat had a rose on it....I declared that was the doll I wanted for Christmas....

"Christmas day was finally here....I opened the box and tore at the tissue. I recall crying out to my mother, 'It's a mistake, it's a mistake, this is not my doll.' I was staring at the doll in the box. This was Grace the discarded doll of my oldest sister in a new pink dress and a pink hat with a rose on it. The youngest child in the family, I was accustomed to wearing the altered clothes of older sisters, but a doll—someone else's doll?"

My mother wrote that she played half-heartedly with Grace for a while, then "the day came when I put Grace back in the closet forever (or so I thought.)" She married and moved and the doll went up into the attic until one day "I opened an old box and found Grace. The pink dress was faded and dusty, the pink hat with the rose on it was missing. Old memories flooded back ...." She reclaimed Grace whose eyes became somehow blue and her hair brown. "She sits in her own small chair next to mine in our living room."

My mother's stories made believers of all her readers. In my collection of her clippings, I found that when *The Weirs Times* celebrated its fifth anniversary and thanked all its regular contributors, they singled out my mother's "zest for life." Although I did not remember that tribute at the time of her death, I used the same word in my eulogy for her. It was the perfect word.

How could I be such a grouch looking for truth when she told such delightful stories? If I parsed the details, there was just enough truth to tug at my heart and just enough falsehood to infuriate me. I felt as if I were trapped in a field of delicate cosmos, one of her favorite summer flowers. Loveliness was all around me, waving gently in a breeze, but I wanted to escape. I knew where I wanted to go, but I could not get there. If I took a step, searching for solid earth to place my feet, I crushed the beauty with my weight.

In her Christmas column for 1993, my mother recalled, "It was a long time ago but I remember standing at the kitchen window with my sisters on a night such as this, searching the sky for 'a miniature sleigh and eight tiny reindeer.' If I listen hard I can almost hear a soft voice calling, 'It's time for bed, girls.'"

If I listened too hard, I had to escape into the bracing prose of Adrienne Rich. In her essay, "Resisting Amnesia," Rich wrote that "nostalgia is the imagination's sugar rush, leaving depression and emptiness in its wake." My mother was addicted to nostalgia. The question that hovered: did the depression and emptiness belong to her or to me?

Rich added, "You do have a choice to become consciously historical— that is, a person who tries for memory and connectedness against amnesia and nostalgia, who tries to describe her or his journeys as accurately as possible...."

Chapter 8
Rita

The small room filled up slowly. Folding chairs were crammed around the long table and on two sides there was a second row of chairs. New to the group, I chose one in the second row. When I had come into the church hall where this adoption support group met on the first Saturday of the month, a cordial team had greeted me and asked me to select a number from the basket. That would be my turn for speaking, they explained, for telling the group news, giving updates on my search, whatever I wished to share. I chose carefully – ten – not too low so I could catch the drift before my own sharing, not too high so I would go last.

I was looking around at men and women, from twenty-somethings to retirees, all talking in small groups, and fingering my numbered tag when another leader said, "If you're new to the group today, you go first so we can all learn about why you're here. That's our procedure. Is anyone new?" Clearly, I was, so I raised my hand and tried a smile. I was to start. But first a young man said he just had to share his good news. He was so excited and familiar to everyone else that when I nodded —of course, he should start—he launched breathlessly into a happy tale of meeting his birth mother for the first time, how she found him, how she looked, his feelings before and during the meeting. As he finished, there were cheers and hugs and smiles and tears.

The immediacy of his story was compelling. In my mind, my story lost its impact and the words I said when it was my turn were dull. I stumbled on the terminology. I am not a member of a triad—the birth mother, the adoptive mother or the adoptee. I am a DOA—daughter of adoptee. Everybody has died, I said, I am searching for information about my grandparents. I started to explain the birth of a Jewish baby on the Lower East Side; her reappearance with a Catholic widow in the Bronx; the secret kept for 80 years; my need to know more. But I had lost their attention. There was no emotional timber in my story or, if there was, I did not convey it well because discussion faltered and the group moved on. Story after story followed, and I came to believe that around that table my story was background noise.

After half of the participants had spoken, we took a break for soda and chips. I mingled a little and made appropriate comments to those whose stories I had heard. No one mentioned my search. As I followed a few others toward the door, a man handed me his card: "I may be able to help you." His card said he was a private investigator and adoption searcher.

Prepared to be suspicious, I checked his website where I found evidence that he was a fine human being, involved in mission work in Guatemala and recipient of an "Angel in Adoption Award" by the US Congressional Coalition on Adoption. He did this kind of investigative work because he sincerely wanted to help. I called him, sent him the information I had gathered, and waited.

Eight months went by before we met for coffee at a local Starbucks. In the interim he had been several times to Guatemala, building houses with other volunteers. He was impressed with the packet of materials I had sent him, he said. He could probably help, but I didn't really need him. He thought I was doing just fine on my own. I nodded, wondering if he were right, and took the rest of my coffee to go.

A friend recommended an adoption attorney in New York. He, too, was generous with his time and advice, but he saw no way he could help. Adoption records, even those from a century ago, were sealed; the Bronx Surrogate Court was, he said, "a rigid place with a Neanderthal mindset" about open adoption records. I would find little sympathy there for my search. He laid out the process. If I wanted to file a petition with the court, I first had to find a New York psychiatrist willing to certify that I had a life-threatening medical or psychological need for the information. Even then, he said, and despite the fact that everyone involved in the case was deceased, there was a high probability my petition would be denied. Why did I want to go through all that? Why indeed? The only psychological impairment I was willing to own was anger at a system that denied me information about myself. I would not play along with those rules even though I understood the subtext—ways to fabricate and embellish my medical and psychological state.

So I set out again on my own, reading, consulting experts, visiting libraries, following up facts wherever I found them. I began to focus my attention on the actual transformation of Rebecca Seidman into Rita Hoefel. The pivotal year for momentous change in my mother's life was 1920; what happened then affected the rest of her life and has resonated through mine.

In 1920 the household of Margaretha Hoefel, 55, included her daughter, Anna, who was 22, and Rebecca Seidman, age 8. But two other little girls were there, too—Gladys Miller, age 7, and Anna Goldstein, 3. All three—Rebecca, Gladys, and Anna Goldstein— were officially described on the 1920 census as "Boarders."

According to the census definitions, "Boarders" were "unrelated household members." Were they foster children? I already knew that at least one of the girls—Rebecca Seidman—came from another neighborhood in a completely different New York City borough. The census taker noted that her parents originally came from Russia and their language was Yiddish. Anna Goldstein's parents also came from Russia and spoke Yiddish; Gladys Miller's parents were born in New York and it would seem they spoke English. But how did these three girls, two of whom were definitely Jewish, wind up in the Bronx household of this German Catholic widow?

I remembered my mother's stories. Always there were three or four little girls. I never knew my aunts' birthdates—only that they were older than my mother—and I never figured out the math. I did sometimes ask why the number of girls in her stories changed and she would say, "Barbara (or Kate) was married by then." But I assumed I knew who the little girls were. Were Gladys Miller and

Anna Goldstein the little girls in her stories? I said the names to myself silently and then aloud. There was no echo. My mother never mentioned a Gladys; and Anna was always the name of the much-loved older sister, who was solidly German and worked as a clerk in the Post Office until she met her husband. Gladys Miller and Anna Goldstein would have been younger than my mother, not the older sisters of her stories.

I wound up with all my original questions: How did a young Russian Jewish father, desperate to find care for his infant daughter, find an impoverished German Catholic widow? How did the Lower East Side interact with the Bronx? How did Rebecca become Rita? How did boarding turn into adoption? But to them I added a layer of deeper questions: how did the events of this one year affect my mother's personality so that she became the woman I knew? And how did those events change my life? What can I understand of all those emotions that we kept submerged for more than fifty years?

When I pursued the possibility of adoption, the first resource that came to mind was the renowned New York Foundling Hospital, started by the Sisters of Charity in 1869 to care for children who had been abandoned after the traumas of the Civil War. In my 20s, I had spent many after-work hours there as a volunteer, playing with the children, reading bedtime stories, giving baths. The President, Sister Carol Barnes, the sister of a friend, was well disposed to believe me, but, she said, such an adoption across religious lines could never have happened in New York in that period. At least not officially. She would consult with one of the oldest sisters whose excellent memory might retrieve such facts.

Sister Rita, who had worked at the Foundling Hospital for decades, was equally amazed. "Place a Jewish child in a Catholic home?" It could not have happened; in those days each religion took care of its own needy infants. In fact, the New York City Welfare Department's rulings required the placement of children "under the control of persons of the same religious faith when practicable. Any deviation from strict religious allocation was to be explained by the presiding judge in the minutes of the court hearing."

And, with my story, Sister Rita observed another problem. "A Jewish baby girl placed with a Catholic mother who was single, even if she were a widow?" No way.

I altered my thinking and pursued foster care, Jewish foster care, since a young father from the Lower East Side, making the terrible decision to board out a baby daughter would likely have turned to a rabbi, his family, or neighbors. And, at first, everyone I interviewed agreed with Sister Rita. No way.

But it turned out that by the time of my mother's birth in 1911 the huge influx of immigrant Jews during the previous ten years had overwhelmed Jewish social services, especially the Hebrew Sheltering Guardian Society (HSGS) and the Hebrew Orphan Asylum (HOA), two stalwart organizations founded in the nineteenth century, to care for "Jewish children of the submerged." Some of the desperately poor newcomers, whose numbers had reached 90,000 a year in the first decade of the twentieth century, found little or no Jewish assistance available when death or desertion forced them to find asylum for their children. Samuel D. Levy, president of HSGS, warned of the problem as early as 1903. "Let the Jewish public of America know that annually 200 of its helpless innocent youths are shut out from Judaism because of the narrowness of our means and through their apathy."

His speech served, as it was meant, as a catalyst for fund-raising, but in the years following, the need still outstripped the Jewish agencies' resources. The orphanages did expand, but more and more frequently, the answer to the problem of where to place destitute Jewish children, who in many cases were half-orphans, that is, with one living parent, came to be "boarding out"—or foster care. What had been a necessary temporary solution became, by 1911, a regular practice. HOA Superintendent Solomon Lowenstein had noted, in 1910, that "the children placed in good boarding homes receive, in general, more individual attention and, in the great majority of cases, individual affection, than is possible in the best institution."

Most of these Jewish children were placed in Jewish homes. But the response of the Jewish community never quite grew sufficiently to care for all the needy children. Few Jewish women, even those with some means, stepped forward to become foster mothers. As late as the 1920s, Jacqueline Bernard reported, "Even Jewish widowers who could pay boarded their infants in non-Jewish homes because no mothers of their own religion could be found." I recalled the wording of the Welfare Department's ruling: children were to be placed in families of the same religious faith "when practicable." In my mother's story, a Jewish home must not have been a "practicable" option for Benjamin. Rebecca Seidman became one of those Jewish children boarded out with a Christian foster mother.

What arrangements Benjamin Seidman made with Margaretha Hoefel, how he made them, or which Jewish agency he used—all those details remained unknown because I could not obtain information from the Bronx Surrogate Court. Still, I was satisfied that I knew how it might have happened. There were indeed ways a little Jewish girl from the Lower East Side could have come to live with a German widow in the Bronx.

Because of the cultural disconnect, to say nothing of language barriers, it did not seem likely that Benjamin read an ad that Margaretha personally placed. Or vice versa. Because there were at least three little Jewish boarders, I leaned toward an explanation that involved a Jewish social service agency. But how that agency found Margaretha has remained a mystery. The agencies placed ads in Jewish newspapers but also in public places seeking homes for the children they wanted to "board out." I would love to know where Margaretha Hoefel —or perhaps one of her daughters—might have seen such a notice.

For most of the first two decades of the twentieth century, New York City paid the agencies the same subsidy for foster families as it paid per child for institutional care—$110 a year, which came out to approximately $2 a week. Did $2 a week provide enough money for Margaretha to take care of Rebecca?

The homes the agencies chose were supervised; procedures dictated that a case worker had to visit monthly to be sure the children were healthy. Margaretha must have passed inspection, providing a good environment, because she cared for at least three foster children. There may well have been other little girls before Gladys and Anna in 1920. I just have no similar census data to confirm my hunch.

Foster care, as necessary as it became, was still not popular during the time Rebecca lived with Margaretha. Mary Boretz who, in 1918, became the new director of the Boarding and Placing-Out Department of HSGS, set out to transform the mindset of the agency and the opinions of her foster mothers. She changed the name of her department to the Home Bureau; she advocated for a substantial increase in the monthly payments to foster parents; and she worked to change the attitudes of the mothers she had under her supervision. Many of these women were ashamed to have to board an unrelated child and they kept the arrangement a secret from their neighbors. Boretz wanted the women to be proud of what they did. She wanted them to accept help from their case workers, to understand new developments in medicine and psychology that affected their children. And she wanted the natural parents, often fathers, to not only accept foster care but to visit their children.

I'd love to know how Margaretha felt about boarding little girls. Could she have been ashamed and determined to keep their presence a secret from the neighbors? I have no evidence of that. Did they summon up happier memories when her own daughters were young? At some point financial need morphed into love. I have plenty of evidence for that. How long did it take my grandmother to fall in love with Becky? To determine to keep her close and give her a permanent home? And I wonder if Benjamin ever visited his daughter in the Bronx. He had married Sophie by 1916. I doubt he brought his new wife to visit Becky. But did he linger as he left his little girl? Did he ever try to bring her back into his life? Like larger facts, those emotions are also lost.

The answer to the next obvious question—how foster care evolved into adoption for Rebecca—also remained a secret, well guarded by my mother and the Bronx Surrogate Court. But increasingly more urgent to me were the layers below the facts, depths I had yet to fathom.

I found some helpful guideposts in the work of Betty Jean Lifton, a therapist and writer who devoted a good part of her career to understanding the psychological impact of adoption—first on her own life and then on other adoptees. She has described what she called "cumulative adoption trauma" to explain why adoptees have no sense of self so that they often feel as if they have a "hole in the center of their being." They were not only separated from their parents, perhaps at or shortly after birth, but then as older children or adults they had to deal with the secrecy and lies that denied them the truth about their real heritage. Having been a victim of secrecy and lies in her own adoption, Lipton was blunt about the devastating results on a child. "While some secrets bring people together by giving them a sense of intimacy and sharing, secrets can be destructive if they cause shame and guilt, prevent change, render one powerless, and hamper one's sense of reality."

As I read through her books, I was shaken by the similarities between some of the adoptees she described and my mother. A fellow therapist, she noted, found "impulsivity, low frustration tolerance, manipulativeness, and deceptive charm that covered over a shallowness of attachment" as common elements in the personalities of many young adoptees. There was no longer anyone to describe Rita the child; but despite my reluctance to acknowledge them, many of those traits were part of Rita the adult.

Lipton acknowledged that listing such traits could seem to be unfair generalizations. But her experience led her to believe in "a broad continuum: from mild to serious to pathological" in cumulative adoption trauma. All adoptees, she believed, could be placed somewhere along the continuum. Most would probably be grouped in the "mild" range—which was probably where Rita belonged. She was married, more or less happily, for 53 years. She was an enthusiastic mother and a creative grandmother. She had hobbies, friends, and a late-in-life career. In her early years the Hoefels cherished her and protected her; then it was my father's turn. And mine. Rita was loved. But, with Lifton's prompts, I also recalled many episodes over the years when she struggled with what psychologists describe as a lack of trust and a fear of abandonment.

My mother frequently advised me not to trust my friends, my father's family, and my husband's family. Ultimately, she could not trust either my father or me. As I reflected on her last years, I came to conclude that, far more than most elderly people, she feared authority, expected another dismal intervention in her life, and trusted none of us to protect her. I wish I had known then about cumulative adoption trauma and the hole it caused at the center of her being. Perhaps the insight could have helped all of us who loved her alleviate some of her suffering.

I suspect my mother's life would have been different if she and the Hoefels had shared the story of the adoption that happened sometime in 1920. Would she have been happier? I cannot say. But certainly my life would have been much different. What I saw in Lipton's work about adoptees reflected not only my mother's story, but my own. I had become the seeker, wanting to connect to my heritage, to fill the hole in my own soul.

One day that first year after my mother's death, my father arrived with another small envelope, this one filled with holy cards that were held together with a rubber band. Most of them memorialized the death of someone I knew, at least by name— my German grandmother, Margaretha, my German aunts, their husbands, my cousins.

In the middle of the pack, there was another holy card, older, tattered, faded, slightly smaller. I turned it over and was amazed to read a hand-written inscription: "To Rita in Remembrance of your first Communion." It was signed "Sr. M. Callista" and dated "May 22, 1920." The date rang in my head. When I rummaged through papers I had saved, I soon saw why. The date on my mother's baptismal record was May 21, 1920. She was baptized the day before her First Communion. That year May 21 was a Friday, an unusual day of the week for a Catholic baptism.

I already knew that there were no other baptisms listed in the register for that date, but that fact hadn't meant anything. What did it mean now? Did someone suddenly discover that this eight-year-old girl, who was to receive First Communion on Saturday, probably with her class, had never been baptized? That she was born Jewish?

Catholic babies were baptized young in those days because so many died in infancy and the theology of the time taught that unbaptized babies who died went not to heaven, but to limbo, a "place" the Catholic Church has since disavowed. It would have been assumed that all the children preparing for First Communion had been baptized. But what happened when a young girl, Jewish by birth, was adopted by a German Catholic widow who spoke little English? Who in the family would have known what records were required? Who in Our Lady of Victory could have known they were missing? That no baptism could have occurred at the usual time? I had no facts, but I could guess how it all might have happened— the last minute surprise, the concern, and finally the unusual but welcoming steps taken to be sure this young immigrant girl got to wear her white communion dress on Saturday, May 22.

How did the sacrament of baptism happen for Rebecca? Perhaps it was in the quiet of early morning, before school or work, with only the priest and her sponsor present. Instead of the usual two, the baptismal record lists one sponsor: Anna Hoefel, Margaretha's youngest daughter, who had accompanied her mother and Becky to Germany in 1914 and would have been 22 years old at the time of the baptism. Perhaps they gathered at the font in the evening, with other family members, even Sister Callista, in attendance.

Who chose the baptismal name for this little girl? Rita can be a diminutive for Margaretha, which can be spelled Margarita. So did young Rita choose to be named after her adoptive mother? Did Margaretha choose? Did Rebecca change her name immediately or gradually—or was she already known to her classmates as Rita? Hard to even frame all the questions. The 1920 census listing for a Rebecca Seidman cannot be erased. As of January 1, 1920, my mother was officially a Jewish boarder in the Hoefel home. But, surely, it would not have been possible to baptize a Jewish foster child. A legal adoption must have taken place by May 21, 1920, turning Rebecca into Rita, and laying the groundwork for her to receive sacraments in the Catholic Church.

Strangely, while I do not know the answers to so many important questions, I do know that my mother's First Communion dress was the traditional white with two rows of delicate ruffles at the neck and around the sleeves and four tiers on the skirt. She wore a large white bow at the crown of her head and a wreath of flowers atop her long curly hair. Her high-button white shoes came to mid-calf and were topped with white stockings.

The evidence lies in a studio photograph that surfaced among my mother's papers—once again, something she had never showed me. In the photo, her eyes are luminous and she has a faint smile on her lips; she is solemn, appropriately, but not sad. In her hands she carried a small prayer book. I have the prayer book, too, the one in the first envelope my father gave me. It is not unlike my own from my First Communion—small, about two inches wide by three inches long and perhaps an inch thick. The cover is hard and glossy, almost pearlized after all those years, and the lightly tinted picture is typical devotional art of the times. Jesus, with long dark hair, pale complexion and glowing robes, points to his bleeding heart, which shines through his white vestment.

How cleanly the three items—holy card, photo, and prayer book—mesh together. They delineate only a few hours, perhaps a day, in the early life of my mother. The rest remains mystery. But through them I have made a real connection to the young girl who was on her way to becoming the woman I knew.

I thought I might uncover another connection if I could locate Sister Callista. Dominican Sisters served in many Catholic schools and parishes in the Bronx in the early decades of the twentieth century. I traveled down a few wrong paths before Dominican archivists at the Sparkill and Sinsinawa motherhouses set me straight. The Sisters of St. Dominic, whose motherhouse was in Blauvelt, NY, was the community that served at Our Lady of Victory for many years and indeed I would later meet some of the Sisters, of much younger vintage, at the parish's 90th anniversary celebration. Callista was a rather unusual name, the Blauvelt archivist told me; there wouldn't be many. And she did indeed find a Sister Callista of the right age who died long ago, in 1949, at the age of 70.

She would have been 41 years old when she signed the holy card for Rita's First Communion. But I could still not be positive I had found the right woman. The necrology the archivist sent me showed no permanent long-term assignment for Sister Callista at Our Lady of Victory. Was she helping out in the spring of 1920? Was she there for a year or two between longer assignments? Once again, questions without answers. But whatever her other ministries, Sister Callista played a special role on that Saturday in May when an unusual eight-year-old girl received her First Communion. Her handwritten message has lasted more than 90 years.

Our Lady of Victory still celebrates the immigrant experience. Father Peter Gavigan, the pastor who welcomed me when I first researched my mother's baptismal certificate, invited my husband and me to the parish's 90th anniversary celebration. We sat in the church surrounded by young and old, Hispanic, German, Italian, and African-American faces, all former and present parishioners. The program included an English choir, mostly black men, presenting hymns like "Is There Anybody Here Who Loves My Jesus?" and a Spanish choir, mostly women, singing hymns like *"Yo Tengo Un Gozo En Mi Alma."* The new children's choir had a black director who, the pastor told us, had stopped by the rectory and offered to give free piano lessons. He had then offered to start a children's choir. We were listening to their debut performance.

Downstairs at the reception, we talked with some Dominican Sisters who had once worked in the parish. They were here for themselves, they said, to see some of the older parishioners. But they were also the presence of generations of American nuns who had taught generations of Catholic immigrants around the city.

Welcoming immigrants has always been a delicate balance for Catholic parishes—affirm the old traditions, teach the new. They probably sang some hymns in German at Our Lady of Victory in 1920. Was my mother part of a children's choir? Many years later, when her grandsons were small and we gathered around the piano at our house for Christmas caroling, my husband and I would hear my mother singing *"Stille Nacht,"* but if we commented, she would always deny she was singing the familiar carol in German. As she neared death, she prayed in German. At least that's what my father and I thought. Did she learn those prayers from her German mother, who welcomed her into a faith, a language, and a culture? Did she learn them at Our Lady of Victory?

And who taught her to make distinctions? To share parts of her identity and suppress others? To keep all those secrets?

By the time my mother celebrated her ninth birthday on May 31, 1920, her transformation was complete. She was no longer Rebecca or Beckie or Becky; she was Rita. She had been baptized and received her First Communion. She must have become—legally as well as emotionally—a Hoefel.

When I focused on the events of 1920 and confronted the anger that some days I could not obliterate, I wondered if Rita ever lingered outside my bedroom door wanting to come in and tell me about those long-ago events. Did she choose a time—like my 18th birthday—and then let the deadline pass? And set other deadlines—when I was to be married or expecting my first child—and let them pass? Or did she just bury the news deep within and know that she would never ever tell? From what I understood about my mother, either scenario was possible. And why did she never show me the holy card, the photograph, and the missal from her First Communion? Perhaps she chose not to draw my attention to the event, fearing I'd ask too many questions. Or perhaps she never rummaged to the bottom of drawers crowded with memorabilia and thus never knew what was there and what I'd see after we could no longer talk. Once again, either was possible.

Chapter 9
Rita and John

Sometime in her eighties Rita answered a gardening query in a Boston newspaper. I no longer remember the paper or why my mother came to be reading a Boston newspaper. By that time she was devoted to *The New York Times*, even in New Hampshire during the summers when they had to drive miles to get one. The question had to do with nurturing a caladium bulb indoors, a task my mother had mastered. Isabel Crawford from Milton, MA, who asked the question, was in her nineties. There began a friendship by correspondence that lasted until Isabel's death. The two women, both in the last years of their lives, discovered they had much in common and my mother often spoke to me of Isabel. They never met, but my mother kept a sheaf of her letters.

As in so many correspondence friendships, the evidence I have is only one side of the story. But I can intuit the other side from what Isabel wrote. I know that my mother told her about her cataract surgery. I know she sent "Izzie" many small gifts like notepaper and "eau de toilette." She must have one year sent a card for St. Patrick's Day because in her note Izzie thanks "Mrs. O'Garibaldi." I can hear Isabel's news, but only an echo of my mother's. With one exception. In the packet of Isabel's letters I found one in my mother's handwriting. Dated "1ˢᵗ day of spring, 1994" it is a two-page letter in which my mother wrote, "Isabel, I feel that if I met you in the street I would know you, but I feel that we don't really know each other all the way so I am sending a brief history of me. You can destroy it after you read it."

She then gave a brief biography. "I was born in N.Y., one of four girls. My both parents were of German descent but my father died early and my father's people were somewhere in Germany. We never knew them. My mother whose folks came from Berlin never knew her relatives either. So she had a hard time managing and did all sorts of work to support us. We all went to work very young. Although I would have loved to go to college, I worked in an office where I met my husband. I have one daughter and two grandsons in college. I am so glad they are able to go."

She went on with a charming description of herself, her likes and dislikes. "I love anything that grows but could do without cactus....I loathe snakes but they fascinate me. I <u>hate</u> mosquitoes....I like mashed potatoes and yams and almost all vegetables. I don't like cabbage....a BLT is my all time favorite sandwich....I love to read, history especially. I am not very athletic. I guess sitting is my favorite position."

The details were no surprise to me. I had always known my mother's passion for flowers, animals, needlework, and BLTs. She loved fiction as well as history and she had an eclectic taste, which nourished my own. Her early favorites ranged from *Gone with the Wind* to *Kristin Lavransdatter*. What interested me was why, after telling Isabel to destroy the letter, I found it in the packet. I surmised that Isabel must have died before Rita had time to get to the post office. In the last of Isabel's letters, dated February 12, 1994, she wrote that she had asked a friend to call "those who won't see my death notice in the paper." And then she added, "It isn't morbid, but at almost 98 one feels better to take care of such little matters." She was, by then, in a nursing home—"happy, no, but grateful and contented, yes."

The information my mother wrote in her letter was what she would have wanted a friend like Isabel to know. It was written in her compelling style—animated, descriptive, detailed. How often she sounded breathless with excitement. She could be talking about making Irish soda bread for St. Patrick's Day or the goldfinch outside her window in May or Fourth of July fireworks or the Christmas tree lighting at Rockefeller Center. Unadulterated uncensored enthusiasm for the everyday occurrences that so many of us miss was one of her most endearing traits.

But, also in typical Rita fashion, the details in the letter were not truly revealing. The basic story line was the same she had followed with me. But there was that troublesome and misleading "born one of four girls." And Berlin? To me she had always said her mother was from "Frankfort am Main" and I had uncovered the information about that amazing 1914 trip that Margaretha and Becky/Rita made to Weiskirchen, a small town on the outskirts of Frankfort. I also discovered that she not only did not go to college, but had to leave high school after one year, a fact she had never shared with me.

I learned that for the first time when I looked through her autograph book for 1925 and 1926. At first, simply amazed to find it, I enjoyed the routine rhyming messages of that era. But a closer reading revealed much more. I could reconstruct, for example, that my mother began the book when she graduated from P.S. 56 in 1925. One of her teachers obligingly dated his signature: "John T. Manning, P.S. 56, Bronx, January 27, 1925." One of her male classmates in a weakly rhymed verse gave more description: "Remember the hop/ Remember the flop/ Remember the fun/ With Old Man Manning."

Here was evidence that Rita had not finished grammar school at P.S. 55, so close to those early Webster Avenue apartments where the Hoefel family had lived for so many years. Sometime after 1920 Margaretha and Rita had moved up further in the Bronx, to 3112 Webster Avenue, so my mother would have transferred to a new school sometime after third grade. By the time I caught sight of her again, she had reached eighth-grade at P.S. 56, where she and her classmates were January graduates.

In her autograph book, I found much evidence that Rita was welcome in her adopted family. Sisters Kate and Barbara each took a page. So did "Your loving sister, Ann," whom I knew as Anna. In Ann's handwriting, there was a message from Margaretha: "Dear daughter, May angels twine for thee/A wreath of immortality/ Is the sincere wish of your Mother." Andrew, now married to Ann, wrote: "To Rita Dear: Here's to your future/Your present and your past/ May each day/Be happier that the last. Your loving brother, Andrew

James." Even her cousin, Edna, Barbara's daughter, was there: "To Rita—There is a pale blue flower/Blooming in yonder spot/It wishes all I have to say/which is forget-me-not."

The book was signed by many friends and teachers from P.S. 56, but spaced in between these messages, all dated sometime in January, 1925, were a few others dated 1926, with references to Evander Childs High School. "To Rita, When cupid shoots his arrow/I hope he <u>Mrs.</u> you. Your Evander Chum, Susan." And "To Rita, When you are married/and your husband is cross/Pick up the broom stick/ And say I'm the boss. Jackie, ECHS." And Isabelle M. Murray, probably a teacher, signed in flowing script and dated her page, using the initials for the high school: "January 21, 1926, E.C.H.S."

Evander Childs would have been a relatively new high school when Rita attended in 1925-26. Students and teachers from all over the northern Bronx had only come together into one building in 1918. The new building, Gothic in style, had four floors, a library, a cafeteria, and a swimming pool. With a full roster of dedicated teachers, the academic curriculum included Latin, physics or chemistry; ancient, medieval, modern, and American history; elocution; and, of course, math and English.

My mother would have had a ride on the El—or perhaps just a very long walk—to get from where she lived at 204th Street and Webster Avenue to the building at 184th Street and Creston Avenue. But many of the other students also had long distances to travel. Despite the new cafeteria, Rita would have brought her lunch from home—a sandwich, an apple, perhaps a spicy *pfeffernusse* cookie, the kind the grownup Rita enjoyed with her coffee.

I know Rita would have loved her classes. I'd bet she excelled in American history and wrote imaginative compositions and book reports. After World War I, Bronx schools no longer taught German so perhaps she took Latin. She would have dreaded physical education, especially if it involved swimming. Whatever her preferences, she only got to spend one year in high school. She would have been no different from so many others of her generation. In the first two decades of the twentieth century, only 9% of Americans graduated from high school. Not until mid-century would a majority of students reach that level of education.

When I visited locations from my mother's later childhood, I found glimpses of the past sporadically woven into the present. In the early 1920s the Third Avenue El ran along this stretch of Webster Avenue. The building at 3112, where Margaretha and Rita lived, was a narrow, ramshackle, two-story house, separated from its neighbor on the downtown side by a three-foot alley and bordered on the uptown side by a vacant lot. A few scraggly trees grew close to the side of the house. Steep steps led up to the entrances for the apartments; commercial space on the street level jutted into the sidewalk. The elevated tracks, just yards from the building, dominated the street, absorbing light and air, dispersing dirt and noise.

3112 was, to my amazement, still there. Vinyl siding had brightened the exterior and tiny windows had been cut into the long blank wall facing north; the vacant lot had become a parking lot bordered by cyclone fencing topped with curled barbed wire. The long flight of steps to the apartments remained and the commercial space along the street was occupied by a bilingual licensed real estate agent who also handled divorces, provided Fax and copying services and acted as a notary. Webster Avenue, without the elevated, was brighter, but still noisy and congested.

School must have been an oasis for Rita. After she had walked the few blocks to P.S. 56, where she graduated eighth grade, she would have found herself in a neighborhood far removed from the dirt and noise of the El, a quiet enclave of brick apartments and small houses where narrow circular streets still insulate and protect. The three-story brick building is overcrowded now, but a well maintained and functioning city school. In the 1920s, when Rita attended Evander Childs High School for that one year, it was just off the Grand Concourse, a new facility in a calm neighborhood. When I drove by the latest Evander Childs location, at 800 East Gun Hill Road, the school was sheathed in netting, closing, victim of changing demographics and growing violence.

I had been guessing that this move, much further than any of Margaretha's earlier moves, uphill, to the northern reaches of the Bronx, meant that Margaretha and her adopted daughter were moving up in their world. Perhaps their fortunes had improved. But my visit changed my mind. The opposite must have happened. Barbara and Kate and Anna, with their husbands, had moved out to the suburbs. Margaretha, on her own to pay the rent, could no longer afford to stay in her neighborhood. And she had no choice but to remove Rita from high school. Sometime in 1926, my mother's freshman year, she and Rita left the Bronx and moved in with the McDonalds—Anna and her husband who had just bought a home in St. Albans, in Queens.

Andy, who brought a gentle Irish humor to the Hoefel family, had met Anna at the Post Office where they both worked; they were married in 1924. He was one of thousands of Irish Catholic men who spent their lifetimes working in one of New York City's uniformed municipal services. The 1920s and 1930s were the heyday of that Catholic presence among the police, fire, postal, and sanitation departments. As many as four thousand men routinely attended the annual Holy Name communion breakfasts for postal workers. Anna would have made sure Andy was there.

The extended McDonald-Hoefel family that lived at 194-34 Murdock Ave was entering the middle class. In 1930, even in the midst of the Depression, each of the houses on the block was worth $7000. At #34, my aunt Anna was the mother of two young boys, James and Vincent. Margaretha, by then officially called Margaret, was 64. During the preceding ten years, Rebecca Seidman had disappeared. In her place was Rita Hoefel, 18, daughter of Margaret Hoefel and sister-in-law of Andrew McDonald, the head of the household. Both of her parents, it was now officially recorded on the census, came from Germany and she had a job as a file clerk with a chewing gum manufacturer. That was the American Chicle Company in Long Island City where she had already met my father.

The locale for those charming scenes my mother would later describe in her columns and place in the Bronx was really this house in St. Albans.

I, too, remember that house. I spent many happy times there in my early childhood. That house was as close as I ever came to having roots, to "going home to grandma's."

My Aunt Anna served as my grandmother, a good woman, devoted to her family, but also to Rita and to me. She was never the inspired cook my mother was. She made comfort food—fried eggs and bacon for breakfast on a girl's first overnight away from home. On New Year's Day she made German specialties—pigs' knuckles, sauerkraut, red cabbage, bratwurst, *spaetzle*—my uncle laid in a keg and they welcomed family and neighbors. For a shy only child, the annual gathering was both exciting and intimidating. It's where I got to know my Aunt Kate, her gruff husband whose sense of humor I never mastered, and the cousins from New Jersey.

I remember the landing on the staircase, which overlooked the small living room, where my cousin Vincent, age 11 or so, celebrated Mass and I served as altar girl, bringing Necco wafers to the rest of the family down below. I remember the way the dining room was decorated for my cousin Jim's engagement party after he came home from the Army. And I remember the tiny breakfast nook where my aunt and I would sit and talk in the sunny morning light, eggs hardening on our plates.

The house had an enclosed front porch with rattan furniture and rubber plants that my mother always hated. One night, I was often told, my aunt left her purse on the porch, only to find in the morning that it had been stolen. For all my adult years, wherever I lived, my mother would warn me to bring my bag with me to the bedroom at night.

The kitchen in that St. Albans house was large with lots of windows where a group of four little girls could look out—or in—depending on my mother's story. When my mother wrote about a garden in the backyard, that's where I believe it was. I can see it, too. In my childhood, my aunt had lots of strawberry plants back there next to the one-car garage with the crisply painted swing-open doors.

Murdock Avenue is still a pleasant airy street; the Q83 bus slips by quietly once or twice an hour. Similar two-story houses, some with neatly fenced front yards, line the avenue. The McDonald house needs tending; the driveway and shrubbery in front are overgrown. The cream stucco I remembered has been replaced with siding and faux gray stone, but the front door opens in the same place, reached by the same front steps, matching stone now instead of brick. I have tiny photos of all of us posed on those steps—my father, wearing topcoat, scarf and fedora, with my mother, in a stylish fur coat, one winter before they were married; my aunt and uncle with two young sons; a clearly delighted me with my father and the three McDonald "men."

The scenes my mother created for her childhood were composites: she wrote about when she was six with three young sisters and a loving mother. But the house where she envisioned a front stoop and a cement walkway to be swept, the kitchen where her mother cooked for holidays or made root beer was not in the Bronx. It was here in Queens, on Murdock Avenue, a place she could not have known until she was well into her teens and off to work.

In one column she wrote: "When the days were warming up in the spring my mother always made root beer for us. With the help of my oldest sister she would bring the bottles up from down cellar. Cold water was carefully measured into two large vats on the stove and slowly brought to a boil. At this point we were banished from the kitchen to the back porch where we could watch through the window."

One of her earliest columns, the one about the hobos and the gypsies, always puzzled me. She located the story in her early childhood. "We lived at that time in a part of town still largely undeveloped. There was a wooded area down the road, where the "For Sale" sign had long since disappeared, trees had died and others cut down for firewood, leaving a weedy overgrown patch. It was called the 'campgrounds.'" That's where, she wrote, hobos and the gypsies would gather.

"... scarcely a week passed that a hobo didn't stop at our door. They shuffled around the back of the house and knocked on the screen door....They were always polite to my mother when they asked for a glass of water or something to eat. She was not afraid of them, but I noticed she locked the screen door and kept our dog tied up nearby in the kitchen, while she fixed whatever food she could spare and poured a large glass of water. The hobos sat on the back porch steps in the sun while they ate their meal. I watched them from the kitchen window."

I believe Margaretha would have been kind and generous. But such a scene could not have taken place in any of the apartments where she lived on Webster Avenue. And in St. Albans she was not the lady of the house; my Aunt Anna was. By that time, Margaretha was a live-in grandmother and Anna was a stay-at-home mother. She would have been there if the hobos came. Rita could not have been looking out the window; she was at work.

My mother was always fascinated with gypsies. I remember that on one of my early Halloweens—I was probably six or seven myself—my mother created part of my gypsy costume with an old emerald green taffeta skirt with ruffles at the bottom. It came to my ankles and I felt very grand. I wonder now wherever she found that skirt; it would never have been her style. I wore some kind of a striped vest and I remember a tambourine with flowing multi-colored ribbons, kept from a dancing class recital.

But my mother's column about gypsies was a story from her childhood, not mine. She located them at the "campgrounds" just like the hobos. They arrived suddenly, usually in spring. Neighbors spread the word. "When she came back inside, mother quickly bolted the front door and told me the gypsies had come and then with me tagging along she locked all the windows. She put the leash on the dog and hurried us out to the back yard. I held the dog's leash while she snatched everything off the clothes line."

One day, Rita wrote, "we coaxed mother to go to the grocery store the long way round passing the gypsy camp.... The encampment was large and as we drew closer the noise was deafening, dogs were fighting and barking, and we could hear the whinny of horses. Groups of children stopped playing and stared at us. (We stared back.) They were barefoot and very dirty. The gypsy women wore faded blouses and long full skirts, colored handkerchiefs were tied around their heads. Busy at their large cooking pots they barely glanced at us.

Men lolled around, some playing cards, other sleeping. They wore bright shirts, dark trousers and boots, the many chains they wore shone bright against their swarthy skin. They stared at us boldly and mother hurried us past the camp."

So did the gypsies really camp near where Margaretha and Rita lived, either when my mother was very young, or later in St. Albans? During the first decades of the twentieth century, there were gypsy camps in the Bronx—near Van Cortlandt Park, Westchester Village, and on White Plains Road at the intersection with Pelham Avenue. None of these locations was anywhere close to where Margaretha and Becky lived during those years. In Queens there were encampments in Maspeth and nearby Laurel Hill. Neither of these locations was near enough to St. Albans to be in the Hoefels' neighborhood.

But I don't doubt that gypsy stories were pervasive in both neighborhoods. A schoolgirl from the Upper East Side in Manhattan vanished and, *The New York Times* reported in 1910, the police were searching for her in the gypsy camps. Kate Simon, in *Bronx Primitive*, her memoir of growing up Jewish in Tremont, a neighborhood near the Webster Avenue locations where the Hoefel women lived, wrote, "They came through our Bronx streets from time to time, two or three women in big swinging skirts like colored winds, dusty long black hair, flashing gold teeth, and bold hands that demanded money, unlike the quivering old bums who bashfully begged. We were told to avoid them; they were filthy, they were thieves and they kidnapped children."

My mother would certainly have seen gypsies; she would have heard all the tales about the gypsies; and over the years she would have read in newspapers and books the details she described. But I doubt there's any factual basis for her trip past the campgrounds. And I'm suspicious about that laundry scene, too, as charming as it is. I have always known my aunt did not want any animals around her house. Rita never had a dog until long after she was married and her husband came home one year with a cocker spaniel as a surprise gift.

Whenever I asked my mother if those episodes really happened, she would brush me off impatiently with one of the several tactics in her arsenal. Those methods worked when I was a child because I perhaps didn't care enough or was intimidated by her anger. By her eighties, when she was writing full speed, I was an independent adult, an established writer myself, no longer intimidated but well aware of her erratic responses. I purposely muzzled my questions because I worried that if I trod too heavily with my need for facts I would interfere with her creative dash to the finish. And that seemed unfair. I was trapped between my own wish to know what was true about her family, my family, and the guilt of impeding what she clearly loved to do.

"The point [of a story]," Caroline Steedman has written, "is briefly to make an audience connive in the telling, so that they might say: yes, that's how it was; or that's how it could have been." Rita loved the telling and her audience loved the conniving.

For her daughter the stories presented more difficult terrain. When so much has been embellished or veiled or obliterated it is hard to know when to stop asking questions, when to assume knowledge and when to excuse ignorance, when to be angry or when to laugh.

I was a junior in high school when one of our class assignments was a family history. I dutifully asked my mother to provide what information I didn't know. By some fortunate accident, that paper survived. I read it now and blush for its naiveté, but I hear, in its cadence and choice of detail, my mother's voice. Did my teacher know there was little truth in the neatly typed report? My grade was a B—rare for the studious me in those days. What I wrote is what I heard the spring I turned 17. In the years, even decades, that followed I never came much closer to the truth.

"My great grandparents, on my mother's side of the family tree, were born in a small German village called Weischerchen [sic]. Times were bad and [they] immigrated to America where they settled in lower Manhattan. There my grandmother was born. When she was still very young, the family's love of the country prevailed and they moved to the Bronx which at that time was entirely farmlands. At a church social many years later, my grandmother, Margaret Bauer, met a handsome young man, William Hoefel. He courted her and one year later they were married in the village church. Their marriage was blessed by four daughters, one of whom was my mother. While my mother was still a child, the Bronx became very populated and the entire family moved to St. Albans, Long Island. My mother grew up there, attended P.S. 135, because there were no Catholic schools nearby."

How did my mother feel when she was confronted by a school report demanding family details? Was she angry? Possibly. Was she threatened? Possibly. That would have been of a different magnitude than my pestering her with my own questions. Over the years, when I asked too many questions, she had many ways to end the conversation. Often she'd laugh, change the subject to something silly, and sidetrack me. That was, unfortunately, easily done. Or she'd say she was too busy—cooking dinner, ironing, getting ready to go shopping. That could, I suppose, reflect mostly on my poor sense of timing. Or she'd just get angry—the most befuddling reaction of all, because I didn't understand why.

But the school report must have presented a more difficult challenge. And I can see that she responded with all her creativity. There is almost nothing true in that paragraph, either in the facts I presented or in the implied idyllic atmosphere. I find it almost impossible to reconcile what I know with what my mother's imagination conjured. My grandmother was not born in Lower Manhattan and she did not move with her family to the Bronx while she was still a child. Margaretha and Rita are the ones who moved from the Bronx to St. Albans. In neither place did the family live in tranquil countryside. My mother did not go to P.S. 135. Shortly after she moved to St. Albans she went to work at the American Chicle Company. She never returned to high school. That secret, too, she would keep until her death.

Margaretha lived in St. Albans for nine years, longer than she had lived in any of the Webster Avenue apartments. She was no longer the head of the household; perhaps that was a relief. She was surrounded by family; Barbara, her husband, and two children lived a few blocks away. She had two grandsons under foot, little boys who would have brought pleasure to a woman who had raised and boarded girls. She did not live to see my mother married or have an opportunity to meet me, but she had already transformed Rita's life.

Unlike the silence and fabrications surrounding her childhood, my mother talked freely to me about her working years, her girl friends, meeting my father, double-dating with two close friends, Frances Artale and Arthur Burrows. I've long known that Margaretha didn't want her to marry John Garibaldi. Was it because he was Italian? Because he did not make enough money and could not promise the rosy future she thought Rita deserved? Whatever her thinking, both my parents reported her disapproval. My father said he knew it even though Margaretha spoke no English—at least to him. Margaretha's English was fine, my mother said. They married anyway.

As I looked at their marriage license, I was amused by two discrepancies. My father, who was born on January 26, 1913, listed his birth date as January 26, 1911, thus making himself four months older than Rita. It was a gallant gesture, so typical of his kindness toward my mother. But the discrepancy stayed with him all his life. A few months after he died, a letter from the Motor Vehicle Commission arrived at my home. They had noticed this discrepancy. If he does not correct it, they warned, he will not be able to receive a new driver's license. The letter was timely. My father never had to confront the conflict between his gentlemanly deed and a computer's indelible memory.

The second disconnect was my mother's birthday. Her birth certificate noted May 31, 1911 as her date of birth. But on her marriage license and her Social Security application, she listed May 30. We always celebrated that as her birthday and much later in her columns, she would write about her delight at having parades on her birthday. I have no idea why she made the change—or did she? Perhaps it was someone else's doing, a clerical mistake in her early childhood. Did my mother even know her real birthday?

But her wedding—ah, that was different, indelibly preserved in stories and memories shared over and over, whenever I asked—

and that was often when I was a child. Back then I knew all of the participants. Mr. and Mrs. Andrew McDonald had announced the wedding of their sister on June 12, 1937. In my mother's memory, it was "a perfect June day." The marriage was celebrated at a Mass at St. Pascal Baylon, a large new church, built for the many Catholic families moving into Queens during the 1930s. The McDonalds, living only a few blocks away, would have been among the earliest parishioners, part of the Catholic community even before there was a church structure. St. Pascal's had seating for 900 and room for an additional 150 people in the choir balcony.

But there was only a small gathering for Rita and John's wedding. My father's brother, George, was best man and my mother's friend, Anna Klashus, was her matron of honor. They had no other attendants. The late morning Mass was followed by a small luncheon reception at the Hotel Franklin in Jamaica. My mother and father paid for all the wedding expenses. Because I found the bills in my mother's drawers of paper, I know that the hotel charged $60 for 60 dinners. Ten bottles of wine added $15 more to the total. There must have been six children at the luncheon because six additional dinners cost only 60 cents each instead of a dollar.

The reception was a success. Anna sent Rita a letter, dated June 14, 1937, two days after the wedding. "Everyone seemed to have a good time and I wound up having a beer with your boss and the girls. Margie [a friend of Rita's] almost cried when she heard you had left...." Anna wrote about relatives who left without saying goodbye, not unexpected behavior, I surmised; about "John's father" who "is a lovely man"; and then about the heavy drinking her husband and his male friends did the evening after the wedding. "Really, Rita, I've never seen Andy so drunk...he wasn't even able to go to church so you can imagine." She went upstairs but "didn't sleep all night." She closed by writing "We all miss you Rita, especially when I pass your empty room even if I did have to call you so many times."

Anna sent two more letters during the week Rita and John were on their honeymoon, three hundred miles north, on the shore of Lake Winnipesaukee in New Hampshire.

Correspondence must have been frequent even for such a short vacation. The letters my mother kept made clear that Anna had already received cards and letters from the newlyweds. I would love to have seen those. For her part, Anna included letters from "Your nephew James," who wrote, "Vincent and I miss you very much. If I shine all your shoes for you and bring them over to your new house can I still be your valet?"; from "Your Little Frend Vincent" who said, "I will get you the bunch of flowers I promised you"; and from a young friend, Anne Kelly, who writes that "Father Crowley said the bride was beautiful and the groom tall, dark and handsome."

Anna, too, was clearly enthralled with the life of the newly married couple. She worried that the bill for the wine was too high; she offered to buy pillows for them if they will let her know "what you want to spend." She fixed Rita's pongee and chiffon dresses and she and Andy brought dishes over to the couple's new apartment. She pressed some flowers from Rita's bouquet and put "the white satin ribbon from the flowers in the veil box." She reported that neighbors came over to see the wedding gifts "and think they are grand." She counseled the young bride to enjoy herself as "Rita, this is the happiest time of your life."

My mother would tell me often how unhappy her marriage was—that her mother was right—but I have come to believe that her courtship years and those early married years were among her happiest. When I combined the affection and intimate family details of these letters with the mountains of cards and notes John sent Rita –and she kept—I could see that my mother was surrounded by warmth and affection in those years. Anna and the other McDonalds never stopped loving Rita. They never stopped showing her their love. Neither did my father. But eventually, their love was no longer enough.

A lifetime later, after my mother's death, as I tried to help my father through his grieving, he told me over and over that he did not do enough to make her happy. He should have found other ways. I recounted for him the many creative ways he had shown his love over the years. We laughed about the time he put a gold bracelet, an anniversary present, in the refrigerator. Sadly, she never acknowledged it was there and he eventually took it out and returned it to the jewelry store. Finally, I told him that it was one of the sadnesses of my own life that I, too, had not been able to make her happy. Happiness was something she had to allow herself—and she could not. I could not tell if that comforted my father.

Coda:
Auf Wiedersehen

In 1968, when my mother was 57, she and my father finally bought their own cottage on the shore of Lake Winnipesaukee. My mother decided that the floors should be covered in traditional New England-style braided rugs. They were not to be factory-made, but handmade. In the summers she traveled country roads, finding places to buy wool scraps; in the winter, she dyed them, cut hundreds of strips and braided. My father constructed a yard-high duck-billed contraption that held tight to one end of a braid while my mother moved her chair further and further away as the length of braid grew. Christmas reds, shades of blue, tweeds of gray, woven together, made their way onto an old ping-pong table in ever widening circles. The centers she made tight and flat, stitching in heavy-duty black thread. She finished one rug, large and oval, then two round, smaller, then another oval, all destined for the living room. For the bedrooms, she moderated her palette, branching into rust, golds, browns, and creamy tweeds.

It was my father's job to transport the rugs to New Hampshire. For decades my role has been guardian of the rugs, first with our sons, then with our grandchildren.

"Be careful with that juice!"

"Your grandmother made those."

"Don't wrestle there."

I've also become the one who repairs. I've bought the requisite heavy-duty rug thread and hunkered down to mend a fraying edge

164

or reconnect separated strands. Always I've found myself irresistibly drawn to the center and I've marveled how my mother made the circles so round and flat. Recently, when I walked a labyrinth, I thought of the rugs my mother braided. I was walking a stone-lined path in the shade of high oaks, but I moved toward the center on the twisted strands of my families.

The first time I walked the labyrinth I was indoors where the path had been stenciled on a very large canvas mat. I had no idea what to expect. It was 1999 and I was still mourning my mother. What I wanted from the labyrinth experience was a peaceful interlude, a walking meditation that might let me find perspective on loss. Unlike a maze, a labyrinth has no dead-ends; it is a continuous path inward, but a meandering one that often takes you away from the center of the circle even as you progress inevitably toward it. It can blur your ideas of reality and subdue your sense of progress.

That day, on my journey into the center, I was alone; the way seemed long and aimless and tedious. I felt no centering or peace. I wondered if I had walked too quickly. But I stayed awhile in the center. While I stood there, gathering myself, I felt a breeze from a door opening behind me. A tall, slender woman, gray-haired, wearing a long flowing skirt, entered the path. She came along toward me almost ceremoniously. Her steps were rhythmic, dance-like. At each step, she brought her back foot into position just behind her front foot and paused there before moving into the next step. Her body swayed as she shifted her weight. As I again centered myself and stepped into my return journey, a group of women, all young and all but one African-American, also entered the labyrinth, walking slowly, one after another. They were part of a YMCA retreat, wearing identifying sweatshirts. The silence remained unbroken. As we passed each other on a curve, one or another of us stepped aside. Our heads were bowed, eyes inwardly focused. I felt an amazing kinship with these women, all of us traveling together. I was joined to them, sharing the journey, but going my own way.

The way out from the center of a labyrinth is the same as the way in, meandering and illusory, but that day, instead of seeing the same tedious detours that had irritated me on the way toward the center, I felt whole, finding clarity even in the ambiguity of the journey. Time passed and it was not possible to hold on to the clarity. The journey has continued. As I would struggle to learn, life goes in only one direction, despite endless detours. When you walk a labyrinth, your path starts out straight; you feel as if you're headed directly into the center. Only then do the disorienting curves and loops begin.

It was a freezing day in January when we had the Memorial Mass for Rita. The parking lot of the church was solid ice. My husband and sons and even the pastor escorted people from their cars over the slippery surface to the door of the small chapel where we gathered. We were only my father, my husband's family and a few friends of mine; my parents had moved so recently to New Jersey that there had been no time for my mother to make new friends. I was the last of her family.

The Catholic liturgy comforted my father and the pain eased a bit for me when I spoke her eulogy. I wanted to try to capture the Rita who had been—not only for the family gathered in front of me, but also for myself. So I recreated for all of us the early Rita, the mother I knew when she was still, I thought, happy.

"I was very young when we went one year to the Mineola State Fair and she discovered that the jars of peaches and green beans and sweet pickles that other women displayed were no better than hers. She took careful note of what won and began entering her own. She won blue ribbon after blue ribbon for her canning. Then she noticed that her pies and cakes looked better, too—and she was right, of course. She entered and won there, too....

"Most of you know how much care she lavished on her gardens in New Hampshire, both her vegetable garden where she did serious battle with the groundhog who dared to eat her beans, and her flower gardens. You may not know how many other gardens she tended earlier. She had first a beautiful rose garden and then a perennial garden, long before growing perennials was as prevalent as it is now. She called them all by their proper Latin names, and naturally they rewarded her with good behavior....

"I do not need to say much, I think, about my mother's incredible energy and her zest for life. She took intense pleasure in so many things and shared her pleasure with all of us. Coloring Easter eggs. Spotting a deer in our woods. Watching the MV Mount Washington steam past their cottage in New Hampshire. Hummingbirds. The Olympics. The Iditarod. She never, ever got bored or lost interest in the world around her."

Her grandsons had put clippings of all her columns into two scrapbooks. We displayed them, with photographs of Rita, at the reception following the Memorial. On our last drive up to New Hampshire, only seven months earlier, I had suggested that we publish a book collection of her columns. She brushed off the idea, but I like to think she was pleased. The scrapbooks were all we could manage.

The weather was far finer on May 30, when we had another memorial service for Rita. She would have been 88 that day, a spectacularly beautiful day, the kind she called a typical New Hampshire day. There were just the four of us—her daughter, son-in-law, and two grandsons—as we took her ashes out on the lake she loved. The box was covered with a white cloth that had long tasseled fringe; I had chosen it from her collection of antique fabrics. We steered the boat to a sheltered spot near the cove where she and my father had spent their first vacations together. We said a few short prayers, my husband eased her ashes into the lake, and I placed two purple blossoms from her favorite lilac bushes on the water.

We had done the best we could for her. Her daughter would have to pay attention to herself. After I had walked through the early painful days of letting my mother go, the rest of the path, winding and unknown, like the labyrinth, brought me deeper and deeper into my families' stories, deeper and deeper into my own story. There were many detours but the three strands, like those in my mother's rugs, remained tightly braided. Part of the struggle has been to accept each of the three strands as family.

The summer after my mother's disabling strokes, when we closed up the house in Merrick, we held a tag sale. The day before the crowds arrived, dealers were invited for an early look. All the closets had been emptied and everything we had not transported to my parents' new apartment in New Jersey or to our own garage was piled on the rugs or leaning against the walls. One dealer, slightly disgruntled, made his way from room to room without showing much interest in anything. Upstairs in my old bedroom, we had removed three very large portraits in heavy gold leaf frames from a closet.

"I'll take those," he said suddenly. "People like ancestors. Are you sure you don't want them?"

I looked at him in surprise. I had no idea who those distinguished people, two women and a man, were. When we had first dragged the portraits out into daylight, I had guessed that my mother, in her antique buying period, had bought them for the frames and stashed them in my closet, unused. But now I felt compelled to look more closely. I saw no family resemblances. I could not imagine either the Hoefel family or the Garibaldi family had been wealthy enough to have such impressive photographs taken. I also had to confront my quick analysis of my mother's motives. Was this more than another example of her passion for antiques? Was she also trying to claim ancestors—even if, as she would have known, they weren't at all, by any stretch of fact, connected to her?

I stood there, feeling all I didn't know close in around me. But deeply, intuitively, I knew these people were not my ancestors and I didn't care about keeping their portraits.

"Take them," I said.

Pursuing the Seidman thread had been far from easy, but it was my search alone, begun after my mother had died. Connecting with my Jewish family, learning the names of grandparents, great grandparents, even great great grandparents, and claiming my Jewish heritage, were independent adult choices, frightening but also exhilarating. The mother I met in that search was Beckie the baby, silent and innocent. Following the Hoefel strand has meant going deeply into the complex adult Rita, the mother I knew. When I revisited my childhood, I had to re-interpret my memories, comparing them with hers, parsing the many contradictions she bequeathed me.

As she was writing her columns over the years and sending them to me, my husband and I often joked about "Rita's World," an alternative present that we often did not recognize. I came to accept that her ideas of narrative truth were totally different from mine. My mother and I had two different interpretations of events and hers seemed innocuous enough. She made us laugh; the stories were charming. But the alternative past she created eventually became much more problematic for me because it was my heritage that she altered and obscured as well as her own.

Rita, at her core, must have been ashamed of being Jewish. Given the virulent anti-Semitism of the times during which she was a child and so vulnerable, that seems understandable. She was also, I believe, ashamed of being German, at least for some middle decades in her life which would have corresponded to other prejudices in American society. She was ashamed of being poor and not having graduated from high school. And she was ashamed of not having a Norman Rockwell family, either as a child or an adult.

None of her life experiences matched the ideal family model she would have absorbed from novels or radio or eventually television. What I have recovered of her Bronx years is far different from the *Little Women* milieu she found more acceptable. The poignancy of all the stories she wrote about four little sisters reveals to me the depth of pain she felt at not being part of a "real" family. What I remember of my childhood years shows me that she was still in a family far from what her wider world viewed as ideal. Across the street from where we lived in my early childhood were the Reillys and the Reeses, two very large Irish Catholic families. There were eight children in the Reilly family; seven in the Reese tribe. Or was it the other way around? They each owned big rambling houses on our still tree-shaded street in Queens. We rented the lower floor apartment in a two-story house. While I remember happy times, playing tag and chasing bumble bees with whichever Reese or Reilly was available, my mother remembered that she was frequently asked why she had only one child. That question came to haunt both of us as I progressed through Catholic schools dominated by the Irish and partial to large families.

My grammar school, St. Catherine of Siena, was part of a large parish where the rectory housed four or five priests and the convent must have had more than twenty sisters in residence. They were all Sisters of St. Dominic from the motherhouse in Amityville, New York. Most of them were young; some would have been only a dozen years older than their students. They were students, too, going to college on Saturdays and during the summer months. Usually it took them 17 years. Some of them could have received their degrees the same June as I did.

The parish had been established in 1920 and grew along with the sturdy Catholic population of Queens. By the mid-1940s, the grammar school held more than 1000 students. My first and second grade classes were split into two sections; we had 80 to 85 students in each section. Usually the arrangement was five double rows across the room and eight rows front to back. By the time my sons were in first grade, no teacher would ever have been expected to teach in such a situation. But I remember no objections among the parents and the Sisters had as yet no voice in their personal or professional lives. I also remember we spent a lot of time sitting in silence with our hands folded on our desks while Sister patrolled up and down the aisles.

Ours was a pious religion, marked by confession and novenas and Communion breakfasts, but we were also part of a church triumphant, which staged large public demonstrations of our faith. In May, elaborate processions culminated in crowning an outdoor statue of Mary. In June, on the feast of Corpus Christi, another procession circled the large city block that held all the parish buildings. When I was in fourth grade, we moved and I transferred to another Catholic grammar school, in the suburbs, much smaller, but with the same traditions. My mother and I were enthusiastic participants in both parish and school activities.

But as I look back, I don't think my mother ever felt secure and comfortable. Her temper would flare and her behavior would turn erratic at the mere hint of a slight. She loved the Sisters until she didn't. The Catholic Church of my childhood would have been just one of the institutions that impinged on Rita's reality. She was a strong imaginative woman, but no match for the pressures a poor New York City neighborhood, a country at war, or a church triumphant could bring to bear on an individual who did not fit in. People without power have few resources; they can remain silent, preserving their inner core for themselves or simply keeping it secret from outsiders, even family members. They can also create alternate worlds. During her long life, Rita chose both options, using them long after the threats had disappeared.

The alternative universe Rita created for herself, and for me, was a safe haven, a happier place, she thought, than the realities she was suppressing. Ironically, the more I have learned about the hidden facts of her childhood, the more lovable she becomes. I wish she could have taken pride in all she accomplished. I wish she could have accepted that in her real story she and Margaretha were both admirable and courageous; she did not need to invent a palatable past. We would have loved her all the more. Instead, she spent most of her life hiding sadness and anger and guilt and loss—to her detriment, I think, and certainly to mine.

I have thought often of all the times, stretching probably over a 20-year period, when I would ask her to have lunch with me—just the two of us. Usually we were in New Hampshire, the boys growing from toddlers to teenagers and beyond. I'd suggest that we leave "the men" alone and go off for a while by ourselves. Lunch and shopping for antiques or a drive to a favorite farm stand. Every year she had a different reason why she couldn't go. She was tired. She had a hair appointment. She wasn't sure the boys should stay alone with their father and grandfather. Who would make their lunch? I had asked her too early or too late. And the most defeating: she wasn't in the mood.

I countered each argument with one or two of what I hoped might be persuasive arguments. I won, as I remember, only once in all those years. We went to lunch at a nearby restaurant and were back in probably ninety minutes. It was lovely, I thought, pleasant and uneventful, no secrets shared, no boundaries crossed, but she never again agreed.

Back then I assumed her refusals were somehow a judgment on me. At the very least, I believed she preferred to spend time with her grandsons. With all that I have learned, I now interpret those painful memories far differently. Some of those years would have overlapped with the years when she was writing her columns, spinning the lovely nostalgic stories of her childhood. She knew I always asked questions. Perhaps she feared what I'd ask that year or where the answers would lead. Or perhaps she feared herself. What would she reveal if she were alone with me and some hidden defense crumbled? Those lost lunches, times when we might have recaptured our earlier closeness, expose the price she and I paid for the erasure of her true past.

The irony of all her writing is that she gave me something against which to measure the truth. What she wrote is all she expected I'd ever know. What I have learned is ever so much more satisfying. It is not just truth, my family's truth, but it is hidden truth, stories intentionally not told. Finding those stories—and telling them—has mattered a great deal to me. Moving beyond Rita, toward Margaretha, matters not only because she is my grandmother. She is not, biologically speaking, but the affection I feel for her is as strong as that I feel for Minnie. Margaretha must have had the same dreams and aspirations as any newly married woman, immigrant or not, but her finest moments came after she was widowed at 45 and raising three daughters alone. She did not give in to the anti-Semitism rampant in the Bronx; she brought young Jewish girls into her home and treated them as her daughters. She did not give in to poverty, but held on to her independence—and Rita's—until one of her older daughters, married and with a home of her own, could take over the responsibility. She added love to one particular child's life, transformed Rebecca into Rita, and changed the course of her future.

At first, I forged a connection to this German grandmother through torn photographs hidden in drawers, a letter sent from Germany in 1940, disembodied facts on census sheets, city tax photos of her tenement apartments, and my many trips to Webster

Avenue in the Bronx. A far better connection has come through my memories of my Aunt Anna.

Even as a child, I knew she and my mother had little in common. My aunt did not like to cook; she couldn't keep any plant, even a house plant, alive. As soon as her sons were independent, she went back to work and continued working even after her husband retired. She was gentle and generous and unfailingly kind, but she was not vivacious or enthusiastic about ideas like my mother. She was not a reader or a talker. She was a fantastic listener. She would have heard my uncle's jokes a thousand times, but she always laughed as if she were hearing the punch line for the first time. Rita and Anna must have talked just about every day of their lives—in person when they lived together or on neighboring streets and later by phone. I have no trouble guessing who did most of the talking and who did most of the listening. And I have no trouble concluding that despite their opposite personalities my aunt and my mother were as close as any two biological sisters could be.

When I have tried to imagine Margaretha, it is Anna I envision. Anna had the solid characteristics I have attached to Margaretha. After reconstructing those early Bronx years, I can see in both women the same sturdy independence, the primacy of a simple faith that prayed and didn't question, a love that showed in a thousand practical ways. Anna loved me without reservation and without flamboyance. She bragged about me as if I were her daughter and lived long enough to delight in the birth of my two sons. I believe that's the way Margaretha loved Rita. And if my grandmother had lived a few more years until I was born, she would have responded to me with the same warm pride as Anna had for my boys.

I have had no trouble continuing to think of Anna as my family. No matter what secrets I have uncovered these past years, she has remained family because my memories show me she loved my mother and me as if we were family. Without the memories, it has taken longer to understand that Margaretha is family, too—a grandmother, like my other two, who would have loved me and taught me her wisdom had we ever met. She can still nourish me; who she was and how she lived affects who I am and how I live.

When I bring her struggles, her indomitable love, her steadfastness in the face of so many obstacles, into the present, I feel a rootedness that has long escaped me. It has become far more than an obligation to retrieve and tell Margaretha's true story; it is an honor.

My journey to the center of my families' stories is not over. But I can no longer hold on to the artificial distinctions that have for so long hampered my appreciation of Margaretha as a real grandmother. Claiming her as family means I am also at peace saying farewell.

In the language she knew and loved, *Auf Wiedersehen*, Margaretha.

Part III
Hell's Kitchen

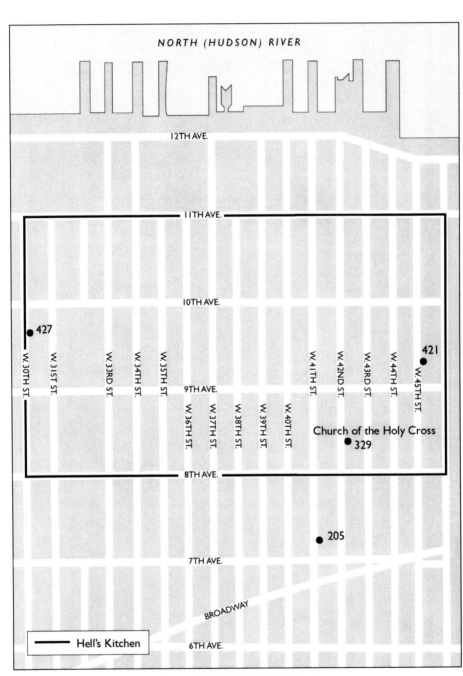

NORTH (HUDSON) RIVER

12TH AVE.

11TH AVE.

10TH AVE.

● 427

9TH AVE.

● 421

W. 30TH ST.
W. 31ST ST.
W. 33RD ST.
W. 34TH ST.
W. 35TH ST.
W. 36TH ST.
W. 37TH ST.
W. 38TH ST.
W. 39TH ST.
W. 40TH ST.
W. 41TH ST.
W. 42ND ST.
W. 43RD ST.
W. 44TH ST.
W. 45TH ST.

Church of the Holy Cross
● 329

8TH AVE.

● 205

7TH AVE.

BROADWAY

━━ Hell's Kitchen

6TH AVE.

West Side, Midtown Manhattan
(looking west)

Chapter 10
Giovanni Angelo

O ne Friday afternoon, as my first year of high school was ending, I boarded the Long Island Railroad for my short ride home. I was sitting at the end of a car with my friends when my father walked through the door, smiling right at me. I was delighted to see him—a pleasure I never outgrew—but since he rarely came home from work before 6 pm, I was also suddenly apprehensive. What was wrong?

"Nothing," he said, still smiling. "I just wanted to see you."

Fifteen and easily distracted, I didn't pursue my questions. Only the next day did I learn that he had come home early because his father, my grandfather, had died.

The memory divulges more than I expect about both my father and me. It is a painful example of his reluctance to share with me information about his family or his early life. Two years later, when my junior English teacher required the paper on our family history, I wrote about my father what I learned from my mother.

"On my father's side, as far as I can find out, Michael, my great-grandfather was born in Genoa, Italy. He married and raised a large family. One of his sons, John, migrated to America as a young man. There he lived with an uncle in the Midwest. Not finding enough employment there he moved to New York where he met my grandmother, Catherine, who lived on the same street. After they were married, they moved to Astoria where my father, John, was born. He was one of eight children. He went to P.S. 6 and then to high school and college."

Some fifty years later I know I relied on an untrustworthy narrator. I can identify the few items I know to be true. One great grandfather did come from Genoa. My grandfather's name, Giovanni, did translate to John. My grandmother's name was Catherine. My father, the third son but the one named John, was one of eight children. And he did graduate from high school. Everything else is either invented or embellished.

What I continue to confront in the early me: that I was not as curious as I should have been about my parents' lives, that I did not have the fortitude or the nerve to pursue uncomfortable questions, that, as an only child, I felt so vulnerable that I did not trust their love enough to anger them. I have sometimes thought that if I'd had a brother or sister, a co-conspirator, I might have been more suspicious, more challenging. Certainly, I'd have been tougher. Perhaps the truth, or at least some of it, would have surfaced earlier. But I know from several of my cousins, who had siblings, that the Garibaldi family's largest secret was well guarded even from them.

By the time I was old enough to remember our visits, my grandfather lived alone in a sparsely furnished apartment in Astoria, Queens. My father visited after work on Tuesday evenings. He would come home late with a Mason jar filled with freshly made sauce for our spaghetti. We didn't call it gravy as other American Italian families apparently did and we didn't have pasta, either. My German-cooking mother, who preferred potatoes or *spaetzle*, used only two shapes of pasta—spaghetti, which went with red sauce, and elbow, which was called macaroni and used only in a salad with mayonnaise, celery, and green peppers. Many the week we did not finish all of Grandpa's sauce and on Monday she would hastily dump the remainder down the drain before a new supply arrived the next evening.

The man I called Grandpa was frail and quiet most of the years our lives overlapped. Even though the time during our visits passed more and more slowly as he and I grew older and it seemed to me that we made the trip as a family less and less frequently, he was the only grandparent I knew and I felt his love. I think all of the grandchildren who knew him were told we were his favorite. I know I believed that.

When my father, my mother, and I visited on weekends, we would stand close together in the tiny lobby of his narrow three-story apartment building, waiting to be "buzzed up." The inner door would open, magically it seemed to me then, and we would climb the stairs. By the time we reached his floor, he'd be at the door of his apartment looking out for us. I can still see his shy smile of welcome. We had to walk carefully down his hallway and into the living room because the rugs were so threadbare and slippery that it was easy to trip and I often did. In the fashion of children who notice odd things at their eye level, the thing I remember most about his apartment is that the pipes under the sink in his kitchen shone gold. We couldn't see the pipes under our sink at home, so discreetly were they hidden behind Formica doors and shelves filled with Brillo and BonAmi. When I asked my father, he said "Grandpa polishes them every week." When I asked my grandfather, he just smiled and allowed as how he liked to keep things clean. He kept his gnarled hands deep in the pockets of his gray cardigan sweater.

Like many Italian men before him, my grandfather left Italy with no skills. Sometime in the 1880s—the dates on his discharge papers are no longer legible—Gio. Angelo Garibaldi finished his military service with the Royal Italian Armed Forces. The discharge shows his home town as Pontori, in the municipality of Ne, the region of Liguria, the military district of Genoa.

Pontori is still a very small town, a *frazione,* what the Italians call a hamlet. When my husband and I drove the tortuous mountain road up to Pontori in 2011, we found two houses, a church, and a small but modern cemetery, which had both large mausoleums and small above-ground crypts. The majority, it seemed, were inscribed with the name Garibaldi. Angelo, Maria, Davide. Domenico, Lina, Cesare. Enrico and Giovanni. There was no way to know if any would have been my relatives; we had arrived in Val Garibaldo, the lands of Garibald, who had been the king of the Lombards in the ninth century. The name has come down through the centuries. This surprisingly remote mountainous region, less than an hour's drive from Genoa or the Italian Riviera, is also the ancestral home of the family of Giuseppe Garibaldi, the Italian patriot who is considered the founder of modern united Italy. We had driven into Val Garibaldo on Via Giuseppe Garibaldi. Not that unusual perhaps in that region of Italy, but in fact almost every Italian town, no matter how small, boasts a *via* or *vialle* or *strada* Garibaldi. Monuments to Giuseppe Garibaldi stand in piazzas in every city. His fame is worldwide.

Not so Giovanni Garibaldi. My grandfather's life took a very different trajectory. He was born on December 5, 1868, the son of Antonio Garibaldi and Maria Ghiotto. The names of my great grandparents were handwritten on one of the last pages of a large gray ledger, which had survived two cataclysmic world wars and now rests securely in the town hall in Conscenti, the municipal center of Ne. When my husband and I, struggling to express our wishes in Italian, made our way to the second floor to request a copy of my grandfather's birth certificate, we were escorted down the hall to the records office where we stood on one side of the glass partition while a cooperative staff person with the ledger stood on the other. She patiently turned the heavy pages until she found my grandfather, but when I asked to see the ledger listing, which I could only read upside down, she smiled and shook her head. *No.* She said *No* again, still smiling, when I asked if she could copy the page she held open. But the rules did allow her to type up and officially stamp two *certificato di nascita*. I slid my passport and two euro into the slot under the glass panel, as she requested, and she slid the documents out. She came shyly around the partition. We all shook hands and I left feeling triumphant.

We walked out into a warm September morning. The mountains of Val Graveglia were etched against a blue sky. At a distance the slopes were a rich green, but a drought had left nearby stream beds dry. Small vineyards and olive groves were dusty and parched. Conscenti is a pleasing town, rather nicely ordinary. Its small houses are painted in warm siena tones; roses, begonias, and petunias bloomed in side yards and on balconies. The few small shops, a *tabachi, pasticceria, panificio,* and *macelleria,* offer sustenance not souvenirs.

We lingered over an espresso at a tiny trattoria on the piazza, talking as best we could to some townspeople. To be a Garibaldi in Ne is hardly worth mentioning. *Trente percenti* of the population is still named Garibaldi and as if to prove their statistic, one of the three men, 92-year-old Angelo, was indeed a Garibaldi. But to have a visiting American named Garibaldi—that was news enough for a quiet Wednesday morning. We were enthusiastically welcomed and repeatedly warned. No busses went to Pontori. It was much too far to walk. To drive was treacherous. We would surely get lost. They gave us careful directions—in rapid Italian, of course—and it turned out we did not grasp all the details. They wished us well. We drove off and promptly got lost on the only mountain road out of Conscenti.

During our hour driving up and down the same steep winding road, looking for a sign to Pontori, we passed only two motorists. The second graciously brought us to our turn, gestured us down a vertical incline, waved, and drove off. We had indeed arrived in Pontori, identified by a sign on the back of an old building, which became visible only when we were leaving town. If you are one of the few families who live in Pontori now, or if you go to San Antonio, the small church, for Mass, or if you visit the cemetery to water the flowers or light a candle, you don't need a sign to know you're in Pontori. We were a rarity: tourists.

My grandfather would have been barely twenty when he returned from his service in the Italian Armed Forces. The glory days of fighting as a "red-shirt" with the great General Giuseppe Garibaldi as he battled to subdue the kingdoms of Naples or Sicily were over. The nation of Italy had been established and the General had retired to live out a quiet old age in Sicily. My grandfather, still young and strong, would have come home to a poor mountain town facing a limited future.

I stood on the small piazza in front of San Antonio and looked out at the view of the valley, trying to imagine what forces impelled Giovanni Angelo to leave Pontori. I cannot find any records to tell me if my great grandparents had other children. Their names, Maria and Antonio Garibaldi, are just too common and nineteenth-century records too scattered to successfully search. The cemetery we visited is relatively new; the location of the cemetery where townspeople from the late nineteenth and early twentieth centuries were interred is unknown.

So I do not know if Giovanni Angelo left behind brothers and sisters when he decided to go to America. Would a large family have made it easier to leave? Or harder? Did he see that there was no way to provide for a family except the risky, hardscrabble life of a farmer? Did he despair of finding a bride in the tiny mountain towns around him? What future did he see for himself? Perhaps his few years away in the Army had made him adventurous. He had seen life beyond Val Graveglia. He had heard stories of young men who had found success in America. Perhaps the mountain peaks themselves had bred into him a willingness to take risks.

Whatever his motives, he said goodbye to his family in Pontori in the early months of 1893 when he was 24. It had not been a hasty decision; he had probably been home for close to four years. In Genoa, after he passed all the health examinations, he boarded the Werra, bound for the United States. He traveled third class, one of a thousand steerage passengers on the Werra, arriving in New York on June 26, 1893. Like so many other Italian immigrants, Giovanni Angelo hoped to find in America a land of *dolci dollari*. But for him, big dreams did not come true.

He married quickly on November 11, 1895. Catherine Prato, his bride, was fifteen. He was just shy of his 27th birthday. The children also came quickly. A son, Emil, was born a year later, in November, 1896. Then came four girls and another boy. By 1910 he had six children. He was a hotel waiter for a while, but for most of his life he worked in the building trades, probably only as a brick layer's assistant. He earned barely enough to house his family in Hell's Kitchen, in two dreary apartments near the Ninth Avenue El, and later, with help from the earnings of his older children, in the upstairs half of a two-story house in Astoria. For years he must have come home to his eight children each night with grit under his fingernails, knees and back and shoulders aching, too tired to talk or participate in family rituals.

In 1930 he worked on the Empire State Building as it rose above the New York skyline, a story a day, completed in one year and 45 days. In one of the few family photographs from that period he stands with his youngest son, my uncle Bob, atop the open frame of the building. My grandfather has his hands in his pockets. He wears a casual jacket over a dark cardigan sweater and open-necked collared shirt and what seems to be a 1930s version of baggy jeans. His face is partially obscured by the brim of his hat—the style my father called a fedora. My uncle, who would have been about 13 or 14, wears woolen knickers and a V-neck sweater over a white shirt and tie. A peaked cap shades his eyes. He carries either a rolled up newspaper or folded notebook under his arm. Their shoes are dusty. The background is cloudy open space with some construction equipment to the right and left. Work must still be in progress, but my grandfather is not in his workday clothing. Even though crews worked seven days a week on the site, this must have been a day off for him. Perhaps it is a Sunday. Grandpa was not a demonstrative man, but he had brought his youngest son with him to see the view from the highest point of the construction and he seems proud to be there. I wonder who else was there with them. Who took the photograph? I want to imagine it was my father, but he never remembered it that way.

My grandfather's trade was not as spectacular as the steel workers who swung out from girders 86 stories above Fifth Avenue or as dangerous as the sky-high teams of riveters who tossed red hot bolts across chasms as they fastened the steel. But, as *The New York Times* reported, bricklayers came in for their share of attention on Tuesday, September 9, 1930 when former New York Governor Alfred E. Smith laid the cornerstone for the new skyscraper. As he wielded a silver trowel, Smith responded to the teasing that came his way from the workers on the site. Reminding the bricklayers who surrounded him that he was a member of their union, he added, "So that there will be no mistake or misunderstanding about it, I declare, and firmly, that I have a right to use this trowel as a member of the union. My dues are all paid and I have my card in my office at 200 Madison Avenue."

I picture my grandfather hanging out with the other men listening to the Governor, leaning against an overturned wheelbarrow, enjoying the repartee, smiling and relaxing for a few minutes during a long brutal workday. Two hundred and ninety bricklayers, plus 384 brick laborers, worked on the Empire State Building. Together, the *Times* recorded, they laid more than 10,000,000 bricks and 200,000 cubic feet of stone.

One blustery morning in October, 2008, I visited the observation deck on the 86th floor. It was 8am, too early on a Monday morning for many tourists, but probably hours after my grandfather would have started carrying and mortaring his day's quota of bricks. You can see Long Island, Connecticut, New Jersey and even Massachusetts from up there. But on that visit I was interested in the foreground—the landmarks of my family's history.

A handful of us stood on the southern side of the observation deck, looking out over New York Bay. Just in front of the Statue of Liberty were the distinctive towers and brick roof of the arrivals building on Ellis Island where Grandpa, traveling as Giovanni Angelo Garibaldi, entered this country in 1893. Shortening my perspective and swiveling west from the Flatiron Building, I focused on the Chelsea neighborhoods, West 16th Street and West 25th Street, where he and my grandmother, Catherine Prato, had each lived before they were married in 1895.

To the west and almost directly below me was the tenement at 427 West 30th Street, just off Ninth Avenue, where the Garibaldi family lived by 1910 and where my father was born in 1913. To the west and fifteen blocks north was the family's final Manhattan apartment, another tenement walk-up at 421 West 45th Street, in the middle of the notorious West Side neighborhood called Hell's Kitchen.

To the east, across the East River, back lit by a still rising sun and softened by an autumn haze, was Queens and what was once called the village of Astoria, now part of Long Island City, where my grandfather and six of his children lived while he worked on this building. Bundled against the stiff breeze, I wondered how he commuted. By subway? Or bus? Either way, he would have had blocks to walk. From this height, distances were compressed and I wondered how much time the trip added to his workday. Also to the east, still in Queens, was Calvary Cemetery, the vast acreage the Catholic Archdiocese of New York reserved as hallowed ground for generations of New York Catholics, including my two Italian grandparents.

As I walked again and again around the perimeter, I suddenly looked not out but down and focused on the floor of the observation deck. Ordinary bricks. They were the first I had seen in this still handsome Art Deco building where the face of the building is Indiana limestone and the lobby walls are marble. They were at that moment behind scaffolding, undergoing one more upgrade. The cornerstone, which Governor Smith troweled into place that September day in 1930 and which I finally located to the left of the main entrance on Fifth Avenue, is a highly polished curved black stone. But there under my feet were bricks. Who could tell if they were the ones that my grandfather might have laid back in 1930 or 1931. It didn't really matter to me. I had found the connection I sought. The bricks led me in a full circle; the spectacular 360-degree panorama of New York was at once historical, geographical, and very personal.

It was perhaps a view that even the young immigrant ushers could appreciate. When I was pressed once too often to purchase a map or an acoustic guide so I could know what I would see from the top, I blurted out to one that I was only there to see where my grandfather had worked. This very young Hispanic man was clearly stunned. Without any obvious trace of mockery and with a gallant gesture more typical of an older generation, he bowed low and ushered me along. His tentative smile accompanied me as I navigated the roped pathways. My grandfather might have smiled like that.

Several months later, I returned. It was the morning of my birthday and as part of our family celebration, we five—my husband, younger son, Matt, older son, Doug, and his partner, Melanie—had come to the top of the Empire State Building. I wanted to show our sons some locations in our family history and also where their great grandfather had worked. But the building was totally fogged in. Every guard on the way up had warned us: don't waste your money. You will see nothing out there.

So we stood by ourselves on the deserted observation deck and looked down—at the bricks beneath our feet. We were talking about what it must have been like up here in 1930 when my toe scuffed the edge of a loose brick. I bent down, loosened it, and held it in my hands. A security guard materialized at our side and I imagined sirens going off as the cameras caught me in the act of vandalizing New York's most famous icon. But the guard was calmed by our family story. He perceived we were no threat and as we talked, I showed him the photograph of Grandpa standing at the top in 1931. A burly man closing in on retirement, he had retained his sense of wonder—and his sense of humor. He had a lifetime of coping with other tourists and their misdeeds. But he had not heard a story from the past like ours.

We remained the only visitors up there; rows of lonely telescopes lined all four sides of the deck. The only view was under foot, what we had come to see. We took a few quick photos of a granddaughter and great grandsons holding one of the ten million bricks. Under the guard's supervision, I replaced the brick, tapping it efficiently back into its niche, amazed and grateful at the way events had conspired to allow me to hold one in my hands.

I was one of the younger grandchildren, too young to have known the small silent man, with the gentle smile, when he was formidable, when his four sons and four daughters all feared an outbreak of his simmering anger and the razor strap he kept on a hook in the bathroom. It is a third-hand story, its power diluted, by the time an older cousin tells me the girls in the family were terrified to tell him that my father had failed a Spanish exam in his senior year of high school.

My father was the second youngest of the eight Garibaldi children. The oldest, Emil, who served in World War I, became a bombastic angry man I barely knew. He and my father were "never close," as my father would tell me years later. Then came the four girls—Mae, Jeannette, Louise, and Catherine. And finally, there were the three young boys—George; my father, finally a namesake for Giovanni Angelo; and Robert, my uncle Bob who became my godfather and my favorite Garibaldi uncle.

I knew all my aunts and my two younger uncles reasonably well in my childhood years, but I recall more stress than jollity on the occasions when we joined the family and gradually those events fell off our calendar. As my cousins and I grew older, I had few opportunities for talks with them. What I learned about the family I stole from overheard phone conversations and late-night arguments between my parents. That's how I knew about the rifts in the family, that some of them concerned money, and that my mother wanted to hire a lawyer for some reason I didn't comprehend. I was well aware that my mother felt badly treated by her sisters-in-law, but she didn't like them very much, either. There was much more in those angry conversations, but it escaped my understanding and as I grew into my teens, I lost interest. My grandfather's funeral during my first year of high school was probably the last family event I attended.

Later, my father will cry whenever he told me about his sisters. Long after their deaths, he talked to me about each of them even though he had never wanted me to attend their funerals. Sometimes neither he nor my mother even told me an aunt or uncle had died. When I mentioned the aunt who frightened me as a child because she seemed so severe, he remembered that she always laughed a lot. I tried harder to recall a twinkle in her eyes. And, yes, it was there. He said they all had a hard time growing up, that his sisters raised him as well as George and Bob. They gave up a lot and he owed them so much. He was crying, he said, because he regretted not keeping in touch all those years.

I have no doubt that my aunts played a large role in my father's early and teenage years. Even before I learned the truth about my grandmother, her absence from all family stories pointed to extra sadness and hardship for her children. And the greatest burden clearly would have fallen on the four sisters. They were not only older than their three younger brothers, but they were girls, expected to run the household and be substitute mothers. Even as my father praised his sisters and his brother Bob, he rarely gave himself any credit for what he accomplished. He never talked about his high school days. When prompted, he would recall the one semester he went to night school at Columbia University, but if I pressed for details, he would only say he dropped out because he could not afford to continue.

Shortly after graduating from Bryant High School in Astoria, he went to work in the purchasing department of the American Chicle Company, which had opened a gleaming new five-story block-square building on Thomson Avenue in nearby Long Island City. He learned to buy heavy machinery as well as packaging materials and ingredients for Chiclets and the array of new products as they came along. The chewing gum manufacturer was a huge part of his life— and mine—for the rest of his working days.

Very early in his career there he met and courted my mother who worked in the cost department, four floors above the purchasing department. Those were stories neither of my parents minded sharing. I knew the names of all their friends and the details of their courtship. In 1932, when my father was just 19, the February issue of the "Current News," the chatty employee newsletter, reported, "Garibaldi and Miss Rita Hoefel have that look of spring's return in their eyes....Rumor has it that John, who lives in Astoria, has been seen wading through the mud in the vicinity of St. Albans." They did not marry until 1937. My mother left American Chicle, as was the custom, but my father stayed on.

My father would have been 28 when the United States entered World War II. I had always been told that he was not drafted, as his younger brother was, because he received repeated deferments for his work "in essential services." But I never really understood what that meant until I looked into the history of American Chicle and learned the role chewing gum played in World War II. It turns out that gum was indeed an essential product for the armed forces and its manufacturers produced and shipped over 15 billion sticks of gum during the war years.

"At night on the front lines, where the glow of a cigarette might betray a position, chewing gum was found by the military to be an adequate substitute for quieting nerves. Packed in K rations and survival kits, gum also served to patch jeep tires, gas tanks, life rafts, radio connections and to fix machine guns, submarines and even the hydraulic landing gear on bombers," Robert Hendrickson reports in *The Great American Chewing Gum Book*.

On the home front, more specifically on Thomson Avenue in Long Island City, the plant was used not only for increased production of chewing gum but also to pack and ship other war rations. Its employees were indeed essential for the stepped-up war effort. The deferments also happened to keep one particular employee at home near his baby daughter.

My visits to the plant would have begun after the war ended and production was once again Dentyne, Black Jack, Sen-Sen, and all flavors of Chiclets for the domestic and increasingly worldwide markets. I remember the mix of scents—clove, licorice, peppermint, spearmint—that greeted us whenever my father brought me up the stairs from his office and opened the doors to the factory. White sugary dust covered every surface, soon including my shoes. Machines whirred; women in white uniforms and caps smiled at me and, as I noticed even then, my father.

Raold Dahl had not yet written *Charlie and the Chocolate Factory*, which decades later meant so much to our younger son, Matt. In his factory Willie Wonka also made fantastic gum. "This gum," as he described it, "... is my greatest, my most fascinating invention! It's a chewing gum meal...This piece of gum I've just made happens to be tomato soup, roast beef and blueberry pie...!" The flavors certainly weren't the same, but I had had my own fantasy factory. And I treasured those Saturday morning visits. My father was supposedly working and I was supposedly doing homework, but I think we both thought of the morning as time off.

I wasn't allowed to chew gum because my mother concurred with Emily Post: it wasn't ladylike. But for all my school years, my classmates delighted in sampling the penny Chiclet packs, from the classic yellow to spearmint green to tutti-frutti pink, that always lay around our house. And they weren't the only ones. My teachers also loved the colorful boxes of gum that my father would frequently drop off at the parish convents where they lived.

In 1949, when we moved to Long Island, my father commuted an hour by the Long Island Railroad. In the 1960s when American Chicle was absorbed into the Warner-Lambert Company and his job was relocated to their headquarters in Morris Plains, New Jersey, he drove four hours round trip, often leaving home at 4am to beat the traffic on the Cross Bronx Expressway.

He turned down many transfers over the years, to Illinois, Mexico, and Puerto Rico, because my mother preferred not to move, and he took early retirement because a fall on an icy train platform during a business trip when he was still a young man left him with life-long back injuries. But he had worked hard and made wise decisions that gave him financial security and some peace of mind in his later years. But, more often than not when we talked, he would focus on his regrets, chief among them that he had not reconciled with his sisters before their deaths.

After my mother's death, my father renewed his bonds to George and Bob, his two living siblings, as well as to those of his nieces and nephews who would accept him. And so I walked with him into another new family, meeting Italian uncles and cousins for what felt like the first time.

My cousin Paul, the older son of Emil, my oldest uncle, became my father's telephone companion. Uncle and nephew, only a dozen years apart, they shared many memories of the old days. For me, Paul became a vital link to the family's past. It was he who gave me copies of my grandfather's discharge papers from the Italian Royal Army Forces, papers that eventually led me to Pontori. And it was Paul who nudged the New York chapters of our grandfather's story back a few decades from my early childhood to his, to the Astoria apartment where the Garibaldi family lived during the late 1920s and early 1930s.

In his vigorous years, Paul often said, our grandfather had a terrible temper. Being the sole parent of eight couldn't have made it any easier to control. His daughters were afraid of him and he didn't know how to talk to them. He was strict with his sons, but he was easygoing with his first grandson. Years later, when Paul reminisced with my father, he would tease, "I got the tamer version."

Paul told me that Grandpa occasionally gave him a quarter and took him on long walks through the neighborhood. "One time we walked from Astoria all the way to the World's Fair grounds in Flushing. Any idea how far that is? We each used to carry a bag. Grandpa picked mushrooms. I picked dandelions." By the time I could have walked with them, the World's Fair had closed, and mushrooms and dandelions were probably no longer there for the gathering. But the distance would have been the same: five miles each way.

Paul had clear memories of life in the Astoria apartment. He described the sleeping arrangements in the small apartment: Grandpa in one bedroom; the three as yet unmarried daughters sharing another; George alone in the third; John and Bob on a foldaway bed in the living room. Mae, the oldest of the daughters, was married in 1928 and out of the household. So was Emil, Paul's father. But after Emil lost his house during the Depression, he moved his family of four in with his father and sisters and brothers. They took over George's bedroom. Times were tough for all of them. Paul slept in a dresser drawer and wore Bob's hand-me-down clothes and an old coat of George's. "It was so thin that I used to freeze on my way to school."

And there were other stories I would never have been told when I was younger. "The family used to sit around the table in the dining room smoking and sometimes drinking whisky. Grandpa smoked those small cigars, the ones where he cut off the tip." Paul paused. "They smelled awful." In the fall, the family made wine in the backyard, turning the grass purple where they crushed the grapes and angering their landlord. All these decades later, he still thinks of his grandfather when he goes to buy a bottle of wine. "Grandpa loved his red wine."

The 1930s were a decade when my grandfather, perhaps under the influence of his adult children, filled out many legal papers.

After he filed his naturalization papers, he received his certificate of citizenship in May, 1934. He was 66 years old, five feet, five inches tall, with a visible scar on his forehead. He is staring straight ahead in his official photograph, scowling slightly, sporting a trim mustache, and wearing white shirt, tie, and dark suit. In his stern unsmiling expression, I see the strict father; I do not see the gentle Grandpa I came to know decades later.

In October, 1934 he received a certificate of literacy from P.S. 70 and the University of the State of New York. And in 1936, he applied for a social security card. He was working for Cauldwell Wingate, a construction firm that had already built some New York landmarks like Saks Fifth Avenue and the majestic Temple Emanu-El at Fifth Avenue and 65th Street.

All the documents attested that my grandfather lived at 28-51 45th Street in Astoria. That was the upstairs apartment Paul had described to me and the house that appears in the background of a few photographs from that period, showing my father, my uncle Bob and a very young Paul. In 1999, when I pushed my father for more information, he said the family moved there in 1923 when he was ten. That was practically all he said—except to rehearse his debt to his sisters. One time, he recalled, a high school friend invited him to go to Yankee Stadium to see Babe Ruth play. He went even though he had been told not to go—for what reason he did not remember. He did remember that his sisters once again shielded him from his father's wrath.

My father remained Yankee fan all his life. And he remained a model of parental patience as he waited for his only daughter to root for every other team in the American League before she finally gave in and became a Yankee fan with him. Together we went to Yankee Stadium. It wasn't quite the era of Babe Ruth, but Mickey Mantle, Phil Rizzuto and Yogi Berra were legends aplenty for us. In the last months of his life, which corresponded to World Series time, I scoured websites for articles and stories about the old days of the New York Yankees and I could always get him to smile as I read to him. "Yes," he would say, "I remember that."

The few remaining facts I have about my father's childhood years are scattered like so many pinholes of light in a family's curtained past.

When he finally shared his birth certificate with me, I learned that his middle name was Adolph—something I had never known. He had always referred to himself as John T. Garibaldi. I was quite young when I first asked what the "T" stood for. He said, "Thomas," his confirmation name. (When I had asked my mother, she had pursed her lips and said abruptly, "He doesn't have a middle name.") I can guess that by the late 1940s and 50s when I might have started asking, the name Adolph meant Hitler to most people and a middle name with such unpleasant connotations was just one more secret my parents kept.

I also learned that he was born, apparently at home, when the family lived at 427 West 30th Street. His mother's name is listed as Katie, maiden name of Prato. Seeing my grandmother named Katie—I had up to then only seen her formally called Catherine—reminded me that she was still young, 33, when my father was born. He was her ninth child, seven of whom, including the baby John, were living in 1913. She will have one more baby, my uncle Bob, in 1917.

My father told me he was baptized at Holy Cross Church at 237 West 42nd Street. "Father Duffy's church," he remembered. Father Francis Duffy, a name I recognized from the familiar statue at the north end of Times Square, was a military chaplain in World War I, serving with the famous New York regiment, "The Fighting 69th," as part of the Rainbow Division. Father Duffy came home from the war a hero, was appointed pastor of Holy Cross parish in 1920, and soon became known as the priest of Broadway. I wrote to the church offices for the baptismal certificate but they had no records for my father. "Oh," he said when I told him, "Maybe that was Bob."

I found five other Catholic churches near the Garibaldi family address on West 30th Street and contacted each in turn. St. Michael's, at 424 West 34th Street, sent back what I was seeking and I saw once again my grandparents names, John and Catherine Garibaldi. The godparents were Anthony Prato, the baby's uncle, and Mary

Garibaldi, probably the baby's oldest sister, whom the family called Mae.

Sometime between 1913, when my father was baptized at St. Michael's, and 1917, the family moved from 427 West 30th Street to 421 West 45th Street, which would have put them within the boundaries of Holy Cross parish. After my father died, I found at the bottom of a carton a large four-color certificate, creased years ago into five narrow envelope-sized panels. Unfolded and carefully assembled, it became a "Remembrance of the first Holy Communion" that John Garibaldi received at Holy Cross Church on May 7, 1921. It was signed by Francis P. Duffy, Pastor. My father's memories of receiving an early sacrament at Holy Cross Church were indeed correct. But it was First Communion, not Baptism.

No matter how much I nudged him, my father told no more stories about the first ten years of his life before the family moved to Astoria in 1923. There, he remembered, he went to P.S. 70 and then to Bryant High School. Down in the carton, wedged under the First Communion poster, I would find his high school graduation photograph. It had been rolled up for so many years that as I opened it ever so slowly, it cracked into so many thin shards that I cannot repair it. And I cannot find him now among the severed rows of solemn graduates.

Missing in all the documents I assembled and the few facts I extracted from my father were not just the details of his childhood years, the stories that would bring a family to life. A central figure in the narrative was absent. My grandmother, Catherine. Until I pried open that secret, I could not begin to envision the family's life during those earlier decades.

Chapter 11
John and Catherine

Several years after we moved from the downstairs apartment of a two-family house in Queens to a house of our own in the suburbs of Long Island, my parents decided that our television needed an upgrade from the boxy faux wood set we had brought with us. So a sleek mahogany console sat under the front window of the living room, just inside the entry foyer. Its smooth surface, empty except for an occasional vase of flowers or a holiday decoration, became a handy place to pile the mail. It was there, probably sometime between the years I was 11 and 14, that I began to notice the thin white envelopes with the return address of Central Islip State Hospital.

The envelopes had a glassine window, like many bills, and through the window I could read my father's name and our address. Above his name was always "Catherine Garibaldi."

"Who," I asked my mother, "is Catherine Garibaldi?"

While my mother always had her arsenal of weapons ready to avoid answering my questions, this one finally, some year or other, elicited an answer. "She's your father's mother." But she added the warning I had occasionally heard about other things: "Don't ask your father about it. He will get angry." Intimidated as usual, I did not ask.

Still, over the years I came to understand that Central Islip State Hospital was a mental institution, that my father paid the bills that kept his mother there, and that no one in the family, least of all my parents, would answer questions about Catherine. I learned

195

nothing substantive until the summer of 1994, forty or so years after I first saw those envelopes.

During a visit to see my parents at their cottage in New Hampshire, I sat with my father down on the dock. It was one of the few quiet places we had to talk. The lake was still; there was no wind. The boats that kept the water churning during the day had gone to their buoys. Night comes early in New Hampshire by mid-August and across the lake the mountains my father loved so much were already turning from green to purple. My mother, my husband, and our sons were all up at the house. My father wanted to talk about his will and his wish to be cremated. He said that he could not talk about these things with my mother, but that he was so grateful he could talk with me. I was taken aback by their wishes to be cremated, which I had never heard, and questioned him closely. He was amazed they had not told me and promised to have my mother confirm her decision to me. When he finished, we sat silently for a few minutes. In the enveloping dusk, I sensed an opportunity to ask my questions about Catherine.

"Can you tell me about your mother now?"

I tried to be gentle, explaining why the time had come to give me some information. I needed to know, I said, what illness she had, what caused her death. Such information is important for children and grandchildren. He agreed. When he acquiesced so easily, I had to wonder what really would have happened if I'd asked my questions directly those many years ago.

And so I heard for the first time what I would come to recognize as the family's story about Catherine. I would hear similar versions more than ten years later as I got back in touch with some of my cousins.

"We were very poor," he told me as we each looked out at the lake. "She raised all of us, eight of us, in poverty. That's why I abhor large families." He spat out the word "abhor" and my mind wandered away for a minute to wonder if that was the real reason I'm an only child.

He continued in what seemed a calmer voice, saying that his brother Emil had been gassed and was reported missing during the war [World War I] and that his mother couldn't take the news. He didn't have any more details to share. But then he started to cry and his voice went high before it broke. He tried again to speak and he cried again. I was in tears, too, feeling guilty for putting him through the ordeal, but afraid to move or speak because I so much wanted him to tell me more.

He was still angry at my mother, he said then, because she never once went to visit Catherine. He had told her about his mother and where she was before they were married. The left hemisphere of my brain registered the math: he had stored inside him more than 50 years of anger at my mother on this one subject alone.

I asked if he went to see his mother.

"Oh yes," he said.

I asked if she knew him when he visited. "Oh yes," he said again. "I was her favorite."

We were called to dinner and walked slowly up the hill to the house. I managed to get in one more question.

"What did she die from?"

He shrugged with that familiar yet irritating gesture I knew so well. "Old age. She wore out."

He caught my impatient response and added, "Her heart."

We were at the door where my mother stood waiting. The conversation was over.

It was so appropriate that my father would tell me the deepest secret of his life as we sat by the lake. The shore along Lake Winnipesaukee was where both my parents were always happiest. I could go even further. This was where they found home. It was not just the scenery and the good times and the memories. At the lake they early on found substitute parents in Lela and Dick Lancaster, an acerbic Yankee couple with no children of their own, and my parents created an alternative past that might have soothed the pain of their own troubled childhoods.

Rita and John first visited the lake in August of 1936, the year before they were married, the year after Margaretha had died. Rita had spotted a small ad in a New York newspaper—neither of them was ever able to remember which paper—describing "Fairview in the Pines," a guest house that offered comfortable lodgings, three meals a day, a pristine lake with gentle beach and mountain vistas. For a young couple without a car, New Hampshire was an exotic destination, a long way from New York City. They were embarking on an adventure when they took first a subway from Queens to Grand Central Station, then a train to Boston, a bus between South and North Stations, and another train to Laconia, where Dick Lancaster, the proprietor of the guest house, picked them up for the fifteen minute drive to "Fairview." My father remembered that not having a car in those days presented no problem; they could swim, hike, and follow meandering mountain brooks right from the front door of the house. They also had time to begin their lifelong friendship with Lela and Dick.

I grew up knowing more about New Hampshire genealogies than about my own New York ancestors. I heard frequently that Lela was a Morrill. The sandy shore the Lancasters owned was called Morrill Beach after her father who, although he lived for a time at The Poor Farm, had received the Winnipesaukee shore property as a land grant from "the King." (Make that "a King"; no one was ever too specific about that claim.)

Rita and John stayed only a week that first year, in separate bedrooms, but returned on their honeymoon the following summer. That year they traveled from New York to Boston by boat, one of the last times the Eastern Steamship Line made that run. In New Hampshire in June, the weather was much cooler, my father remembered, and there were fewer guests. So Lela and Dick, relatively free from housekeeping chores, took the young couple sightseeing—to the Maine seacoast and to the White Mountains. Years later, my parents would return the favor, chauffeuring the elderly Lela and Dick to the same destinations.

There was one more vacation, in the summer of 1938. My father told me that his brother Bob accompanied them for a few days and they tried very hard to fix him up with a rather large, strong-jawed female guest. Bob never returned. No wonder, my father would laugh much later when he told the story. But Rita and John didn't either—for ten years. During those intervening years, I was born and World War II changed everybody's lives. But my mother and Lela wrote faithfully to each other and exchanged Christmas cards. My father sent the occasional box of Chiclets to Dick and the stage was set for a return, with daughter, in 1948.

By that time, my parents had a car, but the trip was still arduous. Without interstate highways or air conditioning, my father drove through steamy downtown traffic in more than a half-dozen New England cities—New Haven, Hartford, Worcester, Leominster, Nashua, Manchester, and Concord—before we reached the cool temperatures of the mountains. I was prone to getting car-sick; so was the cocker spaniel with whom I shared the back seat. My parents had to love New Hampshire to put up with those endless hours in the car.

Life had changed at "Fairview," too. The Lancasters, growing older, rented cottages along the lake shore instead of running a guest house. I never knew the bountiful meals Lela had served at two large round tables in the big house up on the road. Each year my parents negotiated the rental of a different cottage. We had our favorites, like the Skipper, which had a front sleeping porch that I quickly claimed because the bed was only inches from the lake. But Lela had her schedule and her other regulars and since my father's vacation was inflexible—all American Chicle employees went on vacation when the plant closed for the first two weeks in August—we stayed where we were told. One year, the tiny Casino. Another, the Innisfree. Or the Four Winds. A few other cottages were interspersed along the beach, but they were deemed too large for us, a family with only one child.

Those idyllic summer vacations lasted throughout my childhood and early teenage years. I knew my parents had stressful conversations with the Lancasters from time to time—Lela was brutally outspoken and proud of it; Dick was thrifty to a fault and proud of that—but all was invariably patched up by the time we left. Then one year the State of New Hampshire took a liking to the place, bought the entire shore, one of the last available sandy beaches on the Big Lake, and created Ellacoya State Park.

My parents stifled their disappointment and searched for other places on the same side of the lake. More vacations came and went. For two weeks each summer, my parents balanced past and future. Dick died in 1966. My mother made casseroles for Lela and they drove her to the cemetery where Dick was buried next to his first wife, only a row away from the lake. Lela would join them in 1972. As my father neared retirement, my parents bought their own cottage, less than a mile down the same country road—the one where I sat with my father on the dock looking across at the Ossipee Mountains.

When we were not at the lake, my father and I occasionally talked about Catherine in our Thursday morning telephone conversations, the hour when my mother went to the hairdresser, the only time he felt free to call me. When I asked again why his mother was committed to the state hospital, he said it must have been depression because she couldn't cope with the news that Emil was missing in action. When I asked if he had any early photographs, he said he would look. In 1997 when I told him that I was writing to Pilgrim Psychiatric Center, which had taken over the records from Central Islip State Hospital after it closed in 1996, to request my grandmother's records, he did not object. But, even though I had supplied a patient record number, my request was rejected by a form letter saying there were no such records.

Not until after my mother died in 1999 did I again bring up the subject of my grandmother. I asked him to request her death certificate from the State of New York Department of Health. He agreed and I typed up a letter for him to sign. Three months later, he handed me the envelope he had received.

The copy of the death certificate was bureaucratic gray tinged with pink; the information was properly typed, signed by the attending doctor, and embossed with the seal of Department of Health—an ordinary official document. But what I read was stunning.

Catherine Garibaldi died on November 8, 1957. I was chagrined to remember that I had never asked my father when she died. It was easy to place that date in my life: two months into my first year living away from home at college.

"Do you mean to say that I was 18 when she died and you never told me?"

He sheepishly admitted that he and my mother had gone to the funeral. They didn't want to bother me, he added. I saw myself in my small freshman dorm, tossing pillows at my roommates, toasting popcorn in the kitchen, being incredibly silly and doing absolutely nothing that could not have been interrupted for a grandmother's funeral. I did not try to hide my disbelief and my anger. Unlike the first secret—my mother's adoption—which he had shared less than a year earlier and which had so shocked me that I felt no emotion whatever, this news infuriated me, instantly bringing a whole range of feelings, none of them pleasant, kind, or understanding.

I sought to regain some balance by analyzing the other information on the certificate. I learned that Catherine's parents were Antonio Prato and Jeannette Lagoria, that she was 78 when she died of "arteriosclerotic heart disease." Then I focused on a small rectangle that asked for the "length of stay in town, city or village." And I saw that my grandmother had lived at Central Islip State Hospital for 38 years, seven months and three days. I could not absorb those numbers and I grabbed a pencil to do the math. Catherine had been admitted to the hospital on April 5, 1919. She had been 40 years old; my father, six.

The date would fit with Emil's being reported missing in action during World War I. What did not fit was the information typed in the box labeled "Other significant conditions contributing to death but not related to the terminal condition." There it was reported that Catherine had "Dementia Praecox; Hebephrenic Type."

I spent time with dictionaries of mental illness, learning the terms, tracing the history. What we have come to know by its Greek-rooted word, schizophrenia, was until the mid-twentieth century called by its Latinate name, dementia praecox. Hebephrenic schizophrenia, the literature said, was "characterized by severe disintegration of personality including erratic speech and childish mannerisms and bizarre behavior." My grandmother did not land in a mental hospital because she was mourning a soldier son missing in action although that would certainly have been horrific news for any mother, especially a woman who had already lost a younger brother a decade earlier. Fear for Emil may well have been a trigger for a deep depression, but Catherine also had schizophrenia, the kind that affected her early in life, perhaps as early as her 20s, certainly by her 30s, her prime years of child-rearing, and the kind that caused her to be institutionalized for more than thirty years.

Schizophrenia was in those years the most common diagnosis of patients in mental hospitals. As I would continue to read in the psychiatric books of the time, commitment to an institution was the only treatment available for severe cases in the years before drug therapy became widely available and gradually emptied mental hospitals around the world. My grandmother died in 1957, the decade when those drugs first began to have a significant impact on the inmates of institutions like Central Islip. It was the beginning of the end of most of the large state hospitals.

But in my grandmother's lifetime, the institutions were like small cities, no matter that promotional literature called them "farms" or "farm colonies." I got a sense of the numbers of patients when I examined the 1920 census. One hundred and eight census sheets were devoted to listing the "inmates" of Central Islip State Hospital. With 50 names to a page, that added up to a population of 5,400 inmates. I found Catherine at the bottom of a page of phantom women—Margarets and Marys, Sylvia, Josephine, Wilhelmina, Helen. And Catherine Garabaldi. Mamie was 32; Eliza, 66; Bridget, 33; Estella, 47. Catherine was 39. They had been born in New York, Austria, Ireland, Russia, but all of them had landed in the same place. Some of them had an occupation like "laundry" or "ward work." In 1920, so soon after her arrival in 1919, Catherine had none.

In the years that followed I talked about our grandmother with several of my cousins. Paul, the first of Catherine's fourteen grandchildren, told me that he was the only one in our generation who knew about Catherine in the early years. Paul, too, believed that when his father was reported missing in the war, it caused Catherine's mental illness. That was the story my youngest cousins, two of my uncle Bob's children, born too late to have known either of their Garibaldi grandparents, said they had been told.

Gradually I learned that Catherine had not been forgotten during those 38 years. There were family visits from her husband, her sister Louise, her son George, the brother just older than my father, her daughters. Mae, her oldest daughter, sometimes drove out to Central Islip with her daughter, my cousin Ruth. Ruth remembered no details, but envisioned for me a "cloistered environment," where three generations, grandmother, mother, and daughter, sat together in a day room. And after many questions, my father would tell me that, yes, in the early days he, too, had visited with Catherine.

Kathy, another cousin, had done what I did: sent for a death certificate. She knew the family story differed from other facts, but neither of us knew how a diagnosis was made in those days. How might Catherine have behaved that it required she be separated from her husband and eight children for more than 38 years? How long was she ill before they signed commitment papers? And who signed those papers? When we talked, Kathy was as appalled as I was that our grandmother's story had been hidden from us for all our lives.

Kathy was 13 when Catherine died. She had come home from school and found her mother unusually quiet. She had to ask several times before she got an explanation.

Her mother, my aunt Kay, youngest of the daughters, said, "Well, if you must know, my mother died today."

Kathy replied that she didn't know she had a grandmother who was alive. Her mother told her then that Catherine had been in a mental hospital for a long time.

"Do you remember those Sundays when I was gone for the whole day and never said where I was? I was visiting her."

"Did she know you?"

"Sometimes she did and sometimes she didn't."

"Did you tell her about me? That you had children?"

"Yes. Sometimes she remembered and sometimes she didn't."

Well into his 80s, my father would recall that two of his aunts—

his mother's sister, Louise, and her brother Anthony's wife, Helen—were very good to the Garibaldi children when he was growing up. Tears would come to his eyes as he told me he had become estranged because he didn't keep in touch as they all grew older and he didn't go to funerals as he should have.

I kept wondering if there was anything in Catherine's earlier life that pointed to her illness, alarmed the family, and led to the moment of separation. There had to have been problems more burdensome than too many children with too little money, as my father had suggested. Those would not have been uncommon difficulties elsewhere in Hell's Kitchen, or for that matter in the tenements on Orchard Street on the Lower East Side or up on Webster Avenue in the Bronx. Schizophrenia is its own disease with its own causes and its own trajectory. In those days, doctors offered no treatment options except institutionalization. What behavior forced Catherine out of her family and into a state hospital?

I puzzled over the stories during long sleepless nights and then in conversations with my cousins. There was no longer any one to answer our questions or supply details, to confirm or contradict any of my suppositions. I could only reconstruct my grandmother's life, as lovingly as I could, from evidence I had found.

Chapter 12
Catherine
Before 1919

When Catherine left home that April day in 1919, did she understand that she would never come back to her family? Did the children left behind on West 45th Street know what was happening? Emil, 23, was still missing in action, somewhere in Europe, but would return to the family. Mae, who would not turn 20 for another four months, was the oldest at home; Bob, only two, the youngest. My father was six. Catherine's mother, my great grandmother, Jeannette Prato, was still alive; so were a younger sister, Louise, and a younger brother, Anthony, and perhaps even an older sister, Mary.

For almost all of her married life, Catherine had lived in Hell's Kitchen, a notorious Manhattan neighborhood dating back to the second half of the nineteenth century when it was the territory of Irish gangs and mobsters. A *New York Times* account, written on September 22, 1881, called the place "Hell's Kitchen," among other pejorative terms. "The entire locality is probably the lowest and filthiest in the City, a locality where law and order are openly defied....The whole neighborhood is an eyesore to the respectable people who live or are compelled to do business in the vicinity [and] a source of terror to the honest poor...." A few decades later, my grandparents were among the respectable folk, the honest poor who were compelled to survive there.

By 1900, new immigrant nationalities, including the Italians, had joined the Irish in Hell's Kitchen and gang violence had subsided, but the harsh realities of tenements, saloons, railroad yards, slaughterhouses, and factories still dominated people's lives. The boundaries of the neighborhood, always porous, expanded and contracted, sometimes described as stretching south to 28th Street and north to 59th Street, but always west of Eighth Avenue and centered along Ninth, Tenth, and Eleventh Avenues.

These north-south corridors gave the neighborhood its grim character: on Ninth Avenue, the Elevated blocked sunlight, adding deafening noise and swirling grit as it sped through the neighborhood; on Tenth, pedestrians trying to travel east-west needed a bridge, which arched up and over the dangerous confusion of freight trains and heavy horse-pulled carts; on Eleventh, once called Death Avenue, more trains traveled to and from the slaughterhouses using New York Central surface tracks; further west were the docks and the refuse-filled North River, as the lower Hudson used to be called.

The side streets did not escape the overall gloom. They were oppressed by foul odors, thanks to an array of outhouses, slaughterhouses for pigs, sheep, and cattle; breweries; and burning coal at the freight yards. They were noisy and always dark, relying on widely scattered gaslights at night and deprived of sunlight during the day by the El, the smoke from ships arriving and departing their piers, and the constant traffic of locomotives.

"My family and I grew up together on Tenth Avenue, between Thirtieth and Thirty-first Street, part of the area called Hell's Kitchen," Mario Puzo remembered. "Our tenements were the western wall of the city. Beneath our windows were the vast black iron gardens of the New York Central Railroad, absolutely blooming with stinking boxcars freshly unloaded of cattle and pigs for the city slaughterhouse...."

Social workers who studied Hell's Kitchen in the years before World War I minced no words in their reports. Woven among their stories are graphic descriptions of the world they saw. "In street after street are the same crowded and unsanitary tenements; the same untended groups of children playing; the same rough men gathered round the stores and saloons on the avenue; the same sluggish women grouped on the steps of the tenements in the cross streets. The visitor will find...only square, dull, monotonous ugliness....The very lack of salient features is the supreme characteristic of this neighborhood. The most noticeable fact about it is that there is nothing to notice. It is earmarked by negativeness. There is usually a lifelessness about the streets and buildings, even at their best, which is reflected in the attitude of the people who live in them. The whole scene is dull, drab, uninteresting, devoid of the color and picturesqueness which give to so many poor districts a character and fascination of their own."

This was to be my grandmother's world. "Katie" Prato had married Giovanni Garibaldi on November 11, 1895 in a ceremony performed not by a priest in a Catholic Church, as I had somehow expected, but by an alderman, a city official whom they may or may not have known. The marriage certificate says my grandfather was 27; my grandmother, 18. Actually, Catherine was only 15. She had been born in New York, the eldest of five, to parents who had emigrated from Italy. At the time of her marriage, she had been living with her family at 115 West 25 Street, in the neighborhood called Chelsea.

These days 115 is a four-story building, on the north side of the street, with commercial space on the ground floor and apartments and businesses on the top three floors. On our family tour of Chelsea, Hell's Kitchen, and the Empire State Building in 2009, Continental Die Company shared the storefront with Westpfal scissor sharpening services. The white brick had been cleaned, new windows inserted, and the whole building was much improved from its dowdy appearance in the 1930s WPA photograph I have. But I wonder what 115 looked like in 1895. Possibly this structure replaced another that deserved to be torn down; or possibly, in the trajectory of a building's history, that was its best time and the Prato family lived in modest comfort.

When we visited, the street was a mixture of gentrification and light industry. The six-story apartment building on the east side of 115 had been scrubbed, the iron fire escapes removed and trees planted on the sidewalk. On the other side, a dingy two-story had been brightened with red awnings proclaiming "Fine Vintage

Clothing and Antiques." Across the street a parking garage adjoined an assortment of small storefronts, most of them occupied, with rental apartments above. I walked the neighborhood, stood across from 115, and stared, but there was little to help me visualize what life was like for Katie Prato before she left home to marry when she was fifteen.

By 1900, five years after her marriage, she had two living children and she had lost another. She and Giovanni, who had Americanized his name to John, lived at 205 West 41 Street, between Seventh and Eighth Avenues, which placed them just outside the boundaries of Hell's Kitchen, in what was called the Tenderloin district. The Tenderloin was certainly no better a neighborhood, and not at all removed from violence.

An editorial in the New York *Herald* captured the climate of the times. "That the Tenderloin is infested with depraved and vicious Negroes is obvious to pedestrians who by day note the groups of flashily dressed colored men who swagger idly about the street corners, or who by night are accosted or even held up by the female associates of these loathsome wretches....But the whites are equally degraded and even more numerous."

The seeds for a major riot, bred of interracial tensions, were sown on the evening of August 12, 1900 when Robert J. Thorpe, a white police officer tried to arrest Arthur Harris, a black man whom the police believed to be a pimp. Harris stabbed the officer on the corner of Forty-first and Eighth and when the policeman died, rage engulfed both Hell's Kitchen and the Tenderloin. Anger percolated for a few days until the evening of Officer Thorpe's wake when two white women were assaulted by a black man who objected to some remarks the women had made after leaving the wake. No one was injured in the melee that ensued, but in less than 30 minutes, the violence had spread, aided, later evidence suggested, by the police themselves. "From Broadway west to Ninth Avenue, and in all the side streets between Thirty-fourth and Forty-second, mobs of whites assaulted with fist, club, and boot every Negro they could catch—women as well as men and even a few children."

Just down the block from the stabbing, Catherine and John

were raising their young family. Barely out of her teens, Catherine had not only to care for her babies, but protect herself and them from the violence and crime in the streets.

Sometime within the next ten years, between 1900 and 1910, the family moved to 427 West 30th Street, a four-story tenement, west of Ninth Avenue, in the shadow of the El, well within the dismal markers of Hell's Kitchen. The street rises a little west of Ninth and the Palisades across the river in New Jersey are visible. What would Catherine have thought as she looked across to such peaceful green hills, so far beyond her reach? But even on a warm spring morning she probably didn't have the time or energy to raise her sights. In that decade, Catherine gave birth to four more children—Jeannette, Louise, Catherine, whom the family would call Kay, and George—and lost another. They were now a family of eight, with still only one wage-earner.

Rents for a cold-water flat in Hell's Kitchen ranged from $6 to $9 a month. The upper floors were cheaper because tenants had to lug groceries and coal up the flights of stairs, but in return they sometimes had easy access to a roof for fresh air, such as it was, and an occasional breeze. No matter what floor, garbage accumulated in the halls; rats and cockroaches foraged everywhere. The usual pattern of the rooms was "railroad flat": the front room and the back room had windows. In between were the bedrooms with no outside ventilation. Fire escapes came down the front of most buildings; outhouses, looking like a row of metal lockers, but smelling far worse, ruined most backyards.

A cold-water flat also meant no central heating; sometimes there was a coal stove at one end of the flat and an oil stove at the other. No heat reached the middle rooms. While summer was oppressive, winter in Hell's Kitchen was even more punishing. Rattling windows with loose panes, cracks in the walls and ill-fitting doors allowed freezing winds off the River to penetrate the flats. Darkness came early. A lamplighter came each night at dusk to light the four lampposts on each block, but they spread little light beyond their arcs. Dirty snow piled up. Trips to work and school and the market became feats of endurance. I wonder how my grandmother, often pregnant, got to any of the shops along the Avenues. Probably she relied, like most her neighbors, on the peddlers and pushcarts who roamed through the streets.

Paddy's Market, under the Ninth Avenue El, stretching from 38th Street to 42nd Street, was a lively scene on Saturday nights as pushcart vendors gathered to sell bargain foods at week's end prices. I imagine my grandfather or more likely the older children watching the younger ones as Catherine walked to the corner and turned north, up Ninth, to buy loaves of day-old bread for five cents and putrid chickens for 39 cents. Or perhaps Emil went with her to carry a basket home. Was she feisty enough—and healthy enough—to bargain with the vendors? It was not hard to imagine Margaretha Hoefel holding her own in street negotiations. But I am unsure about Catherine.

I wonder too how she managed all the obligations of mothering six, then seven, and then eight, children. My cousin Kathy gave me a few cherished old family photographs. In the first are only three children, Emil, Mae, and the baby Jeannette. I'm guessing the photograph dates to 1903 or so when Emil would have been seven, Mae, four, and the baby between one and two. Taken at O'Connor Studios, on Eighth Avenue, between 24 and 25th Streets, it is a charming posed shot with amusing grownup props for the children. Emil holds a walking stick; he wears a cravat with white shirt and knickers. Mae, her long hair parted in the middle and held back with two bows, wears a pastel-colored dress with darker sash. She carries a basket of flowers. The toddler Jeannette, standing in a long white dress, rests one elbow against a table and holds the handle of another basket of flowers, which is almost as big as she is. The children look well cared for; they are clean and groomed; their hair brushed, their shoes polished.

In the next photograph, there are five children. The clothes are simpler but still clean. The baby here is Kay; she too wears a long white dress and is perched on a high table between Emil, standing, looking worried, and a solemn Mae. Jeannette, a sprig of flowers in her lap, and Louise, holding a stuffed animal, sit on stools in front. None of them looks relaxed. But it's possible to read too much into photographs, I think, especially when you're trying to compensate for family secrets too well kept. Perhaps this photographer, Bromberg, a few blocks north on Eighth Avenue, was just not as good with children.

The final photo, from yet another Eighth Avenue photographer, showing six children, is the last in the decade before my father's birth. Emil, close to a teenager by now, and Mae are still solemn; but the others seem more relaxed—except for the baby, George, who clearly would rather not be there. The background shows a stained glass window; there are no props.

I conjecture that over these years, Catherine functioned at least some of the time as a proud parent. Someone gathered the children together, made sure they had baths, brushed their hair. Someone selected a photographer and herded the family to the studio. Was each photograph to celebrate the arrival of the newest baby? I want to embellish the scenes. Was the photograph taken on a special day? Did the children come home from the studios more relaxed, even laughing? Did they share stories of the experience with their father at dinner? Did Catherine try to prepare something special to eat that night, even if there was little money for a celebration? Perhaps she did none of this. Early onset schizophrenia often strikes in the early twenties. Catherine turned 30 in 1910. So she may have had symptoms of mental illness as early as the years of these photographs. If it were one of her bad days, was she hiding in a bedroom, fearful, crying, alone? What role did my grandfather play? Did her mother or sisters rally round? They would have comforted the children, dressed them, hustled them off to the studio. They would have put a good face on things. They would probably not have told the neighbors.

As I assembled what few pieces of information I had from those years, 1900 to 1910, I found not just grinding poverty, and the possibility of her mental illness, which I expected, but an early tragedy in Catherine's life.

While she was busy with her young family, the Prato family faced its own difficulties. As my cousins and I shared information about our grandmother, I heard several times about Victor, Catherine's oldest son, they told me, who was born before Emil and killed as a teenager in a confrontation with the police. My father said he had never heard this story and I could not find any trace of Victor Garibaldi. Finally, late one night, as I examined the 1900 census for the Prato family, I found a Victor Prato. I re-checked the 1910 census; he did not appear there. And, ever so slowly, a story emerged.

Victor Prato was not Catherine's son, but a younger brother, unmarried, living at home with his parents at 353 West 25th Street, a five-story tenement between Eighth and Ninth Avenues. Victor worked as a florist and he died on May 17, 1909, at the age of 24, after spending 11 days in Flower Hospital. Death came from "cardiac and respiratory failure due to general peritonitis following perforation of stomach wall by a gastric ulcer."

A cousin and I discussed the conflicting reports. A family remembers violence on a street corner; a death certificate attests that the complications leading to Victor's death were the result of a gastric ulcer. How do we reconcile the two? If the family stories we have heard confused Catherine's eldest son with her younger brother, perhaps the encounter with the police was wrong, too. But that seemed an unlikely embellishment for a family so intent on keeping unpleasantness under wraps.

We searched newspaper records from that year. Beginning on May 3, under a headline, "Battle in the Camp of Striking Bakers," *The New York Times* reported on a bakers' strike that caused some violent outbreaks on the Lower East Side, around Delancey Street, on the night of May 2. Coverage continued in the following days and on May 6, the day that Victor was admitted to the hospital, the violence spread. In stacked headlines, *The Times* proclaimed: "Police Club Rioters in Bakers' Strike: Six Beaten Down and Two Sent to the Hospital....Innocent Onlookers Hurt..."

The article goes on to describe how the detectives "drew their blackjacks and jumped into the fight." The two seriously injured men were taken to Gouverneur Hospital and the other four, who were brought before a magistrate, were identified. None was named Prato.

The Times also reported, "In addition to the strikers who were clubbed, reports were received all day of onlookers, who declared that they, too, had been beaten." One of the detectives on the scene "did not deny that such might be the case, declaring that the police had been compelled to act promptly and firmly to prevent serious trouble and had been compelled to disperse crowds at any cost."

Victor lived on the far West Side, not on the Lower East Side; he was a florist, not a baker. But young men in one trade have friends in other trades. Was he in the neighborhood to support a friend? Was he learning to be a union organizer? Or was he simply a young bystander who got caught up in the melee? He spent 11 days at Flower Hospital, from May 6 until the night he died. That year, Flower Hospital was still located at 63rd Street and York Avenue. Why take him there if he had been injured on Eldridge Street or Delancey or Essex when there were other closer hospitals, like Gouverneur, which was already caring for some of the injured? Were they overwhelmed with emergencies on the night of May 6? City geography works even less well if Victor took sick at home on West 25th Street. It seems quite likely that from West 25th Street, he might have gone or been taken to St. Vincent's Hospital, much closer at Seventh Avenue and 11th Street, and which had, since the mid-nineteenth century, had as its mission to serve the poor.

There were isolated pockets of violence at bakeries elsewhere in the city, including Harlem and Yorkville. Was Victor at one of those other locations? Or was he simply part of another altercation with the police—a small random confrontation that did not even make the news?

I could not resolve the details of his last days. Whatever the cause of his death, illness or violence, the tragedy of losing a son and brother so suddenly, at such a young age, even in that precarious environment, would have been profound. Victor was buried from St. Columba Church, 343 West 25th Street, on Thursday, May 20, 1909 at 10am. Mourning him were his parents; his two married sisters, Mary and Catherine, my already fragile grandmother, caring for a newborn as well as five older children; a younger sister, Louise; and the youngest in the family, his brother, Anthony, who would have been barely ten.

The Prato family lived on West 25th Street for more than twenty years. When Catherine had left to marry in 1895, the family address had been 115, between Sixth and Seventh Avenues. By 1900 they had moved two blocks west to 353. Their immediate next door neighbor, at 355, was Engine Company 19, rooted deep in New York history as one of the original paid engine companies and dating back to 1865. Only a few steps to the east, at 343, was their parish church, St. Columba, where Victor's funeral would be held.

I cannot be sure if the move west brought them up the economic ladder or down, but it seems likely that it was down. Clearly, 353 would not have been a desirable location. Engine Company 19 was a very busy hub, answering alarms around the clock for tenements and commercial buildings in the surrounding area. For families whose apartments shared an adjoining wall with the firemen, alarms and departing trucks would have created constant background noise.

Engine Company 19 remained active at 355 until 1947. When I walked the street more than 50 years later, several buildings, including 353 and 355 had been razed and replaced with a peaceful neighborhood park. Looking north and east over the trees, I could see the top of the Empire State Building. Along the south side of the street were high-rise apartments set in the midst of green spaces and modern playgrounds. St. Columba, built in 1845 and one of the oldest Catholic Church buildings in the city, still stands as it was, a sturdy brick immigrant church with masses now in English and Spanish.

Anthony, my great grandfather, was a chocolate maker. So was his nineteen-year-old daughter, Mary, still at home in 1900. Years ago, there was a family rumor that my great grandmother was French. So, as I pursued the research, I allowed myself to indulge in images of Juliette Binoche in "Chocolat," imagining Mary, my grandmother's sister, making chocolate at home and selling to neighbors on the street. But reality quickly enveloped me as I read about the numerous candy factories in New York City and the working conditions there. "The chocolate rooms are generally cooled by refrigerating pipes, and their temperatures are sometimes as low as sixty degrees....The lower temperature may seem comfortable for a time, but it is found to be chilling when the worker sits from ten to twelve hours without exercise...." Young Mary was not making chocolate in her own little shop; she was toiling, like so many other young immigrant women, in a factory. Hers happened to make candy instead of shirtwaists.

The Triangle Shirtwaist fire in 1911, which killed more than one hundred young immigrant seamstresses, served as a rallying cry for labor activists in the city. But the candy factories had their own horror stories. On December 4, 1897, at D. Auerbach & Sons, on West 39th Street, a plant close enough to West 25th Street, that the Pratos, father and daughter, may have worked there, a large cauldron of syrup exploded and scalded six workmen as they prepared a batch of Christmas candy. Despite the dangers and unhealthy conditions, Anthony was still working as a candy maker in 1910. Perhaps he moved with Auerbach to their new block-long factory, on Eleventh Avenue, between 46th and 47th Streets. He would have had a longer walk to work, and hours just as long, but the new factory boasted safety features like sprinkler systems and fireproof staircases and elevators, and employee perks like wash rooms with showers, lunch rooms, and a hospital room for emergency care.

Mary Prato was married to Cassius Maroney at St. Columba on March 30, 1902. Because I have paper evidence—the date was a Sunday and they were married by the pastor, Rev. Henry Prat—I can envision a happy church wedding for her, with perhaps a white dress and veil, as Catherine probably did not have. But I cannot know because Mary then dropped out of family memory. My great-grandparents with their two youngest children, Louise and Anthony, continued to live on the same street and attend the same church. They would have known their neighbors and fellow parishioners well. They would still be living there six years later when Anthony died of stroke, or apoplexy, as it was called then, at the age of 63. Only three Pratos—my great grandmother, Louise, and young Anthony—would be left to buoy up the Garibaldi children during the tragedy to come.

The following decade brought two more babies into Catherine's life—John, my father, born in 1913, and Robert, born four years later.

When my father arrived, the family was still living at 427 West 30th Street.

Their parish was the Church of St. Michael, which was built in 1906 and which still stands at 424 West 34th Street. The parish itself dates back to 1857; by the turn of the century when the Garibaldi family was living on 30th Street, it was largely an Italian community, more proof of the changes that had occurred in the ethnic mix of Hell's Kitchen. Irish Catholics no longer dominated as they had only a decade earlier.

When I first visited St. Michael, the parish was celebrating the 100th anniversary of the church. This building would have been open only seven years when my father was baptized there on March 27, 1913. As I walked up the steps, through one of the three arched doorways and entered a large Gothic interior, I envisioned my grandmother as she carried her newest infant into the church. When did she hand the baby over to her 13-year-old daughter, Mae, serving as godmother? The godfather, standing nearby no doubt, my grandmother's younger brother, Anthony, turned 14 that year.

A church as large as this must have been awesome for its poor immigrant parishioners. Even a century later, it is still impressive. Marble columns and rows of dark wood pews lead to the altar. Statues, with stands of flickering votive candles, are spaced along the side aisles and at side altars in the front. I found the Infant of Prague, Saint Anthony, the Sacred Heart of Jesus, Saint Jude, and the parish's patron saint, the archangel Michael with his sword drawn and bouquets of white roses at his feet. Stained glass windows filtered late afternoon light.

I was drawn to the dark wood baptismal font placed about midway down the nave. Its carved pedestal base and octagonal shape intrigued me. I wondered if it was original. It certainly looked worn, but could it really be one hundred years old? How many infants had been gently held over its waters? One of them would have been my father. I saw the family gathered round and I have placed my grandmother there, happy and proud, beside her newborn, who is nervously held in the arms of her oldest daughter. But I had to catch myself. Was Catherine able to come? Or was she too sick? Was she having a bad day? Suffering again from what they might have called postpartum depression? By 1913, six years before she would be taken from her home, were symptoms of dementia praecox already evident? Had the others already learned to cope without her?

From my cousin I have formal First Communion photographs of all my aunts and uncles. So I can guess that the Catholic faith was important to the family. Was it the kind of home piety that many Italians of the era had with statues of St. Joseph and other saints placed all around their flat? Did Catherine go to novenas or participate in street processions? Did she have a particular devotion to St. Anthony or St. Jude, as many Italian women did? There can be no answers to those questions now, with all the memory keepers gone, but at the very least John and Catherine saw to it that all of their children were baptized and received First Communion.

First Communion probably happened for each of the older six children at the Church of St. Michael where my father was baptized. Boys and girls were carefully dressed for their formal studio photographs. The four girls each had a crown of flowers on top of the long white veils that they wore with lacy white dresses. There may have been one hand-me-down dress for the three older girls, but a clever seamstress had made unique sashes and altered the necklines for Mae, Jeannette, and Louise. Kay, as the youngest, got to wear a totally different dress. Emil, George, and my father all wore dark suits with long belted jackets and matching knickers. George and my father wore high white collars with floppy bow ties. George had a white armband, a lapel pin, and a boutonniere. Only Bob, who would not make his First Communion until the mid-1920s, wore the short white suit so typical of later young communicants. All eight held rosaries or their First Communion prayer books.

The Garibaldi family remained on West 30th Street until sometime after 1915. This location, overwhelmed now by mail trucks and industry and snarled traffic from the Lincoln Tunnel, was, a century ago, only steps from the Ninth Avenue El. All local trains stopped at 30th Street. Like the Hoefel family in the Bronx, who also lived near a station, the screech of brakes and the vibrations as trains slowed, stopped, and then accelerated must have constantly intruded on their lives.

The 1915 New York State census sheets capture a single day in those years. Five families lived in the narrow four-story building at 427. Narrow means the width of three single windows, a fire escape descending in front of two. Because there was commercial space on the first floor, the five families would have shared three floors. So John and Catherine and their seven children may, or may not, have had a full front-to-back flat to themselves. Garibaldi was the only Italian name; the other families were probably German and Irish. Most everyone, except my grandfather, had been born in the United States. Giovanni, who had become John and a citizen, was working in the building trades as a laborer. But by 1915 he had other wage earners in the family who could help him pay the bills. Emil, 18, worked in an office. Mae, 15 by then, was a dressmaker. Jeannette, Louise, Kay, and George were in school; my father was two.

By the time Bob was born in 1917, they had all moved to the five-story tenement at 421 45th Street, once again just steps from the raised tracks of Ninth Avenue El. I cannot think life was much easier here, especially for my grandmother. How did she manage clean clothes for her eight children? Did she hang the wash out—in the midst of cinders and ash, garbage and grime? Smoke still rose from the ships approaching their piers; freight trains still traveled on the surface of Tenth and Eleventh Avenues; slaughterhouses and breweries still operated.

Did she buy the children's clothes in the shops along Ninth and Tenth Avenues? Or did she try to save money by making them? Many immigrant women in the neighborhood bought sewing machines on the installment plan. But could Catherine make decisions like that? And remember the payments? All my aunts, when I knew them decades later, were accomplished seamstresses. Did they learn at home from their mother? By 1915 Mae was already a "dressmaker." As they grew older, the other girls must have joined her. By 1930, Jeannette was also listed as a dressmaker. And Kay worked as a milliner at a hat shop. I think Louise was not well as she grew up; there were no jobs listed for her in the census. From my earliest childhood, I remember that Aunt Kay designed wonderful hats; and Aunt Louise transformed scraps of fabric, yarn, and beads into imaginative dolls for me.

Life could not have been easy for these four young women. They worked in the same punishing environments as other girls of their era and when they came home they assumed responsibility for their younger brothers. How was Catherine behaving by then? Was she getting violent? Was she talking to voices she heard in her head? Or was she simply catatonic, lying in her bed day after day? None of my aunts married young, as so many other girls did, rushing to escape their bleak lives. That certainly seems to be a testimony to their loyalty and determination, but perhaps it is also a tribute to my grandfather.

I wonder what role he played in those years while Catherine was still at home. Italian fathers in Hell's Kitchen had the reputation of being strong disciplinarians. Their sons did not run with gangs; their daughters did not loiter with friends on street corners. Was this true in the Garibaldi household as he tried to hold the family together? Was his temper in evidence then? Directed at Emil, his oldest, and his four daughters instead of his three very young sons?

When the Garibaldi family moved to 45th Street, they changed parishes. Which of my grandparents approached the priests at Holy Cross to register the family as parishioners? Was that my grandfather's decision? Did he gather the family together and walk with them to Mass on Sundays? In Italian immigrant families, fulfilling religious obligations was normally the mother's role. But what if Catherine couldn't? Their youngest child, my uncle Bob, was baptized at Holy Cross in 1917. And when my father received his First Communion there, the family marked the special day with a photograph, as they had with all the other Garibaldi children. He is dressed formally like his two older brothers, but I am delighted to see that, unlike them, he is smiling. He looks shy and tentative, but still smiling.

His is the only formal photograph I have that is not taken in a studio. And that's a wonderful bit of serendipity because he stands next to a distinctive cast iron post and railing which marked the front steps of 421 West 45th Street as late as the 1930s when the WPA photograph was taken. During our family visit to Hell's Kitchen in 2009, his daughter and grandsons stood on the same steps. The two ornate posts are gone, replaced with simple functional ones, but the steps and the doorway with its side columns and decorative pediment remain the same. So do the fire escapes and the etched designs in concrete that trim the red brick façade. The apartments now are two to a floor, east and west, each with access to the fire escape through one window.

The building is at the eastern edge of a row of similar brick buildings, all gentrified from the tenements they once were, and its eastern wall abuts a parking garage, open 24 hours. I think the garage must have once been a taller building, probably another five-story tenement. Add the shadow of tracks from the elevated just behind where we stood, and my father's time at 421 would have been much darker and noisier than ours.

It was midday on a Saturday in May when we turned into this relatively peaceful side street from Ninth Avenue, where the famous Hell's Kitchen Flea Market was in full bloom. Shoppers and vendors here are a world away from those at Paddy's Market, under the El, back in the days when my grandmother might have shopped there. This market, open every Saturday and Sunday around the year, is filled with the kinds of bargains that attract tourists but also native fashionistas. Looking for vintage clothing or antique jewelry or anything crafted from glass, leather, or straw? T-shirts, cell phones or a weekend subscription to *The New York Times*? A gyro to give you sustenance for the blocks to come? Ninth Avenue is no longer the place for day-old bread and rotting poultry. At the Holy Cross Church booth, I talked with parishioners, enjoying their banter, and came away with an apron that proclaims in not-to-be-missed yellow: "Something Good's Cookin' in Hell's Kitchen!" Holy Cross Church, it says, is "at the Crossroads of the World."

The smiling communion portrait of my father on the steps of 421 makes me ache for more images of him as a child. When our sons dressed up for Halloween trick or treat and he watched their antics, he would sometimes talk about Ragamuffin Parades. I knew that the parades of his childhood were connected to Thanksgiving, not Halloween. But he never shared any memories and I didn't really understand until I read some histories of Hell's Kitchen. Ragamuffin Parades would have been a big deal in the life of a little boy.

On Thanksgiving morning, the children of the neighborhood would dress up in homemade, colorful costumes and walk through the streets in a Children's Rag Parade. Anticipating pennies, not candy, from the spectators was no doubt a large part of the morning's fun. But the real excitement came that evening, after family dinners, when a brass band led a parade of costumed adults up and down the side streets and the avenues of Hell's Kitchen. The festivities lasted late into the night as thousands fell in step behind the band. Those who weren't in the streets, including little children like my father, who should have been in bed, watched from the windows, rooftops, and fire escapes of their tenements.

How disappointing to recognize that I knew nothing about the other 364 days in any of my father's early childhood years. He would only have gone to primary grades in Hell's Kitchen. What was first grade like for him? Was it an escape from the troubles at home? What did his teachers know about this quiet boy, who was already tall for his age? Were they good to him? What were his summers like? Did he have to stay inside while his sisters were off at work? Or did he play outside with the other little boys in the neighborhood? Sit on the stoop and watch the older boys play stick ball? Fly kites from the rooftops? Visit with the old men as they cared for their pigeons? He was four when Bob, the last of Catherine's children, was born. How did he feel about having a baby brother? As young adults John and Bob were as close as brothers could be. Did their affection, I wonder, date to those very early years? And how did my father feel about his mother? He was six when she was sent away to Central Islip State Hospital, but I suspect now her schizophrenia separated them even while she lived at home.

Four years after Catherine left the household, the family would move to Astoria. Her sons and daughters would grow up, marry, raise families of their own. Her husband, living as if he were a widower, would continue to work as a laborer in what official documents called "the building trades." He would learn to have conversations with his adult children. He would see his grandchildren often. By the time Catherine died in 1957, she had more than a dozen grandchildren, but she could not be a part of their lives.

Chapter 13
Catherine
After 1919

Early April, 1919, was unusually cold in New York. The winter had seen practically no snowfall, but spring was very late in coming. No teasingly warm breezes off the river broke the chill on West 45th Street. Easter, too, was late that year. During the first week of the month, statues in Catholic churches were still shrouded in the purple of Passiontide. Did the lasting cold or the dreary penitential season finally fracture Catherine's equilibrium? Did the Hell's Kitchen landscape seem a prison to her? More likely, none of that mattered. The trouble was inside, in her soul. Outside timing was irrelevant; inner rhythms collided.

Surely the news that her oldest son was missing in action could have provided a trigger for all that followed. News that would crush any mother's spirit would have done so much more damage to a woman whose psyche was already fragile. Who was with her when she received the telegram? How long a time elapsed between that episode and her final departure?

I try to envision how that happened. Perhaps during a weekday morning, when my grandfather was at work and the older children at school, neighbors clustered on the street outside 421, listening to Catherine scream and wail. One of them, alarmed for the young children she knew were in the apartment, summoned the police and they took Catherine away. Or it happened in the evening when Grandpa was home. He had to send one of his daughters for the cop on the beat because he could no longer protect his wife from herself. Did she weep uncontrollably? Or perhaps laugh incessantly—and so inappropriately? He had to protect his children. The little boys were shut behind a bedroom door. Bob, the baby, was asleep; George and my father, at 6, were wide awake and terrified at what was happening out of their sight. Were the neighbors there, too, clustered in semi-darkness in the hall or on the landings as Catherine was carried out? Perhaps this was just the last of the times she was taken from the apartment.

Before, the mad times would have been followed by peaceful interludes when Catherine seemed sane and lucid. She was teary, quiet, and withdrawn, preferring corners of rooms to the melee of her family. But she acted like their mother and wife. Still, my grandfather must have waited, tense, fearful, wondering when the next outbreak might come. That night she would have gone from the protectiveness of her family, a familiar apartment, and her own neighborhood, however grim, to a lineup of strangers and the harsh lights of a city emergency room. What could that have been like for her? Did it induce more terrors?

And why, this time, did she not go back to her family? Instead, she was taken 46 miles east to Central Islip State Hospital, one of the new institutions that doctors and city authorities believed were best for people like Catherine. Someone signed official documents. Someone committed her to a new life in a state hospital with 5000 other inmates. Someone began the process that transformed my grandmother from Catherine, sometimes called Katie, wife and mother, to Catherine, inmate, number 113108.

In 1919 schizophrenia was still known as *dementia praecox* and psychiatrists used the term to describe patients who exhibited any of three behaviors. They might be catatonic or in the language of the day, suffering from stupors. They might act silly, laugh senselessly, or otherwise behave in a bizarre manner; that was called hebephrenia. And they might have hallucinations or delusions. Or any combination of the three. They also might have calm lucid times, lasting hours or months, which lulled their families and their doctors into hope. None of the scientists could say just what this mental illness was. "...'schizophrenic' is a concept wonderfully vague in its content and terrifyingly awesome in its implications," Thomas Szasz observed in 1976. I doubt Catherine's children found her disease wonderfully vague.

From the time the term *dementia praecox* was first used in 1898 through its evolution decades later into schizophrenia, psychiatrists disagreed among themselves about the causes and the symptoms and the treatments, but they never doubted they could deal with the disease. During the forty or more years Catherine suffered from schizophrenic behavior, their solutions changed dramatically. As an "inmate," or later, a "patient," confined to a state hospital, she might have experienced many of the treatments—all except the last, the miracle of Thorazine, the drug that became available in the 50s, as she was dying, and might have allowed her to return to life in the world outside an institution. It was my grandmother's fate to suffer through what has been called the darkest period of modern psychiatry.

In the early decades of the twentieth century, the preferred treatment for *dementia praecox* was compulsory hospitalization or institutionalization. What were the correct criteria for committing someone? The classic medical answer at the time was when a patient became too dangerous for her own good or when she posed a threat to the rest of the family. In other words, when conversations no longer persuaded and it became necessary to use restraints.

I have to accept that my grandmother was not just silly or silent but intractable and probably violent while she was still at home on 45th Street. Why else would the father of a poor family consent to sending his wife, the mother of eight, away? Her departure would only have increased the burdens on him and his daughters. He never divorced Catherine to remarry so it seems highly unlikely he wanted her out of the way for a romantic interest of his own.

My grandmother does not fit the stereotypes that have come to surround mentally disturbed women of that era who may have been wrongly confined. She was not young and single, inappropriately romantic, perhaps a worry to her family. She was not old and alone, widowed, a burden to society. She must have met the criteria; she was committed.

Today's scholars, applying contemporary wisdom, ask if institutionalization really served the patient's wellbeing. That argument would never have swayed the minds of psychiatrists or reformers or bureaucrats back then. By 1910 New York State had chosen what it considered an enlightened path and had institutionalized 31,280 mentally ill patients, more than any other state.

Like so many other poor patients sent from the city's boroughs to what were euphemistically called "the farm colonies," Catherine was probably transported to her new home by train. Nowadays, the trip from Penn Station to Central Islip, via the Long Island Railroad, takes about an hour and fifteen minutes. Her journey would have lasted much longer and was probably far less comfortable. The hospital had nearly five miles of rail track on its property, mostly for delivery, maintenance, and construction, and it operated its own small train with an engine, baggage car, and passenger coach. On what the institution called "transfer days," its passenger car linked up with a regular morning train leaving Central Islip for New York City, picked up new patients in the city and returned again to Central Islip in the evening. Patients stayed in their car, behind the barred windows, as it was uncoupled from the rest of the train and pulled onto the hospital tracks. When they exited at the last stop, these new inmates had arrived securely inside the grounds. I doubt any of them had noticed the small wooden five-sided guardhouses they had passed as they crossed the edges of the hospital's property.

I wonder who traveled with Catherine that day. It seems unlikely anyone from her family could have accompanied her, but no doubt hospital aides were aboard. Were there many other new patients? Was she restrained? Medicated? Did she look out through the bars and take in the unfamiliar countryside? Did she ask where they were going? So many questions pile up.

Catherine arrived at her new home on Saturday, April 5, 1919. Were they in time for dinner? Was she hungry? Or even conscious? What kind of procedures awaited these new inmates? Who showed them to the dormitory rooms where they would sleep for the first time? The years went by for Catherine, as they have for me, but I am still haunted by images of my grandmother's arrival in that new world.

That first morning in the ward Catherine opened her eyes before any light came through the distant windows, wondering what had awakened her. Was the baby crying? Were the little boys up already and fighting just outside her door? As she struggled to get to her feet, she looked over at the figure hunched up in the next bed and did not know her. Frightened, she sat back down, reaching for her pillow. But a woman in uniform had flipped a switch and the light bulbs in the ceiling far above her head had spread dim light through the room. As Catherine's eyes adjusted, she saw other figures beginning to move slowly. The figure standing at the door called again.

"Ladies, let's hurry up. We'll be late for breakfast."

Catherine sat where she was. The woman came to her side.

"Catherine," she said. "You have to follow what I say. Get up now."

She turned to the woman in the next bed. "Bridget," she said, "Bring Catherine along with you."

She retreated to her place at the door and the women filed past her into the hallway. Bridget took Catherine by the hand; she was rough, pulling her along, not letting go of her, but saying nothing.

The women formed a straggling line to the toilets. Catherine felt groggy and confused. She thought she should be in her kitchen. She would like her coffee. But the doors along the hallway were closed and she did not see a place to turn. Where was she? No one seemed willing to say anything to her. Even Bridget did not talk. In the next room a woman handed her some clothes she did not recognize. She held them tightly in her arms.

"Get dressed, Catherine."

She still hesitated and someone said, "My God, do you need help with that now?"

She started to cry. "Where are my clothes?"

Her arms went to her head; she thought she needed to protect her face. The unfamiliar clothes dropped to the floor. And quickly

Bridget was there. She picked up the day dress and the underwear, ushered Catherine to a bench along one wall and pulled her night dress over her head.

"Better me than her," Bridget said, nodding at the young woman frowning at them from across the room. Together they managed the dressing even though Catherine had not stopped crying.

"Where are my children?" she called out.

No one answered or even looked in her direction as they lined up once again in the hallway.

"Where are my children?" she could not keep from shouting.

The matron was at Catherine's side. "You'll feel better after you eat," she said. "Come along."

Her day was a series of lines. For the bathroom. For medicine. For food. Walk and wait. She had never walked so far for a meal. She had never waited for cereal or soup or meat and potatoes to be ladled out to her. Bridget, she found, was always there. Grumpy, silent, holding her elbow, shoving her around corners, leading her to a chair in the corner of the day room. From there Catherine watched the other women, tried to recognize a familiar face. She looked for neighbors. Her sisters. Her daughters. Once she saw someone she knew, she would ask all her questions.

By late afternoon she was impatient. "I'm going home now," she said loudly to no one and she started toward a door. Suddenly figures surrounded her.

"You can't leave here, Catherine."

"Go back and sit down, Catherine."

"This door is locked, Catherine."

"It's late, Catherine. Why don't you stay until morning?"

And she allowed them to usher her back to her seat in the day room. Maybe tomorrow would be a better time to leave. She remembered good night hugs from her little boys, longed for them and her arms ached. She massaged them restlessly. She decided to sing. She did not see the matron frown.

Between that first day and her last were all the other days— 14,087 of them, to be precise.

Kathy, daughter of my father's sister Katherine, also wanted to understand how our grandmother spent her days. We talked about the frustration of never knowing any details and the emptiness we felt. We agreed that a visit to the grounds of the old hospital would be good for both of us. Our cousin Paul had already visited. It was still a beautiful property, he said, "peaceful."

As we drove onto the campus of New York Institute of Technology, I got a sense of the magnitude of the task we had set for ourselves. Central Islip State Hospital in its prime years covered 851 acres, had 98 buildings, housed 9,500 patients, and employed a staff of 2,100. The NYIT campus spans only 350 acres of the original site and contains many of the early brick buildings. Kathy and I struggled to make the old numbers real in the present context. We could see that some of the buildings are once again busy places where now students and faculty gather. Old structures have been refurbished with new windows and entrances and embellished with new landscaping. We checked out The Epicurean Restaurant, which had a sophisticated menu showcasing the work of faculty and student chefs. Only later did I learn that the same space was once a dining room where far less elegant meals were served to Central Islip inmates.

The buildings that drew our attention were the ones that stand almost as they were. Massive three and four-story structures were deserted. We could see cracked panes and the remains of grills that covered the outside of the windows. Another abandoned complex of low, connected, almost charming, buildings curved into the landscape. Windows and doors had been boarded up and the grass grew tall.

We wandered freely around the campus, moving at will from sunlight to shade, down this path, up this road, wondering what it would be like to be here and not be free. I envisioned Catherine walking these paths in summer and sitting in the cool shade of these huge trees. As we sat there, I looked up into their arching branches, knowing they would have been here even in Catherine's first years. I thought back to the few words about Catherine that her sons and daughters shared. "Gentle" is the one that clings.

Later I would recall something my father had finally said when I prodded and pushed him for memories of his mother. When he first visited with his father, he said, they went by train. But later they must have driven because he remembered, "We used to take her for rides in the car. She liked that." He never spoke about the hospital or the grounds or was able to give me any other details.

Central Islip State Hospital had opened in 1887 as a better place for New York City to hospitalize its mentally ill than the filthy and mismanaged overcrowded county asylums then operating on islands off its shores. It was designed by the State of New York to house 300 inmates. By the 1920s, Catherine's first years there, Central Islip, too, had far too many residents for its facilities.

Some of the original 1880s wood frame free-standing buildings, one-story wards grouped around a common dining room, remained in use for more than 50 years. Gradually, in later decades, Central Islip saw the construction of much larger buildings that were identical in structure to those at many other state hospitals. These buildings housed 400 inmates in large dormitory rooms on three floors.

Rarely, in Catherine's time at Central Islip, would she have known uncrowded buildings. As soon as new buildings were built, more patients arrived and the dormitories were again so filled with beds that only the narrowest of walkways separated one bed from its neighbor. There were usually no curtains on the windows; no rugs on the floors; no lamps—only harsh ceiling lights; no drawers or cabinets for personal possessions. Some improvements in dormitory life came in the 1960s—partitions for more privacy, under-bed drawers for personal items, smaller bedrooms for three or four women—but they happened too late for my grandmother.

Between 1919 and 1957 Catherine must have lived in many of the different buildings Central Islip constructed. It was not only new construction that brought change. Most patients, especially those who never got well enough to leave, were frequently moved from one ward to another, as their mental state deteriorated or improved. Catherine would have known the early "string of pearls" dormitories where she had to walk through long corridor buildings for all her meals and then found herself in one of the "newer" wards where she trekked to breakfast, lunch, and dinner through damp and dark tunnels. Eventually she would have found herself in one of the massive brick buildings still standing when Kathy and I visited. There, she might not have left the building for months or years at a time. Each floor was divided into a men's side and a women's side and both sides had a dining hall, a day room, showers, toilets, and dormitories. In some buildings, those designed for patients who had severe mental disorders, a central core also held tub rooms and pack rooms where patients were given prolonged hot baths or placed in hot and cold packs, treatments that were once thought to calm troubled patients.

When Catherine first arrived, Central Islip, like the other farm colonies, followed a therapeutic philosophy sometimes called "O&O and R&R"—Occupation and Oxygen, Rest and Relaxation. Doctors hoped a structured environment would "cure" their patients. The patients, who were still called inmates in 1920, learned crafts or trades and were kept busy, away from the situations and stimuli that were thought to have caused their disease.

The men worked in the fields, gardening and felling trees, and assisted with road building. They also repaired shoes and made furniture, birdbaths, baskets, and brooms to sell at the annual crafts fair. The women worked in the wards, in the gardens and greenhouses, and as seamstresses. At machines lined up in long rows, not unlike city sweatshops, they repaired the doctors' surgical gowns and bed linens from the patients' wards. Or they made women's clothing, dresses and undergarments, not only for the patients' use but also for sale to the public.

For all the years Catherine had lived in Hell's Kitchen, she had probably not worked at a sewing machine in a sweatshop. I wondered if that was her assignment at the hospital. Perhaps she liked it better than mopping floors or cooking. Those days of working in the mornings and afternoons might have been good days. She was busy and following a routine. I wondered if she was assigned outdoor work, sitting in the garden with the other women, learning to weed or plant seedlings. I see her on her knees, wielding her trowel carefully. How could she know weeds from flowers when she had lived all her life in a city tenement? Did she learn to like the feel of the soil in her hands? Did she welcome the responsibility of watering plants in a greenhouse?

Holidays were big celebrations at all the state hospitals. Whatever the era, staff and patients decorated the day rooms with balloons, flags, or crepe paper streamers. Together they decorated Christmas trees and wrapped packages. Perhaps Catherine joined in. Perhaps not. Safe to assume that for some of those 38 Christmases, she was not well enough to care. And how did she fare on Christmas Day or Easter Sunday? Did she have visitors? Did she notice when the other women did and she did not?

I like to think Catherine enjoyed small pleasures on her good days. An attendant read to them during a break in their sewing. She found a favorite dessert as she walked through the cafeteria line. She sat on a bench in the sun. She went to a concert on the lawn or a parade or a picnic with the other women in her ward. She went to Sunday Mass, comforted by familiar hymns and prayers. Her husband or a daughter or son visited and she could ask about their families.

In 1919 she would have spoken both English and Italian. I wonder when she lost the ability to use Italian. She had only the basics of an education. Did she remember during those 38 years how to read or write? Did she even try? George, the last of the uncles to die, told my cousin Paul that Catherine wrote poetry. What an intriguing detail. He did not say if it was before she was committed or after. I see Catherine sitting at a table in the day room, scribbling on paper torn out of a notebook. On a good day, words appeared and someone, perhaps a kind nurse, told her the poem was good. "Keep writing, Catherine."

But for Catherine there was no escape from bad days. I cannot avoid them either. Sometimes the bad days were not of her making. Central Islip was a huge institution. Overcrowded wards meant fewer attendants, longer lines, fewer places to sit alone, more pungent odors. A cruel matron could terrorize an entire ward. Food could be mushy, tough, or inedible. A doctor impatient. The work too hard; idle hours alone in the day room too long.

But other days would have been nightmares all her own. Sundays when unfamiliar faces at Mass in the assembly hall so terrified her that she could not hear the hymns. Dances and picnics and holiday parties when they expected her to smile and join in and she could not. Family visits when they hoped she'd recognize them and she did not. Times perhaps when she tried to write poetry in a notebook but there was only gibberish on a tissue. Days when a friend like Bridget disappeared and she could not find her anywhere. Times when she crashed and regressed so far that she was moved to another ward, one with more restrictions, more treatments, more medications, and all new faces. Perhaps there were even times when she found herself totally alone in a small "isolation room" where very disturbed patients were placed, supposedly for their own good, on a mattress on the floor.

In these wards Catherine knew real madness, her own and what she saw in her fellow inmates. Here the nurses kept close scrutiny, becoming of necessity more like jailers. I do not think patients in these wards ever went outside. I fear they soiled themselves. They were force-fed when necessary and with their screams they kept each other awake at night.

As the years went by, the early twentieth century emphasis on treating inmates with O&O and R&R gave way to other methods. The use of medications like paraldehyde and barbiturates increased. For hydrotherapy, a patient was sealed into a steam-heated cabinet with only her head exposed. Or she was wrapped in sheets, arms and legs restricted, while she was placed for hours, or sometimes days, in a warm bath. Doctors had observed that such baths calmed disruptive behavior. Alternate therapy called for immersion in a cold pack, leaving patients frigid, teeth chattering. A nurse was supposed to stay with a patient during treatment. I wonder how often they slipped out for a smoke, leaving a terrified patient unattended.

Electroconvulsive shock therapy began in the 1930s and came into wide use at Central Islip. I have to assume that in all those years Catherine endured at least one course of these treatments.

Electrodes were attached to the patient's head and low doses of electricity were shot through her brain. Doctors monitored the dosage while nurses and aides tied or held the patient firmly against the bed to limit fractured bones as arms and legs convulsed. A treatment might entail as many as 12 or even more sessions. The psychiatric community believed that patients had no memory of their experience. The few patient memoirs that exist belie that assumption. The word "shock" or even "downstairs" summoned fear and anxiety as patients understood, however dimly, what was waiting for them.

The most invasive of all psychiatric treatments during Catherine's era was prefrontal lobotomy, first performed in 1935 in Portugal. It involved drilling holes into the patient's forehead, inserting a surgical knife and severing the prefrontal cortex from the rest of the brain. All patients who had undergone the surgery displayed changed personalities. The doctors argued that a quieter patient was an improved patient, especially if she could be released from an institution. But the surgery decreased many parts of a personality, frequently making patients into non-functioning zombies. Lobotomy is now considered a barbaric surgery, a tragic short-lived episode in the history of mental illness. But medical statistics show that between 1939 and 1951 more than 18,000 lobotomies were performed in the United States. The doctors who worked in large state mental institutions were most likely to do the operation. Revisionist histories of Central Islip do not admit that doctors there performed lobotomies. However, photographs that show the operations being performed still exist.

Was my grandmother a candidate for a lobotomy? I do not want an answer to that question. Just as I do not want to think too much about how close she came to the era when drug therapy that "eased anxiety...without fogging the mind" allowed so many schizophrenic patients younger than she to go home.

During all those years of her institutionalized life, I wonder how many times Catherine longed to go home. And how many years went by before she stopped yearning to see her babies. Many of the experts admitted that the institution did not cure the disease.

In fact, life in a mental hospital brought with it an increasing dependence on the institution. Life outside its walls became more and more difficult to achieve. How many times did my grandfather hope to bring her home, only to face repeated disappointments when she couldn't manage to leave the ward?

The railroad tracks in Central Islip are still at ground level. Trains to and from New York City come through frequently. As I drove the short distance from the grounds of the hospital to Central Islip's small downtown, I glanced down the tracks to my left, westward, and allowed my focus to switch from my grandmother's daily life to my grandfather's. The tragedy was his as well as hers.

I know now that shortly after Catherine was formally admitted to Central Islip State Hospital in April, 1919, my grandfather would have received a form letter that read:

Dear Sir:

This is to inform you that M [fill in the blank] was committed to this Hospital on [fill in the date]. Central Islip is accessible by the Long Island Railroad from Long Island City via East 34th Street Ferry from New York City or from Brooklyn, Flatbush Avenue Station. Railroad tickets at reduced rates may be had at the hospital ....Trains leave Long Island City and Flatbush Avenue Stations at 8:00 A.M. and 10:00A.M. on weekdays and 9:00 A.M. on Sundays.

Yours respectfully...

Attached was a set of rules and regulations that applied to visitors.

The Superintendent shall regulate and determine the times at which patients may be visited by their friends; and no visitor shall be allowed to see a patient without his consent....

Visitors are expressly forbidden to furnish money, wine, liquor or tobacco to any inmate of the Hospital, or

236 • HIDDEN LIVES

to deliver to, or receive from a patient, any letter, parcel or package without the knowledge and permission of the Superintendent....

The Physicians attached to the Hospital will attend in the offices at the usual visiting hours and will cheerfully and fully answer all questions addressed to them, as to the condition and prospects of the different patients....

Regular visiting days are Tuesdays, Thursdays, Sundays and Holidays.

The one-half price excursion tickets were good for any of the three state hospitals—King's Park, Pilgrim, and Central Islip—that were served by the Long Island Railroad. I wonder how many times someone in the family made the trip.

Now, looking at the train schedules, and seeing the Hunterspoint Ave. station in Long Island City as the departure point, I wonder if being closer to the trains for Central Islip had any influence on the family's decision to move to Astoria in 1923. Perhaps in the early years, Grandpa traveled out frequently.

I see him on the LIRR, handing over the tan round-trip "excursion ticket," which covered his "continuous passage" from Long Island City to Jamaica, connecting there to "Special Hospital trains" bound for one of the three mental institutions. The other passengers would all have been visitors on the same journey. Mothers, fathers, husbands, wives, sisters, brothers; the rules didn't encourage visits from friends. I wonder when my grandfather began to recognize familiar faces. He would have heard a mélange of languages—Italian, Yiddish, German, brogue-lilted English. The families would have brought food from home to sustain them through the day, but also perhaps to comfort a patient. Perhaps some Saturdays Grandpa brought some salami with bread his daughters had baked. A slice of homemade *bobka* around Christmas. Some candy-coated almonds—a memento of a daughter's wedding, an event Catherine surely did not attend. Did he find Italian families and pass the time with them or did he sit solitary at a window? Perhaps those long trips were the source of the anger he loosed too often on his children.

Some days Grandpa returned to Astoria with good news. The doctors saw some improvement and he was hopeful that Catherine would soon be home again. When did those hopes begin to fade and they all became resigned to the separation? Life moved on without her. Each decade brought changes she would never know. In the beginning of the Twenties, women gained the right to vote. By the end, movies had sound tracks; Charles Lindbergh had crossed the Atlantic solo; and the country had become mired in the Great Depression. Yankee stadium had opened; Babe Ruth and Lou Gehrig had captured the city's attention with their home run battles. Her two youngest sons, so small when she left them, had started their lifelong love affairs with the Yankees. Mae, Emil, and Jeannette had married and the first grandchild had been born.

Catherine did not know about the celebration when the Empire State Building, where her husband had worked, opened in 1931. She did not know the name Franklin Delano Roosevelt or the hope he brought to so many other Americans when he was elected President in 1933. She did not know when World War II began or that her youngest son, Bob, enlisted in the Army and served at the Battle of the Bulge. She did not know when my father was married or I was born.

As the Forties grew into the Fifties, the family moved on and up into the middle class. In lives carefully constructed, their secret held. Catherine was not allowed to emerge from their past to cloud the future. For my father and mother, even Catherine's death and funeral were events to be kept hidden. I have come to understand that living with the tension was far from easy among the siblings or between husband and wife. It led almost inevitably to my parents' late night arguments and fractured family relationships.

On December 26, 1956, when Catherine was 77, Dr. Robert Boyle began to treat her for what would be her final illness. Something specific happened on that day after Christmas. Her death certificate says the cause of death was "arteriosclerotic heart disease" so perhaps she had a heart attack or a stroke.

She probably spent the rest of her life in an infirmary ward together with all the other inmates who needed acute medical care. Was she able to get out of her bed into a wheel chair? Sit in a geriatric chair for a few hours each afternoon? Perhaps her ward had curtains between the beds for a little privacy. But probably not. The 1950s was another decade for overcrowding. Beds in the infirmary were crammed as close together as they were in the institution's other wards.

Catherine died at 1:45pm on November 8, 1957. It was a Friday. The family buried her on the following Tuesday. I cannot remember where I was that weekend. I was not home and I was certainly not at her funeral.

Decades later, after Paul and I talked about Catherine, he sent me an itemized bill from the funeral parlor, which his father had kept. The family had paid for a Mass at Most Precious Blood Roman Catholic Church, for pallbearers and gratuities, newspaper notices, a landau for flowers, and also for one lady's dress costing $28.84. With the bill was a letter from the Director of Central Islip State Hospital, dated January 22, 1958, more than two months after my grandmother's death, and addressed to Emil, Paul's father, Catherine's oldest son.

The letter is an inventory of Catherine's possessions at the time of her death:
one bathrobe,
one duster,
four coats,
eleven cotton dresses,
two pairs of socks,
two handkerchiefs,
one hat,
four pairs of hose,
one pair of mittens,
fifteen nightgowns,
five pairs of panties,
one pair of shoes,
two slips,
one sweater,
one vest

The Director wanted to know if the family wanted the items sent collect or if they want them distributed to other patients who "would appreciate having them." I can guess the family's choice. For me the list only raised more questions about Catherine's life. She had mittens, a hat, and four coats. Maybe she wore one of those coats when she went for a ride in the car on visiting day. Did she wear her socks or her hose with the same pair of shoes? She had panties and slips, but no bra? Did she have so many nightgowns because she spent a lot of time in bed? Or because they were frequent Christmas gifts over the years? She would have spent 38 birthdays at Central Islip. Nightgowns made good presents. She had eleven cotton dresses but none appropriate, I guess, for her funeral.

As we walked around the grounds that long afternoon, Kathy tried to reconstruct the funeral for me. She remembered our grandmother was dressed in blue lace at the wake. I held on to the image. That must have been the dress the family purchased for $28.84. Catherine would have had no occasion for wearing blue lace in any of the buildings we saw.

The day's excursion left me unsettled and unsatisfied. When George Colt wrote in his family memoir, *The Big House,* of his proper Bostonian grandmother's mental illness and her times in Butler Hospital, one of the oldest psychiatric facilities in the country, he recalled that the family always said she was away "for a much needed rest." During that time his grandfather never mentioned her to his children or to anyone else. None of the children was ever taken to see her. "Mental illness was a subject to be avoided or talked about only in whisper." If that was the way the story was told—or not told—in a wealthy educated Boston family of that era, it is surely asking too much that a struggling Italian immigrant family would not also keep insanity a secret.

Still 38 years is a long time.

One day could not fill the gap. I was not able to connect with my grandmother. Yes, it is good that a college campus and a courthouse and a shopping center stand where once there was a mental hospital for tens of thousands of people. But these new and valid uses for the acreage of an old institution did not dispel my mood. On an overgrown pathway at the edge of the property, near some woods, I picked up a piece of crumbling terracotta. My small fragment lay near another much larger fragment of what was once probably a gate post or a hitching post—a large iron ring was still embedded in one side. I held the clay fragment in my hand, fingered it gently, felt its edges crumble, leaving fine red dust on my hands. I kept it, my only memento of my grandmother. A few years later I would read in a Mary Oliver poem, lines that demanded my attention: "What we love, shapely and pure, is not to be held, but to be believed in."

Coda:
Ciao

I have been growing a metaphor for my Garibaldi family in our backyard garden. When my husband and I were leaving the cemetery in Pontori, my grandfather's home town in Italy, I saw a large cluster of hen and chicks, the small ubiquitous succulent plants I remembered from my own childhood. I dug out two with my fingertips and carried them home in a zipped baggie. The ground was hardening when we returned so I planted them in a pot, left them in a sunny window and nurtured them through the winter.

In early spring I moved them to the garden. But then the weather turned frigid, there was a long drought and I overwatered them in their new environment. They dropped their tiny leaves and I lost hope for their survival. The almost invisible leafless shoots hung in there. They were clearly struggling. It took a while but finally they grew and spread.

Then disaster struck. An errant lawn mower strayed into the garden and churned them up. I rescued one small shoot and nurtured it. I am once again hopeful.

Hen and chick plants usually transplant easily and grow most anywhere. Mine has just barely survived. I see in its hardiness and adaptability a reflection of my Italian ancestors. For them, unlike some more fortunate newcomers, the New York environment was never easy. They struggled and they survived. Eventually their roots grew deep and spread. I and my cousins are the result. So are my sons.

As I was learning about my grandfather and my grandmother, living for 38 years in Central Islip State Hospital, I finally recognized how short a distance from their troubled lives to mine. The link became something important to acknowledge, not hide.

On the Thursday before Easter, the year my mother died, I was driving my father from his apartment to my home for the Easter weekend. We were about four minutes from his door when he said, "Well, I've started."

I had learned that the most important things he wanted to share with me always came out within minutes after we saw each other. Whether he was angry or sad or puzzled or excited about a new idea he'd had, these were the times when he did not need to be prompted to talk.

"I've been getting in touch with my family," he continued. "It's time I did that." That was far from any answer I might have anticipated.

"Who, for instance?"

"This week I called George."

George, his next older brother, was one of his two siblings still living. I knew they had not spoken in years although I also knew that my mother had occasionally called George's wife. She and Rita had something in common; they both felt as if they were outsiders, not part of the core of the Garibaldi family.

My father said his conversation was difficult – I can imagine!— but he was glad to have it over. He planned to reach out to some nephews and nieces, to whomever he felt would talk to him. As the months went by, I would hear about the phone calls that went well and those that didn't. After decades of silence some links were too broken to be repaired.

I would also find out that he had regularly been in telephone contact with his younger brother Bob. All those Thursday mornings, when he had called me while my mother was at the hairdresser, he was also calling Bob. Those conversations with Bob and with me were among his rare private moments, times he had relished and never shared with my mother.

I had many questions, but that morning was not the time. It was almost Easter. His mind had moved on to other topics. He wanted to know if Jeri, my husband's sister, would like hyacinth or tulips. He wanted to call a florist and send her some Easter flowers.

That conversation set the tone for my father's last seven years. For him it was all about reconciliation. One spring day, a year later, two of his nephews and his brother George, a recent widower like my father, traveled from Long Island to join us for lunch at a restaurant near my father's apartment. My father had always allowed that he and George "were not close." George saw the half-empty glass; John preferred the half-full. It was a small difference that revealed larger fissures and it took its toll over the years. In their young days, Emil, the much older brother with the fiery temper, and George teamed up together. My father and Bob, with much more in common than just their status as the two youngest, formed a separate duo. But that day at lunch, George tried and my father tried and they were both quite charming. My cousins and I, who had worked hard to pull off this luncheon, relaxed. A few months later Paul, son of Emil, and Kathy, daughter of Kay, came to my home for a visit with my father. For me, those two afternoons provided the foundation for a new relationship with some of my cousins.

A few months before my father's 90th birthday, in 2003, I suggested a party. At first he demurred. How could we ask people to travel during January to celebrate with him? But once he agreed, he was a happy participant in all the planning. When his brother Bob arrived, it was the first time they had seen each other in more than 40 years. Mirrored in my father's happiness, I knew my own as I met again a favorite uncle from my childhood.

As my father negotiated old age and increasing frailties, his family was never far from his thoughts. The telephone was a constant companion. He told me how he and Bob talked frequently, with as much strength as they could each muster, until Bob's death only ten months before John's. He talked often with Paul; they shared memories and laughs and probably a few tears.

I do not know if these conversations brought my father a measure of peace. With me he only rehearsed his regrets. But I found his efforts admirable. When the time came for me to give another eulogy, as I reflected on his last years, I quoted from a sixteenth century mystic, who was also named John: "At the evening of life, we shall be judged on our love."

And John Garibaldi had indeed loved. I could just as appropriately have quoted from the many letters he wrote all of us over the years—or my most treasured note, one he left for me to find among his papers. "When something happens to me," he wrote, "please remember how much I thought of you but most of all how much I loved you and how proud I have been of you, your husband, and your wonderful Doug and Matt. No one ever had a finer daughter."

We scheduled his Memorial Mass, not in the small chapel we had used for my mother, but in the auditorium of Heath Village, a large space where his family and all the friends he had made in his last seven years, many of whom could not have made the trip to the church, gathered to say goodbye. We filled that room and celebrated the life of a man who was not a joiner or an extrovert, but who had managed to touch people's lives, one by one, with extraordinary insight and kindness.

Later, at the reception, we arranged the many photographs we had collected of John over the years. There could be no scrapbooks filled with articles he had written to capture his past as there had been with Rita. But both his grandsons shared their memories of him. It was Matt who told the story that captured his grandfather's last days. Home from Costa Rica for what he knew might be his last visit, he was telling his grandfather about his work, about all he wanted to do and some of the obstacles he faced. He was, he said, just about sinking and he gestured to his forehead with a sweeping cross motion of his hand. My father, who had always been passionately interested in all our lives, had not been very responsive that day and there was an exceptionally long silence. I was about to suggest Matt repeat his story, but before I could stumble into the conversation, my father turned to look at his grandson.

"You'll get taller," he said.

My father had grown taller, too. And he had brought all who knew him, especially his daughter, along on the journey. We scattered his ashes on the lake that July, in the same cove where we had left Rita's seven years earlier. The same four of us said goodbye, in the same boat, on a similarly beautiful morning. Instead of lilacs, we floated a branch of the weeping willow he loved, a tree that had lived on where he planted it, despite all attempts to cut it back or transplant it.

To find the truth about my Hoefel grandmother, I had gone through, around, and beyond my mother. To uncover information about my Garibaldi grandmother, I had to go around and beyond my father. The difference was that he was still healthy, alert, and very much a part of my life.

I had tested the waters early on. When I probed for his memories of his mother, his answers had provided no new information and the pain emanating from his eyes shot down any more inquiry. He had agreed to send for her death certificate, but when he gave me the envelope I could tell that he had not looked inside. When I told him that state officials said they had no records of a Catherine Garibaldi as a patient in Central Islip State Hospital, he pursed his lips and said nothing. So I never told him about my research into the symptoms and treatment for schizophrenia in the 1920s and 30s. I never told him that Paul had sent me the list of Catherine's last possessions. I never shared the photographs I had found of inmates' lives in the Central Islip wards. The idea for this book did not coalesce until after my father's death and nothing could have been written before it. But I, too, followed a family tradition; I kept secrets.

All my life I had been proud to be named Garibaldi. Growing up in a world of Irish ascendancy, if one had to be Italian, it was at least helpful to have a famous name that people could spell, pronounce, and perhaps even recognize. I was often asked if I were related to the General; I knew enough family history to say No. But the name alone was sometimes magical. When I traveled in Europe with three college classmates, bottles of wine mysteriously arrived at our table whenever the *maitre d'* learned my name.

My pride in an Italian name never translated into family pride. The secret surrounding Catherine bred a shame that was handed down through generations, afflicting all of us, and it became essential for me to not only get to know Catherine and grieve a grandmother I had never known, but also to accept what I learned.

Paradoxically, it was my father's gestures of reconciliation, extended not toward the absent Catherine, but to his siblings and the next generation, that provided the path for me to reach out to my hidden grandmother. My cousins Paul and Kathy offered not only their memories, photographs, and documents, but became companions on the journey. Still, it took a long time to catch even a glimpse of the Catherine her sons and daughters saw.

When Kathy and I visited the vast acreage that once was Central Islip State Hospital, we talked throughout the long sunny afternoon about what Catherine's days must have been like. It was extraordinary for me to have a cousin to share the emotions, but we both recognized we were on our own with no parents to comfort us. Despite the soothing conversation, the peaceful grounds we walked, and the fragmented memories we compiled, I could not dispel the sadness.

The first anniversary of my father's death caught me by surprise. What was I waiting for? It was time for my own reconciliation. It was time to speak the truth about the past and lay the old family embarrassments to rest. But it was also time to forgive myself for not knowing, for not asking more questions.

I understand now why Catherine's children could not talk about her, why my father had shielded me from knowing the deepest secret of his life. The pressures on Rita to keep her secrets had been enormous. In the end, she could not overcome them. So, too, society had laid a burden on my father. His childhood and young manhood passed during the silent years when parents could consider blind or mentally challenged children a disgrace, even a punishment for their sins, when families hid their disabled or aging members out of sight in back bedrooms.

As Catherine was born too early to benefit from the drugs that could have treated her mental illness and allowed her to live a normal life, so her sons and daughters had to face her condition decades before such an illness could be acknowledged, shared, and perhaps become more bearable. They kept the secret not only from their children, but from friends, neighbors, and employers. I am the beneficiary of a later, more enlightened era where psychiatric medications can heal or at least soothe and changing societal expectations have removed some of the stigma of mental illness.

So many secrets kept; so many families fractured by the effort. After all that pain, it's sad to recognize that I can heal only myself. I should have been there to say goodbye at her funeral. But that choice was not mine to make. Now it is.

Ciao, Catherine.

Postlude:
Final Gifts

Is the journey over? By some measures, yes. Although I confess to late night doubts, wondering what I might find if I searched for Minnie just one more time, I've allowed my membership in ancestry.com to lapse. I've tossed the DNA sampling kit, knowing that without brothers or maternal uncles, through whom to search Y chromosome lines, I cannot learn anything specific about my ancestors. I've checked a final time on the procedures at the Bronx Surrogate Court; New York remains a closed adoption state. I've packed away what documents and photos I was able to retrieve and will preserve them for another generation.

Where does that leave me? I continue to feel alone and angry and sad when I remember all the years I knew nothing and asked no questions. But often now when I think about my three grandmothers, I smile. I have crested the taboos. I understand what it means to have roots. I know these women and I know I am made of sturdy stuff. I can feel the stability that comes from finally knowing my heritage; the knowledge may have come late, but the identity is now mine to claim. Accepting this gift of myself is the end point of the journey.

Unwrapping that gift has allowed me to see some of the other extraordinary gifts that have tumbled into my days...connecting to new Jewish relatives...reconnecting to Italian cousins...embracing a new understanding of what family means...sharing stories too long hidden...relaxing into truth and celebrating unknown ancestors... pursuing work that summons old skills and teaches new ones.

When I began to research my grandmothers' lives, I thought of my work as a task that had to be done, the anthropologist's "duty memory," something that fell to me as their granddaughter. But over the years I have come to love these women. As I have begun to share their stories, I see in faces across the table that others, too, find worth and beauty in Minnie and Margaretha and Catherine.

For many years the work of theologian Elizabeth Johnson has offered me powerful inspiration. Her books lay out feminist insights into God, but she constantly reaffirms the value of women's lives and the importance of remembering. "The act of remembrance...does not revisit the past in order to dwell there with nostalgic sentimentality. Rather it brings the witness of past lives forward into the present as challenge and source of hope....By daring to evoke the suffering, the beauty, the defeats and victories of people who struggled before us, it nourishes our own wavering commitment in the present."

It is one thing to grasp this intellectually by reading the work of a theologian focused on Biblical women. Writing about my grandmothers is a quite different exercise; recognizing their defeats and victories has been far more painful. But if telling the stories nourishes my own wavering commitment in the present and leads me to hope for the future, I can add two more gifts to the lengthening list.

My grandmothers never admonished me or imparted words of wisdom or taught me traditions. I never heard their voices at all. Who they were is still struggling to emerge in who I am. If I can know I am both Jewish and Christian and integrate that news into the person I have always been, then I must accept ambiguity and praise porous borders that do not insert walls between people or religions. If I reveal the details of a grandmother's hidden 38 years in a mental institution, then I must be strong enough to absorb the horror and skepticism I sometimes see in my listeners.

I have said goodbye to Minnie and Margaretha and Catherine. I have let go of my wish for perfection, my need to know every last answer, to close every last link. I must also let go of the anger and the hurt. And so I hesitantly unwrap one final gift—the opportunity for forgiveness.

When my father left our home at the lake for what I suspect we both knew was the last time, he walked up the hill, leaning heavily on his cane, but with a steady gait. As I followed a few steps behind, I noticed that he never turned around, never looked back at the lake, at the view he had so loved. His face was set uphill where difficult times lay and he just walked on. He, too, was made of sturdy stuff.

He, like my mother, had hidden his past from me, his only child, and prevented me from knowing my grandmother. It was the way he survived the trauma he had endured and he wanted to spare me. In her efforts to survive her own troubled childhood and shield me from what she believed was its disgrace, my mother kept me from knowing a heritage as well as a family. She wrapped away her private core and substituted an alternate world that she truly believed would sustain us both. She taught me to cherish the activities of home—baking cookies, tending gardens, decorating for holidays. But she never managed a deeper coming home—to herself. That remains for me to teach myself.

I have no doubt my parents deeply loved me and I, in turn, deeply loved them. I miss them even now. This gift of myself, claimed belatedly, without their knowledge and perhaps without their approval, is still the best gift parents could have given. It is time to say what people say whenever they receive gifts—even those less wonderful than these.

Thanks, Mom and Dad.

Bibliography

Albright, Madeleine. *Prague Winter: A Personal Story of Remembrance and War, 1937-1948.* New York: HarperCollins, 2012.

Antin, Mary. *The Promised Land.* Boston: Houghton Mifflin Co, 1912.

Behar, Ruth. *The Vulnerable Observer: Anthropology that Breaks Your Heart.* Boston: Beacon Press, 1996.

Bernard, Jacqueline. *The Children You Gave Us: A History of 150 Years of Service to Children.* New York: Jewish Child Care Association of New York, 1973.

Bernstein, Nina. *The Lost Children of Wilder: The Epic Struggle to Change Foster Care.* New York: Pantheon Books, 2001.

Bershtel, Sara and Graubard, Allen. *Saving Remnants: Feeling Jewish in America.* New York: The Free Press, 1992.

Brendle, Mary. *Clinton/Hell's Kitchen and its Women.* New York: F.A. Printing, 1997.

Carvajal, Doreen. *The Forgetting River: A Modern Tale of Survival, Identity and the Inquisition.* New York: Riverhead Books (Penguin Group), 2012.

Christiano, Gregory F. *Riding the High Tracks: The Bronx Remnant of the Third Avenue El.* http://www.myrecollection.com/christianog/bronx3el.html

Cohen, Jocelyn and Soyer, Daniel, editors and translators. *My Future is in America: Autobiographies of Eastern European Jewish Immigrants.* New York: New York University Press, 2006.

Cohen, Rose. *Out of the Shadow: A Russian Jewish Girlhood on the Lower East Side.* With an introduction by Thomas Dublin. Ithaca, NY: Cornell University Press, 1995. Reprint of Cohen,Rose, *Out of the Shadow.* New York: George H. Doran Company, 1918.

Colt, George Howe. *The Big House.* New York: Scribner, 2003.

diDonato, Pietro. *Christ in Concrete.* New York: Penguin Putnam, 1993.

Diner, Hasia R. *Lower East Side Memories: A Jewish Place in America.* Princeton: Princeton University Press, 2000.

Dolnick, Edward. *Madness on the Couch: Blaming the Victim in the Heyday of Psychoanalysis.* New York: Simon&Schuster, 1998.

Eisendrath, Charles R. "An Identity and Family History that Are Inextricably Linked." *International Herald Tribune,* June 16, 1999.

Epstein, Helen. *Where She Came From: A Daughter's Search for Her Mother's History*. New York: Little, Brown and Co., 1997.

Epstein, Lawrence J. *At the Edge of a Dream: The Story of Jewish Immigrants on New York's Lower East Side 1880-1920*. San Francisco: John Wiley & Sons, Inc, 2007.

Ewen, Elizabeth. *Immigrant Women in the Land of Dollars: Life and Culture on the Lower East Side, 1890-1925*. New York: Monthly Review Press, 1985.

Freedman, Samuel G. *Who She Was*. New York: Simon & Schuster, 2005.

Freemont, Helen. *After Long Silence*. New York: Delacorte Press, 1999.

Friedland, Susan R. *Shabbat Shalom: Recipes and Menus for the Sabbath*. Boston: Little Brown, 1999.

Friedman, Reena Sigman. *These Are Our Children: Jewish Orphanages in the United States 1880-1925*. Waltham: Brandeis University Press, 1994.

Frommer, Myrna Katz and Frommer, Harvey. *Growing Up Jewish in America: An Oral History*. Lincoln: University of Nebraska Press, 1995.

Goldman, Ari L. *Being Jewish: The Spiritual and Cultural Practice of Judaism Today*. New York: Simon &Schuster, 2000.

Green, Hannah. *I Never Promised You a Rose Garden*. New York: Holt, Rinehart and Winston, 1964.

Hannon, Jane Colleen. *Saints and Patriots: Catholicism in the Bronx, 1920-1940*. Ph.D diss., University of Notre Dame, 2000.

Hendrikson, Robert. *The Great American Chewing Gum Book*. Radnor: Chilton Book Co, 1976.

Herries, Bill. *The Old Westside Hell's Kitchen*. New York: 1954.

Heschel, Abraham Joshua. *The Sabbath: Its Meaning for Modern Man*. New York: Farrar Straus Giroux, 1951.

Hibbert, Christopher. *Garibaldi and His Enemies: The Clash of Arms and Personalities in the Making of Italy*. Boston: Little, Brown and Company. 1965.

Homes, A.M. *The Mistress's Daughter*. New York: Viking, 2007.

Howe, Irving. *World of Our Fathers: The Journey of the East European Jews to America and the Life They Found and Made*. New York: Harcourt Brace Jovanovich, 1976.

Howe, Irving and Libo, Kenneth. *A Documentary History of Immigrant Jews in America: 1880-1930*. New York: Richard Marek Publishers, 1979

Jackson, Kenneth T., ed. *The Encyclopedia of New York City*. New Haven: Yale University Press, 1995.

Jacoby, Susan. *Half-Jew: A Daughter's Search for Her Family's Buried Past*. New York: Scribner, 2000.

Johnson, Elizabeth A. *Truly Our Sister*. New York: Continuum, 2003.

Kagonoff, Benzion C. *A Dictionary of Jewish Names and Their History*. New York: Schockin, 1977.

Kesey, Ken. *One Flew Over the Cuckoo's Nest*. New York: Signet, 1963.

Kessel, Barbara. *Suddenly Jewish: Jews Raised as Gentiles Discover Their*

Jewish Roots. Boston: Brandeis University Press, 2000.

Kravel-Tovi, Michal. "Rite of Passing: Bureaucratic Encounters, Dramaturgy, and Jewish Conversion in Israel." *American Ethnologist*, 39:2 (May 2012) 372-388.

Lifton, Betty Jean. *Journey of the Adopted Self: A Quest for Wholeness.* New York: Basic Books, 1994.

Lifton, Betty Jean. *Twice Born: Memoirs of an Adopted Daughter.* New York: McGraw Hill Book Company, 1975.

McConnon, Tom. *Angels in Hell's Kitchen.* Garden City: Doubleday, 1959.

Miller, Arthur. *Timebends: A Life.* New York: Grove Press, 1987.

O'Connor, Richard. *Hell's Kitchen: The Roaring Days of New York's Wild West Side.* Philadelphia: Lippincott, 1958.

Oliver, Mary. *Evidence.* Boston: Beacon Press, 2009.

Penney, Darby and Stastny, Peter. *The Lives They Left Behind: Suitcases from a State Hospital Attic.* New York: Bellevue Literary Press, 2008.

Polaski, Leo. *The Farm Colonies: Caring for New York City's Mentally Ill in Long Island's State Hospitals.* Kings Park: The Kings Park Heritage Museum, 2003.

Puzo, Mario. "Choosing a Dream: Italians in Hell's Kitchen." In: *Visions of America: Personal Narratives from the Promised Land*, Wesley Brown and Amy Ling, eds. New York: Persea Books, 1993.

Remen, Rachel Naomi, M.D. *My Grandfather's Blessings.* New York: Riverhead Books, 2000.

Riall, Lucy. *Garibaldi: Invention of a Hero.* New Haven: Yale University Press, 2007.

Rich, Adrienne. "Resisting Amnesia: History and Personal Life." In *Blood, Bread and Poetry.* New York: W.W. Norton, 1986.

Roiphe, Anne. "Taking Down the Christmas Tree." *Tikkun*, 4:6 (Nov-Dec 1989) 58-60.

Roskies, Diane K and Roskies, David G. *The Shtetl Book.* New York: KTAV Publishing House, 1975.

Schoener, Allon, ed. *Portal to America: The Lower East Side 1870-1925.* New York: Holt Rinehart Winston, 1967.

Simon, Kate. *Bronx Primitive: Portraits in a Childhood.* New York: The Viking Press, 1982.

Sklarew, Myra. *Over the Rooftops of Time: Jewish Stories, Essays, Poems.* Albany: State University of New York Press, 2003.

Smith, Betty. *A Tree Grows in Brooklyn.* New York: Harper & Brothers, 1943.

Smith, Denis Mack, ed. *Garibaldi: Great Lives Observed.* Englewood Cliffs: Prentice-Hall, 1969.

Steedman, Carolyn Kay. *Landscape for a Good Woman: A Story of Two Lives.* New Brunswick: Rutgers University Press, 1987.

Sternlicht, Sanford. *The Tenement Saga: The Lower East Side and Early Jewish American Writers.* Madison: University of Wisconsin Press, 2004.

Szasz, Thomas. *Schizophrenia: The Sacred Symbol of Psychiatry*. New York: Basic Books, 1976.

Trevelyan, George Macaulay. *Garibaldi and the Making of Italy*. London: Longmans, Green and Co., 1911.

Ultan, Lloyd and Hermalyn, Gary. *The Bronx in the Innocent Years, 1890-1925*. New York: Harper&Row, 1985.

Ultan, Lloyd and Unger, Barbara. *Bronx Accent: A Literary and Pictorial History of the Borough*. New Brunswick: Rutgers University Press, 2000.

Ward, Mary Jane. *The Snake Pit*. New York: Random House, 1946.

Weil, Simone. *The Need for Roots*. Translation of *L'enracinement* by Arthur Wills. New York: G. P. Putnam's Sons, 1952.

Weinberg, Sydney Stahl. *The World of Our Mothers: The Lives of Jewish Immigrant Women*. New York: Schocken Books, 1988.

Ziegelman, Jane. *97 Orchard Street: An Edible History of Five Immigrant Families in One New York Tenement*. New York: Harper Collins, 2010.

Carole Garibaldi Rogers is a journalist, oral historian, and poet. For more than 30 years, she has published numerous articles and essays in national newspapers and magazines, including *The New York Times* and *America*. Her poetry has appeared in a variety of small-press journals and in anthologies. She has a Master of Arts degree in theology. This is her eighth book. She and her husband live in Morristown, New Jersey.

CPSIA information can be obtained at www.ICGtesting.com
Printed in the USA
BVOW032135010713

324861BV00002B/102/P

9 780985 849559